The Dance of the Intellect

The Dance of the Intellect

Studies in the Poetry
of the Pound Tradition

MARJORIE PERLOFF

Northwestern

University Press

Evanston

Illinois

Northwestern University Press

Evanston, Illinois 60208-4210

Printed in the United States of America

ISBN 0-8101-1380-5

Library of Congress Cataloging-in-Publication Data

Perloff, Marjorie.
    The dance of the intellect : studies in the poetry of the Pound
tradition / Marjorie Perloff.
        p.   cm. — (Avant-garde and modernism studies)
    Includes bibliographical references (p.   ) and index.
    ISBN 0-8101-1380-5 (paper : alk. paper)
    1. Pound, Ezra, 1885–1972—Criticism and interpretation.
2. Pound Ezra, 1885–1972—Influence. 3. American poetry—
20th century—History and criticism. I. Title. II. Series.
PS3531.082Z7857 1996
811'.52—dc20   96-19344
                                                          CIP

The paper used in this publication meets the minimum
requirements of the American National Standard for Information
Sciences—Permanence of Paper for Printed Library Materials,
ANSI Z39.48-1984.

Contents

	Preface	*page* vii
	Acknowledgments	xi
1	Pound/Stevens: whose era?	1
2	The portrait of the artist as collage-text: Pound's *Gaudier-Brzeska* and the "italic" texts of John Cage	33
3	"Letter, penstroke, paperspace": Pound and Joyce as co-respondents	74
4	"To give a design": Williams and the visualization of poetry	88
5	"The shape of the lines": Oppen and the metric of difference	119
6	Between verse and prose: Beckett and the New Poetry	135
7	From image to action: the return of story in postmodern poetry	155
8	Postmodernism and the impasse of lyric	172
9	"Unimpededness and interpenetration": the poetic of John Cage	201
10	The Word as Such: L=A=N=G=U=A=G=E poetry in the eighties	215
	Index	239

v

Preface

The revolt against Victorianism meant to the young poet a revolt against irrelevant descriptions of nature, the scientific and moral discursiveness of *In Memoriam* . . . the political eloquence of Swinburne, the psychological curiosity of Browning, and the poetical diction of everybody. Poets said to one another over their black coffee – a recently imported fashion – 'We must purify poetry of all that is not poetry', and by poetry they meant poetry as it had been written by Catullus, a great name at that time, by the Jacobean writers, by Verlaine, by Baudelaire. Poetry was a tradition like religion and liable to corruption, and it seemed that they could best restore it by writing lyrics technically perfect, their emotion pitched high, and as Pater offered instead of moral earnestness life lived as a 'pure gem-like flame' all accepted him for master.
  – W. B. Yeats, Introduction to *The Oxford Book of Modern Verse 1892–1935* (1936)[1]

Yeats' succinct and eloquent account of the ethos of his poetic generation ("The Tragic Generation" as he christened it) has an ironic import today, as our own *fin de siècle* approaches. For in an odd way, Yeats' characterization of poetry is still the popular one: poetry as the art that avoids "irrelevant descriptions," "scientific and moral discursiveness," and "psychological curiosity"; poetry as the language of feeling ("emotion pitched high"), written in verse that is, whether metrical or "free," "technically perfect"; poetry to be declaimed at readings in a special "poetry-reading" voice, "a tradition like religion and liable to corruption."

But, as Yeats puts it in the paragraph that follows the one quoted here, "Every light has its shadow, we tumble out of one pickle into another, the 'pure gem-like flame' was an insufficient motive" (p. ix). The very "impurities" denounced over black coffee by *les jeunes* of

Yeats' circle were to return, in startling new guise, in the second decade of the new century. Indeed, one of the great poetic memorials to the nineties was written by an American poet who was to make "scientific and moral discursiveness" and "much that is not poetry" seem newly poetic. I am thinking, of course, of Ezra Pound's *Hugh Selwyn Mauberley* and the stage it sets for the *The Cantos*. Yeats, who shared the Yellow Nineties' distrust – a distrust inherited by the early Modernists – of Victorian "rhetoric," had no use for Pound's encyclopedic poem, which was not only blatantly didactic in places but also seemed willfully disorganized. "Like other readers," Yeats says of *The Cantos*, "I discover at present merely exquisite or groteque fragments." And he wonders (p. xxiv), "Can impressions that are in part visual, in part metrical, be related like the notes of a symphony; has the author been carried beyond reason by a theoretical conception?"

Exquisite or grotesque fragments, impressions partly visual, partly metrical, a poetry governed by a theoretical conception – Yeats, who never wavered in his faith that "form must be full, sphere-like, single," could find no justification for the odd assortment of modes that he rightly perceived to characterize *The Cantos*. What is more curious: today, some fifty years later, Yeats' questions are still being posed at poetry conferences and in the little magazines. Is Williams' *Kora in Hell* a poem, given that it is written in prose? Is the visualization of the poetic text, as we find it in the minimal poems of Williams and Oppen, an aberration from "true" verse structure? Are texts like Gertrude Stein's *Tender Buttons* and "portraits" to be classified as poetry or fiction or personal essay? Is Louis Zukofsky's *"A"* (a collage-text made up of countless interwoven fragments, part lyric, part documentary prose from newspapers and texbooks; part metered stanzas, part free verse) an important poem or merely a tedious and eccentric one? If "form must be full, sphere-like, single," what can we say of Ed Dorn's *Slinger*, a poetic narrative that is at once a parody Western, an exercise in Heideggerian thinking, and a compendium of drug argot, movies, and comic strips? If poetry depends upon the "power of emotional construction" (Yeats, p. xxviii), how are we to respond to the purposely "flat," seemingly emotionless poetic texts of John Cage or to the dispersal of the speaking subject, the unitary ego, which is at the heart of current L=A=N=G=U=A=G=E School poetics?

The essays in this book address themselves to these and related questions. All were written during the past four years and extend – as well as revise – certain ideas put forward in *The Poetics of Indeterminacy: Rimbaud to Cage* (1981). In that book, my main concern was with the way meanings are articulated in twentieth-century poetry and with the dichotomy — in retrospect perhaps too neat — between Symbolist and anti-Symbolist modes of signification. Here, I am more interested in questions of structure, mode, and genre — specifically, the increasingly important role played in twentieth-century poetry by the "impurities" scorned by Yeats and his contemporaries as inimical to the hard gem-like flame of the perfect lyric moment.

The essays are presented roughly in the order of writing: "Pound / Stevens: whose era?" was presented at the Pound Conference in Sheffield, England, in the spring of 1981; the essay on Language poetry was completed in the spring of 1984. But the order is not only chronological: when I came to put these essays together, I realized that they fell more or less naturally into three groups.

The first group deals with Pound's own poetics as that poetics relates to two of his great contemporaries, Stevens and Joyce, as well as to the visual artists with whom Pound had much more in common than is usually thought – the Italian Futurists. For Pound, I would posit, the art of *writing* came more and more to supplant the question of genre. "My one vol of prose," he wrote in 1929 to Joyce, who was trying to arrange for the publication of Pound's collected prose writings, "is no more a series of . . . vols than my cantos are a series of lyrics. . . . the components need the other components in one piece with them."[2] "Canto-structure," that is to say, came to refer to poetic writing in general – whether the text in question was an actual canto, a manifesto, a critical essay, or a personal letter.

The second group of essays deals with the more technical aspects of verse and prose – more particularly, with the way Williams' invention of a particular form of free verse is related to his "reading" of the visual art works of the avant-garde in the years of the Great War; and the ways in which George Oppen, in turn, revised and adapted the Williams model. From the free verse of Williams and Oppen it is a short step to what I call the "free prose" of a writer like Beckett, whose associative monologues have set a standard for a significant body of later poetry, for example, Ashbery's *Three Poems*.

In the last four essays, I take up broader issues as well as more recent developments. A consideration of the renewed interest in narrative in contemporary poetry, for example, in the poems of O'Hara and Ashbery and in Dorn's mock-epic *Slinger,* has led me to question the centrality of the neo-Romantic poem of intense subjectivity, what Harold Bloom calls the crisis-poem. In "Postmodernism and the Impasse of Lyric," I suggest that, belated as the crisis-poem – or, as I prefer to call it, the epiphany poem – may now be, this is not to say that *poetry* in the more traditional sense of verbal art employing some form of sound recurrence may not be alive and well. For contemporary examples of such art, I turn, in the last two essays, to some texts by John Cage as well as to the young poets, male and female, who are loosely associated with the movement called L=A=N=G=U=A=G=E poetry.

And here, we may witness a curious return. As odd and "unpoetic" as the work of such Language poets as Charles Bernstein or Lyn Hejinian or Ron Silliman may seem on a first reading, their "Poetic Diction" (one of Yeats' "impurities"), highly formalized sound patterning (alliteration, assonance, internal rhyme, puns, echolalia, metrical runs), and their foregrounding of political themes recall, of all things, what Yeats dismissed as "the political eloquence of Swinburne." And beyond Swinburne, the calculated artifice of Wilde and the Yellow Nineties.

But of course our own *fin de siècle* is not theirs. The emphasis on sound structure and verbal play in contemporary poetry may recall the nineties, but it does not serve the incantatory purposes of a Swinburne or the emotive rhetoric of a Lionel Johnson. The Romantic and Modernist cult of personality has given way to what the new poets call "the dispersal of the speaking subject," the denial of the unitary, authoritative ego. Here the poets seem to be echoing contemporary theory, a situation hardly surprising given the increasing inextricability of "theory" and what we might call, on the analogy with visual art, conceptual poetry. Pound, whose presence is everywhere in this book, even in those essays not specifically devoted to him, had a term for this new strain in poetry. "Logopoeia," he called it: "the dance of the intellect among words."

NOTES

1 *The Oxford Book of Modern Verse 1982–1935*, chosen by W. B. Yeats (Oxford: Oxford University Press, 1936), p. ix.
2 See *Pound/Joyce. The Letters of Ezra Pound to James Joyce,* ed. and with a commentary by Forrest Read (New York: New Directions, 1967), p. 244. The first ellipsis is Read's and is used routinely to eliminate a four-letter word.

Acknowledgments

The ten essays in this collection were published between 1981 and 1984. Most were written for specific occasions – a conference, a special issue of a journal, or a commission from an editor. Given these circumstances, there is inevitably some overlap: Christopher Clausen's discussion of lyric, for example, which provides the impetus for "Postmodernism and the Impasse of Lyric" (Chapter 8), is also cited at the end of "Between Verse and Prose: Beckett and the New Poetry" (Chapter 6). In the interest of maintaining the integrity of each essay, I have made no attempt to avoid such slight redundancies. Not every reader, after all, will want to read every essay, and so each is kept intact, with full documentation. I have made some minor corrections and added a number of references, but, on the whole, the essays are reprinted in their original form. I thank the copyright holders for permission to reprint.

Of the many editors and conference organizers who made these essays possible, I wish to give special thanks to the following, who raised important questions or offered valuable suggestions for change: Jonathan Brent, Ralph Cohen, Ihab Hassan, Burton Hatlen, Carroll Terrell, Arthur Vogelsang, and Robert von Hallberg. But my greatest debt is to Albert Gelpi, the editor of the Cambridge Studies in American Literature and Culture, who invited me to put the collection together and whose wise counsel and careful reading of the manuscript have been invaluable.

Sandra Stanley prepared the index.

"Pound/Stevens: whose era?" was delivered at the Pound Conference in Sheffield, England, in April 1981; it was published in *New Literary History* , 13, no. 3 (Spring 1982): 485–514.

"The portrait of the artist as collage-text: Pound's *Gaudier-Brzeska* and the 'Italic' Texts of John Cage" was published in *American Poetry Review,* Special Supplement, 11, no. 3 (May–June 1982): 19–29.

" 'Letter, penstroke, paperspace': Pound and Joyce as co-Respondents' " was delivered at the Special Session on Pound and Joyce at the Modern Language Association in Los Angeles, December 1982; it was published in *American Poetry,* 1 (Spring 1984): 20–32, by McFarland & Company, Inc., Publishers, Jefferson, North Carolina.

" 'To Give a Design': Williams and the visualization of poetry" was published in *William Carlos Williams: Man and Poet* , ed. Carroll Terrell (Orono, Maine: National Poetry Foundation, 1983), pp. 159–186.

" 'The shape of the lines': Oppen and the metric of difference" was published in *George Oppen: Man and Poet,,* ed. Burton Hatlen (Orono, Maine: National Poetry Foundation, 1981), pp. 215–29.

"Between verse and prose: Beckett and the New Poetry" was delivered in shorter form at the Modern Language Association in New York, 1981; it was published in *Critical Inquiry,* 9, no.2 (1982): 415–33, © 1982 by The University of Chicago. All rights reserved.

"From image to action: the return of story in postmodern poetry" was published in *Contemporary Literature,* special issue on Poetry of the Seventies, 23 (Fall 1982): 411–27, © 1982 by the Regents of the University of Wisconsin.

"Postmodernism and the impasse of lyric" was delivered in different form at the Postmodern Conference in Cerisy-la-Salle, France, summer 1983, and at the International Association of University Professors of English, Hamburg, Summer 1982. It was published in *Formations* , 1 (Fall 1984): 43–63, © 1984 by the Regents of the University of Wisconsin.

" 'Unimpededness and interpenetration': the poetic of John Cage" was published in *Triquarterly* (Special Section: John Cage Reader), 54 (Spring 1982): 76–88. The special section was reprinted as *A John Cage Reader,* ed. Peter Gena and Jonathan Brent (New York and London: C. F. Peters, 1982).

"The Word as Such: L=A=N=G=U=A=G=E poetry in the eighties" was published in *American Poetry Review,* 13 (May/June 1984): 15–22.

1   Pound/Stevens: whose era?

On 26 October 1955 William Carlos Williams wrote to Ezra Pound at St. Elizabeth's, asking him if he would care to comment on the obituary essay he had just written on Wallace Stevens, then two months dead, for *Poetry* magazine. Pound replied:

> . . . as to yr / pal / Wally S / . . . . it wd / be highly
>   improper for
> me to have opinions of yr / opinion of a bloke I haven't read
>   and DOUBT like all hell
> that yu will be able to PURR-suade me to venture on
>   with such a
> helluvAlot I don't know and WANT to find out.[1]

If this sounds unnecessarily dismissive, compare it to Stevens's curiously similar response to Pound. In 1947 Theodore Weiss invited Stevens to write something for a special Pound issue of the fledgling *Quarterly Review of Literature*. Stevens replied curtly: "Nothing doing about Pound. I should have to saturate myself with the work and I have not the time."[2]

Time for you and time for me – it seems that neither Pound nor Stevens could allow for it. We, reading these two great Modernists in the late decades of the twentieth century, tend to ignore such mutual distrust, positing that *of course* Pound and Stevens are among the four or five great American poets of the century. Literary historians and anthologists continue to give them roughly equal time, thus following the practice established by the New Criticism in the forties and fifties: Randall Jarrell, R. P. Blackmur, Allen Tate, and such of their followers as William Van O'Connor, Babette Deutsch, and Sr. Bernetta Quinn wrote respectfully – if also quite critically – about both poets.[3] So, for that matter, did the great counter-critic of this period, Yvor Winters.[4] Yet by the late sixties, the very real gap between Pound and Stevens – a gap that perhaps no inclusive definition of Modernism can quite close – had become apparent; the alliance posited by the critics but never by the poets themselves was falling apart. "The Pound Era," Hugh Kenner called the first half of our century, dismissing Stevens in 2 of his almost 600 pages as having created "an Edward Lear poetic pushed toward all limits." Kenner wrote: "The gods have never left us. Nothing we know the mind to have known has ever left us. Quickened by hints, the mind can know it again, and make it new. Romantic Time no longer thickens our sight, time receding, bearing visions away. Our books of cave paintings are the emblems of its abolition, perhaps the Pound Era's chief theme, and the literary consolidation of that theme stands as the era's achievement."[5] *The Pound Era* appeared in 1971; in *A Map of Misreading* (1975), Harold Bloom retorted: "Modernism in literature has not passed; rather, it has been exposed as never having been there. Gossip grows old and becomes myth; myth grows older and becomes dogma. Wyndham Lewis, Eliot and Pound gossiped with one another; the New Criticism aged them into a myth of Modernism; now the antiquarian Hugh Kenner has dogmatized this myth into the Pound Era, a canon of accepted titans. Pretenders to godhood Kenner roughly reduces to their mortality; the grand triumph of Kenner is his judgement that Wallace Stevens represented the culmination of the poetics of Edward Lear."[6] And in *Wallace Stevens: The Poems of Our Climate* (1977), Bloom suggests that it is high time to call the period in question "the Age of Stevens (or shall we say the Stevens Era?)."[7]

This is neither an idle quarrel nor a narrow sectarian war between rival academics (e.g., Bloom, Hillis Miller, Helen Vendler, Frank Kermode in the Stevens camp; Kenner, Donald Davie, Guy Davenport, Christine Brooke-Rose among Poundians) who just happen to have different literary and political allegiances. The split goes deep, and its very existence raises what I take to be central questions about the meaning of Modernism – indeed about the meaning of poetry itself in current literary history and theory.

What prompts those who believe in the Stevens Era to ignore or dismiss Pound? In a recent study of Stevens, Lucy Beckett gives us a neatly reductive version of the anti-Pound myth. *The Cantos,* she argues, are a failure because Pound does not sufficiently resist what Stevens calls "the pressure of reality": "The fragments of [Pound's] own experience and of the civilizations, literatures and histories that have caught his attention remain a shifting heap of splinters. . . . Aware of technique only, not of the poet's responsibility to the disciplined use of language, he is hardly aware at all of the poet's responsibility in respect of thought. . . . The problems of belief and value in a world without established systems of truth, the search for 'what will suffice', the poet's task envisaged by such as Arnold and Santayana, concern him very little. In this sense he is a most unmodern poet."[8] A "modern poet," it seems, is one who understands his responsibilities to "thought" rather than to "technique," and "thought" somehow has to do with the examination of "belief and value in a world without established systems of truth." Accordingly, "the *Cantos,* that colossal attempt to master reality with *persistence of method* rather than with *persistence of thought,* remains the saddest of modern defeats."[9]

Naively put as is this argument, Lucy Beckett's assumptions are quite in keeping with, say, Harold Bloom's repeated insistence that, in Emerson's words, "it is not meter but a meter-making argument that makes a poem." And not just any meter-making argument but especially one that entails the search for "what will suffice" in a world "without established systems of truth." "Pound's *Cantos,*" writes Geoffrey Hartman, "remain a nostalgic montage without unity, a picaresque of styles." By contrast, in Stevens "the music left in the wake of the gods' demise is a great poetry, though limited by its very power to console."[10] In a similar vein, Helen Vendler concludes her important book on Stevens by praising "the short late poems . . . those liquid lingerings in which the angel of reality transforms, for a moment, the bleak continuo of life's drone."[11] And Walton Litz observes: "Unlike Ezra Pound's *Cantos* . . . Stevens's final *mundo* is neither eccentric nor private. It is built upon the central reality of our age, the death of the gods and of the great coordinating mythologies, and in their place it offers the austere satisfactions of a 'self' dependent on the pure poetry of the physical world, a 'self' whose terrifying lack of belief is turned into a source of freedom. The final achievement of Wallace Stevens is a poetry of exclusions and denials which makes a sustaining fiction out of the search for irreducible reality."[12] Carried one step further, we get this formulation from Harold Bloom: "[Stevens's] major phase, from 1942 to his death in 1955, gave us a canon of poems themselves more advanced as *interpretation* than our criticism as yet has gotten to be."[13]

But Poundians have never claimed that their poet is great because his work constitutes an advanced form of "interpretation." Indeed, *poetry,* not to speak of *modern poetry,* is defined quite differently in discussions of Pound. Let me begin by comparing the ways critics have talked about two famous texts: Stevens's *Notes toward a Supreme Fiction* (1942), specifically the Canon Aspirin poems (Pt. III, cantos 5–8), and Pound's Canto LXXXI (1945), specifically the first ninety-five lines (see Appendix).[14] In confronting the Canon Aspirin with the Padre José Elizondo of the *Pisan Cantos,* we may come to a clearer sense of why the division between Pound and Stevens continues to haunt our own sense of Modernism.

II

Notes toward a Supreme Fiction is often called Stevens's greatest poem. Of Part III, "It Must Give Pleasure," Frank Kermode wrote in 1960: "These two hundred lines of verse seem to me to give continuously a higher delight than anything of comparable length written in this century." And more specifically, "The complex and majestic Canon Aspirin poems . . . raise the temperature of the whole work and justify not only the sober esctasies of the conclusion but the immense and beautiful claims for poetry made in III. viii: it the poet creates an angel (and he has just done so) is not his joy equal to the angel's?" Kermode now quotes the entire eighth canto ("What am I to believe? . . .") and concludes, "The power of this is great in isolation; in its context, as sequel to the previous poem, it is overwhelming . . . the whole work exists in a radiant and productive atmosphere, saying the words of the world that are the life of the world."[15]

"The words of the world that are the life of the world" – in his first major study of *Notes toward a Supreme Fiction* in 1963, Harold Bloom echoes this judgment: "The Supreme Fiction . . . enters the poem in the exhilarating person of the Canon Aspirin, Stevens' finest invention. The Canon is the cure for our current headache of unreality. . . . In his activity the Canon first becomes the angel of reality, then is tempted too far in his benevolent impositions, and finally is surpassed by the poet himself, who discovers an order that his created angel could only impose."[16] The opening of canto 5 ("We drank Meursault, ate Lobster Bombay with mango / Chutney") is praised for its "deceptive inconsequence," deceptive because the poem's vision is "fiercely Romantic." Bloom goes on to explain the symbolism of this canto: the Canon's sister stands for "seeing the very thing itself and nothing else"; as such, her limited vision must be transcended, as it is in canto 6, whose "thesis" (Bloom's word) is "the Canon's quest toward an integration of all reality, fact and thought together." Further, "Section VII is the antithesis, presenting the Canon's surrender of his quest to the angelic impatience that imposes rather than discovers order. The synthesis is in Section VIII, which one does not hesitate to call Stevens's finest poem, where the poet's discovery of reality is both given and celebrated"(Borroff, p. 92).

The Canon's choice between reality and imagination in canto 6 is, according to Bloom, "heroic," because he ultimately refuses to "reject either order":

> He had to choose. But it was not a choice
> Between excluding things. It was not a choice
> Between, but of. He chose to include the things
> That in each other are included, the whole,
> The complicate, the amassing harmony.
>
> [*Notes*, Pt. III, canto 6]

This choice, says Bloom, is "Wordsworthian rather than Blakean, for it insists that the context of fact or nature can be harmonized with the more exuberant context of the poet's apocalyptic desires." Thus after the "extraordinary emotional progression" that leads the poet to the desperation of canto 7 ("It is possible, possible, possible. It must / Be possible"), Stevens "gives us his ultimate poem, the supreme achievement of post-Romanticism and the culmination of Coleridgean and Blakean poetic theory." The angel poem (canto 8) surpasses the *Prelude* in its courage "to cross into this desperately triumphant poetic humanism" (Borroff, p. 94).

When Bloom returns to *Notes* more than a decade later in his *Poems of Our Climate,* he reads the poem according to the revisionary ratios and the theory of crossings he has formulated in the interim, but his response to it remains essentially unchanged; indeed, he now goes further in relating the Canon Aspirin to "a high Romantic fallen angel, a morning star," and argues that "the name 'Aspirin' probably plays upon the archaic meaning of 'aspires,' the *anders-streben* of Pater's *'All art constantly aspires toward the condition of music,'* or the upward-rising of Blake's 'On what wings dare he aspire.' " Further, " 'Aspire' goes back to the Latin for 'breaking upon, desiring, favoring,' and . . . we can translate 'the Canon Aspirin' as the self-defining, self-describing human desire for a beyond, even if that beyond turns out to be an abyss" (p. 205).

Whether or not we agree with Bloom's interpretation of the Canon Aspirin poem is, I think, less important than what that interpretation tells us about Bloom's central assumptions about poetry. We might note, to begin with, that Bloom's value judgments – his use, for example, of such adjectives as "exhilarating," "moving," "strenuously heroic," "supreme," "splendid," and "extraordinarily emotional" – refer always to what the poet is saying rather than to how he says it. The poem's sound structure, for example, is treated as a mere irrelevancy, as is the syntax of Stevens's cantos and even, to a large extent, their diction. Would it matter, say, if we substituted "poor" or "paler" for "pauvred" in Part V, canto 6? If "closelier" in line 12 of the same canto became "closer"? What is the effect of repeating "paint" three times in the lines, "The way a painter of pauvred colors paints. / But still she painted them"? Such questions are never raised because they have no real bearing on what Bloom takes to be the only question a Great Questioner should ask, namely, what is it that Stevens tells us in this poem? In the Coda to *Poems of Our Climate,* he says: "Why do we read one poet rather than another? We believe the lies we want to believe because they help us to survive. Similarly, we read (reread) the poems that keep our discourse with ourselves going. Strong poems strengthen us by teaching us *how to talk to ourselves,* rather than how to talk to others" (p. 387; italics are Bloom's). Which is to say that the greatness of Stevens's poetry is a function of the "desperately triumphant . . . humanism" that Bloom believes in. *Notes* teaches us "how to talk to ourselves," provided that we happen to share its sense of strenuous quest for the "Supreme Fiction."

There are two corollaries. First, Stevens's poetic truth is a "late plural of Romantic tradition" – a condition assumed to be the only proper one for modern poets. To call *Notes toward a Supreme Fiction* Wordsworthian or Blakean or Keatsian is equivalent to calling the poem Good or True or Beautiful. Secondly, in its belatedness, *Notes* paradoxically betters Blake and Wordsworth and the Keats of *The Fall of Hyperion,* for it "cultivates the highly anti-apocalyptic virtue of patience."[17] We might restate Bloom's doctrine and its corollaries in the language of *Notes*: (1) It must be Romantic. (2) It must question Romantic premises. (3) It must be Visionary Humanist.

When we turn from Bloom's reading of Stevens to the powerful ones of, say, Hillis Miller or Helen Vendler, we find that, despite a number of conflicting interpretations (Vendler regards Part III, canto 7 of *Notes* as more pessimistic than does Bloom, referring to the "repetitive, accumulative and hysterical affirmations [that] mount in a crescendo conveying the fear which is their origin"),[18] the central assumptions remain essentially the same. When Miller traces Stevens's gradual evolution from metaphysical dualism and "representational thinking" to the recognition of the late poems that "man's spiritual height and depth are available here and now or nowhere," he is reading Stevens along Bloomian lines, although he is much less inclined than Bloom to attribute value to Stevens's particular truths.[19] Again, although Helen Vendler does pay close attention to the linguistic and syntactic strategies of *Notes,* her emphasis, like Bloom's, is on the poem's final refusal "to resolve theoretical difficulties," its "strenuous exploration of every possible escape from . . .

self-pity and its literary forms – nostalgia and elegy."[20] Indeed, in a recent essay on Stevens, Vendler has made her personal predilection for his particular vision quite clear:

> Many of Stevens's poems – read from one angle, most of the best poems – spring from catastrophic disappointment, bitter solitude, or personal sadness. It is understandable that Stevens, a man of chilling reticence, should illustrate his suffering in its largest possible terms. That practice does not obscure the nature of the suffering, which concerns the collapse of early hopeful fantasies of love, companionship, success, and self-transformation. As self and beloved alike become, with greater or lesser velocity, the final dwarfs of themselves, and as social awareness diminishes dreams of self-transcendence, the poet sees dream, hope, love, and trust – those activities of the most august imagination – crippled, contradicted, dissolved, called into question, embittered. This history is the history of every intelligent and receptive human creature as the illimitable claims on existence made by each one of us are checked, baffled, frustrated, and reproved.[21]

What begins as loving description of the poetry, drawing upon Stevens's own vocabulary of final dwarfs and the august imagination, abruptly shifts, in the final sentence, to a statement of moral truth not everyone would endorse. For *is* Stevens's "history," however accurately Vendler describes it, synonymous with "the history of every intelligent and receptive human creature"? And, more important, is a given poet's *oeuvre* better for conveying such a history?

I am persuaded that those who regard Stevens as the great poet of the twentieth century would say yes to both questions. Indeed, in adopting such an Arnoldian, which is to say an essentially Romantic, view of poetry, they are, after all, merely giving tacit assent to Stevens's own definition of poetry as "an unofficial view of being."[22] In "The Figure of Youth as a Virile Poet," Stevens observes: "In philosophy we attempt to approach truth through the reason. Obviously this is a statement of convenience. If we say that in poetry we attempt to approach truth through the imagination, this, too, is a statement of convenience. We must conceive of poetry as at least the equal of philosophy" (*NA*, p. 41). Despite the modest disclaimers with which he couches this familiar Romantic distinction, Stevens obviously means it. "The poet's role," he suggests, "is to help people to live their lives" (*NA*, p. 28); "he gives to life the supreme fictions without which we are unable to conceive of it" (*NA*, p. 31). As such, the poet is obviously set apart from all others: "There is a life apart from politics. It is this life that the youth as virile poet lives, in a kind of radiant and productive atmosphere" (*NA*, p. 57). And, most tellingly, "Poetry is a part of the structure of reality" (*NA*, p. 81).

These are aphorisms to which Pound would have taken strong exception, opposed as he was to the belief that "there is a life apart from politics," a special "radiant and productive atmosphere" in which the "youth as virile poet" can retreat when he longs to have a final soliloquy with his interior paramour. Poetry must, on the contrary, relate to the whole of a man's life in the real world, which is not to say that it is "a part of the structure of reality." For how could it be, given that "the medium of poetry" is not thoughts but "WORDS"?[23] Or so Pound construed it.

"The poet," says Stevens, "is the priest of the invisible."[24] It follows that certain discriminations must be made. In "The Relation of Poetry to Painting," we read: "Let me divide modern poetry into two classes, one that is modern in respect to what it says, the other that is modern in respect to form. . . . The first kind is interested in form but it accepts a banality of form as incidental to its language. Its justification is that in expressing thought or feeling in poetry the purpose of the poet must be to subordinate the mode of expression, that while the value of the poem as a poem depends on expression, it depends primarily on what is expressed" (*NA*, p. 168). In the second class we find, says Stevens, too many poems "in which the exploitation of form involves nothing more than the use of small letters for capitals, eccentric line-endings, too little or too much punctuation and similar aberrations. These have nothing to do with being alive. They have nothing to do with the conflict between the poet and that of which his poems are made." And, in casting about for an example, Stevens refers to "the division, say, between Valéry and Apollinaire" (*NA*, pp. 168–69).

Or, we might say, the division between Stevens himself and Pound, a poet more than fond of "eccentric line-endings," "too little punctuation," and "similar aberrations," a poet in many ways similar to Apollinaire and certainly unlike a late Symboliste like Valéry. Stevens applies the same distinction between matter and manner to himself and Williams in a letter of 1946 to José Rodriguez Feo: "I have not read Paterson. I have the greatest respect for [Williams], although there is the constant difficulty that he is more interested in the way of saying things than in what he has to say. The fact remains that we are always fundamentally interested in what a writer has to say. When we are sure of that, we pay attention to the way in which he says it, not often before."[25] Hugh Kenner, who cites this passage in his chapter on Stevens and Williams in

A Homemade World, comments laconically: "This is one of the most extraordinary misunderstandings in literary history."[26]

If so, it is a misunderstanding that Stevens scholars from Robert Buttel to Adelaide Kirby Morris have been eager to perpetrate.[27] A concordance of Stevens criticism, if there were such a thing, would probably show that the following words had a very high incidence: *being, consciousness, fiction, reality, self, truth.* These are, of course, Stevens's own words, and the poet's advocates have adopted them quite naturally. But it does not follow that they have some sort of absolute value as nodes of critical discourse. Certainly they are not the words we meet in discussions of the *Cantos.*

III

One of the most interesting treatments of Canto LXXXI is that of D. S. Carne-Ross, who submits the Canto's first twelve lines to a patient analysis, in dialogue with the students in his Pound seminar. The discussion makes three main points: (1) the seemingly random elements in the Canto do have necessary connections: thus line 12, "and Dolores said, 'Come pan, niño,' eat bread me lad," relates back to the divine marriage of sky and earth in line 1, "Zeus lies in Ceres' bosom," the eating of bread (cereal) being for Pound not just symbolic as in the Christian sacrament but a *real* part of the Eleusinian mystery; (2) such connections are curiously elusive just because Pound "leaves it to us to put the elements together with the force of a personal discovery"; and (3) it is incorrect to assume, as does one student in the class, that "Pound makes this Elizondo say" such and such, for: "We are to suppose that Padre Elizondo really did say this. He is a real man who on two occasions said something to Pound in his own Castilian Spanish. It is a cardinal principle of the poem that the materials it presents must be presented exactly as they are or were. A man's actual words, and as far as possible even the sound of his words, must be reported, the date, location, etc. must be given. As Pound sees it, this is part of the evidence."[28]

In other words, the stress is always on what Pound called "constatation of fact," however disjunctively those "facts" are structured in a given Canto. Indeed, as Carne-Ross concludes:

> What is difficult about Pound's poetry is its "simplicity" . . .
> the whole reverberating dimension of inwardness is missing.
> There is no murmurous echo chamber where deeps supposedly
> answer to deeps. Not merely does the thing, in Pound's best

verse, not point beyond itself: *it doesn't point to us.* The green tip
that pushes through the earth in spring does not stand for or
symbolize man's power of spiritual renewal. . . . Pound's
whole effort is *not* to be polysemous but to give back to the
literal first level its full significance, its old significance. . . .
That green thrust is itself the divine event, the fruit of the
marriage at Eleusis. Persephone is in that thrusting tip, and if
man matters it is because he too has a share in that same power,
he too is a part of the seasonal, sacred life of nature. But only a
part.[29]

A similar emphasis on what Carne-Ross calls "Pound's offense against
the great principle of inwardness, of internalisation that has put us at the
center of things and laid waste the visible world" is to be found in the
criticism of Guy Davenport, Donald Davie, and Hugh Kenner. Davenport, like Carne-Ross a classical scholar, argues that, unlike nineteenth-
century poets "who put everything against the scale of time and
discovered that all behavior within time's monolinear progress was evo-
lutionary. . . . It was Pound's determination . . . to treat what had become a world of ghosts as a world eternally present." The first line of
Canto LXXXI is, accordingly, meant quite literally: "The myth of Persephone is here and now, in civilization's rhythm of inevitable decay and
conscious renewal."[30] Donald Davie, commenting on the "wasp" passage in the neighboring Canto LXXXIII, makes a related case: "At no
point does the wasp become a symbol for something in Pound's predica-
ment, or for his ethical and other programs, or for his personality. The
wasp retains its otherness, as an independent form of life. . . . Pound's
repeated assertion that the paradisal is *real,* out there in the real world, is a
conscious challenge to the whole symbolist aesthetic."[31] And Hugh Kenner refers repeatedly to what he calls Pound's "move out of
Symbolism":[32] "In shifting his interest . . . from the articulation of personae to the observation of epiphanic events, Pound was participating in
the major intellectual *peripeteia* of the past eighty years, the desertion of
the windowless monadic world of pigeonholed 'subjects' for a lively
explorer's interest in particulars, that one can grasp simultaneously, as
from a moving ship, the relative and the continuous."[33]

Which is to say that Padre José Elizondo (whose wise words about
the difference between "catoli*th*ismo" and ReliHion" and about the
probable demise of "los reyes" pick up key motifs from earlier Cantos)
cannot be translated into something else in the sense that Harold Bloom
speaks of "translat[ing] the Canon Aspirin as the self-defining, self-
describing human desire for a beyond, even if that beyond turns out to

be an abyss." As Stevens himself sums up the difference, "The bare image and the image as symbol are the contrast" (*OP*, p. 161). For Stevens, as for Stevensian critics, "Poetry as an imaginative thing consists of more than lies on the surface" (*OP*, p. 161). Poundians, on the other hand, are reluctant to generalize about *poetry;* rather, they want to show how *modern* poetry gives renewed attention precisely to what "lies on the surface."

The first step in dealing with that surface is, of course, to track down Pound's endlessly teasing allusions. Why does "Taishan" appear in line 2 of Canto LXXXI? Because the high peak seen from his prison cell at Pisa reminds the poet of the sacred mountain of China, the home of the Great Emperor.[34] And where does the Mount Taishan motif reappear? Some sixty lines later, when "Benin" (the friendly Black soldier whose face reminds Pound of a Benin bronze) supplies him with a "table ex packing box," a gift "light as the branch of Kuanon." Kuanon is the daughter of the Emperor, the Chinese goddess of mercy. To make connections between references is to discover, not a cluster of possible meanings as in the case of the Canon Aspirin and his sister, but rather the way the *structure* of Pound's long poem works.

"The Structuring of Pound's *Cantos*," M. L. Rosenthal calls a recent essay that describes the "intimate, fragmented, self-analytical, open and emotionally volatile structure" of Pound's poetic sequence.[35] Again, the "open form" of *The Cantos* – form as a "means of discovery – for poet and reader alike" – is the subject of Eva Hesse's remarkable analysis: "In using the objective realities of other human, vegetable or mineral existences . . . the poet has developed the three main technical devices of the *Cantos*: persona, ideogram, metamorphosis. In turn, these represent the otherness of persons or of natural and supernatural things in order to stake out the boundaries of the poet's own being within the 'manifest universe.' "[36] The disjunctive presentation of "factual atoms" is, Hesse suggest, itself a way of saying something about human life: specifically, that, in keeping with the doctrine of such medieval mystics as Richard St. Victor, the soul cannot be its own object; "it cannot 'delight in itself' (Canto XC) but only in its functions or its objects" (p. 26). If the mind can assume the shape of all things, and if "things are really their functions," then, says Hesse citing Fenollosa, " 'All processes in nature are interrelated; and thus there could be no complete sentence . . . save one which it would take all time to pronounce.' So much for the closed form" (p. 47). In the "vast process of becoming" (Frobenius's phrase) which *The Cantos* unfold before your eyes, "Syntax yields to parataxis . . . Pound juxtapos[es] concrete particulars that he considers meaningful in the conviction that they will speak for themselves" (p. 48).

The exploration of the Poundian parataxis is at the center of Kenner's *Pound Era*. For Kenner, Pound is to be seen as the inventor of a new language. Of the *Homage to Sextus Propertius,* he writes: "Something has happened; the tone of time has vanished, and aerial perspective. There is no 'point of view' that will relate these idioms: neither a modern voice . . . nor an ancient one. . . . In transparent overlay, two times have become as one, and we are meant to be equally aware of both dictions (and yet they seem the same diction). The words lie flat like the forms on a Cubist surface. The archaizing sensibility of James' time and Beardsley's has simply dissolved" (p. 29). This, Stevensians might complain, is to focus on the "persistence of method" rather than on "persistence of thought." But Kenner's assumption, like Eva Hesse's, is that the formal structure of a work – in this case, the Cubist surface upon which items are arranged in "transparent overlay" – is itself meaningful. "Language," says Kenner, "creates its characteristic force fields. A whole quality of apprehension inheres in its sounds and its little idioms" (p. 120). Or again: "Pound's structures, like Jefferson's plough, were meant to be useful: to be validated therefore not by his opinions but by the unarguable existence of what exists. No more than Zukofsky, then, does he expatiate, in many passages that tend to set annotators scribbling. Rather, he constellates Luminous Details, naming them, as again and again in the *Cantos* he names the signed column. For the column exists" (p. 325). The constellation of "luminous details" depends, as Kenner explains it, upon the Vortex as "self-interfering pattern" (p. 145) as well as on Fenollosa's concept of the ideogram as the mimesis of vital process (p. 289). The resultant "subject rhymes" create a "polyphony, not of simultaneous elements which are impossible in poetry, but of something chiming from something we remember earlier" (p. 370). Such "chiming" has been explored by a number of other commentators. George Kearns, for example, shows how the Ceres-Dolores (cereal-bread) motif, already discussed, reappears in such unlikely places in Canto LXXXI as in the passing reference to the formality of French "baker and concierge," the cryptic "Some cook, some do not cook" (an allusion to the Ezra-Mary-Olga triangle), and the image of the poet's father in his backyard: "My ole man went on hoein' corn." [37]

Pound's constellation of "luminous details" is related by Herbert Schneidau to the poet's peculiar "contempt for equivalence-structures, and for selection, constrasted with the favor shown to the 'drive' of poetry, which one can only interpret as the combination principle, the surge of one word to the next." And Schneidau reminds us that Pound disliked even the most basic of equivalence structures – rhyme. His preference for the metonymic over the metaphoric function, his belief that "the cherry tree is *all that it does,*" is, Schneidau suggests, "a revolutionary break-away from metaphoric habits in composing poems." And he notes: "The work does not 'imitate' or describe or make a point about something external . . . although its references to the outside world may be diverse and interesting and even crucial. . . . Rather, it would seem the work is more nearly the product of wanting to say things *in a certain demanding way.*"[38]

Note Schneidau's emphasis here on the *how* rather than the *what* of poetic discourse. For such key words in Stevens criticism as *imagination, consciousness, being,* and *self,* Poundians would substitute terms like *precision, particularity, image, technique, structure, invention.* Again, such value tags as *Keatsian, Wordsworthian,* or *Emersonian,* ubiquitous in Stevens criticism, find their counterpart in the Pound annals in such adjectives as *Confucian, Homeric,* or *Provençal* on the one hand; in *experimental, avant-garde,* and, especially, *new* on the other. To unite these two sets of terms is, of course, to MAKE IT NEW. Pound critics, that is to say, are just as likely as are the Stevensians to adopt the vocabulary of their master.

The close relationship of Pound's terminology to that of his critics becomes apparent no matter what critical text of Pound's we choose to look at. Take "A Retrospect" of 1918. The three Imagist principles – "1. Direct treatment of the 'thing' whether subjective or objective. 2. To use absolutely no word that does not contribute to the presentation. 3. As regarding rhythm: to compose in the sequence of the musical phrase, not in the sequence of a metronome"[39] – reappear, whether directly or indirectly, in all the studies of Pound that praise his concreteness and particularity, his precision and radical condensation. Again, in raising the question of rhythm versus meter, Pound prompted critics like Davie and Kenner to analyze his verse forms; indeed, some of the best essays written on Pound are those that deal with his prosodic innovations.[40] This is in marked contrast to Stevens studies: even Helen Vendler, who writes so discerningly of Stevens's verbal and syntactic ambiguities, pleads ignorance when it comes to prosody: "Since criticism has yet to find a way of making notes on cadence, rhythms, and sounds both reliable and readable, I resort to only occasional remarks on these subjects."[41]

On the second page of "A Retrospect," Pound gives us his famous definition of the image as "that which presents an intellectual and emotional complex in an instant of time" (*LE,* p. 4). Not poetry as Stevens's "unofficial view of Being" or "Supreme Fiction" but poetry as a way of getting the job done: "Good writers are those who keep the language efficient," or "Dichten = condensare" (*ABC*, pp. 32, 36). Again, when we compare such typical Pound prescriptions as "Use no superfluous word, no adjective which does not reveal something" (*LE*, p. 4) or "Do not retell in mediocre verse what has already been done in good prose" (*LE*, p. 5) to such Stevens aphorisms as "The thing said must be the poem not the language used in saying it" (*OP*, p. 165) or "Poetry and materia poetica are interchangeable terms" (*OP*, 159), the gulf between the two poetics is seen to be wide. For Stevens, "Form has no significance except in relation to the reality that is being revealed" (*OP*, p. 237); for Pound, form *is* that reality. From this faith in form as itself expressive of the poet's view of identity and culture comes Pound's conviction, stated later in "A Retrospect," that "no good poetry is ever written in a manner twenty years old" (*LE*, p. 11).

Here Pound seems to be anticipating current semiotic theory, which regards the transformation, indeed often the disappearance, of particular genres and conventions as aspects of the inevitable literary change that occurs when the codifications that govern their production break down.[42] Thus Christine Brooke-Rose studies the *Cantos* as a new genre, the poem "as a spiral, whirling with events, which are reiterated at new levels, juxtaposed to new elements and made new,"[43] just as Hugh Kenner examines Pound's departure from earlier modes of translation in his chapter on the Cathay poems called "The Invention of China." *Modernism,* in this context, means rupture – not, of course, with the distant past which must be reassimilated, but with all that has become established and conventional in the art of one's own time. "Literature," declared Pound in a famous aphorism that Stevens could hardly have endorsed, given its capitulation to what he regarded as "the pressure of reality," "is news that STAYS news" (*ABC*, p. 29).

IV

If Poundians take MAKE IT NEW! as their watchword, one might say, without being at all facetious, that those who regard Stevens as the great poet of our time admire his ability to MAKE IT OLD. What matters, to Harold Bloom and Hillis Miller as to Frank Kermode and Helen Vendler, is Stevens's restatement, in chastened, qualified, and ironic form, of the Romantic position his Emersonian (for Bloom) or Coleridgean (for Kermode) or Keatsian (for Vendler) ethos. Stevens carries on the Symbolist tradition, whereas Pound's Imagism and Vorticism constitute, in Donald Davie's words, "a radical alternative to it."[44] For Stevens, poetry is "an unofficial view of Being"; for Pound, it is, so to speak, an official view of becoming: the "VORTEX [is] a radiant node or cluster . . . from which, and through which, and into which, ideas are constantly rushing."[45] Some interesting corollaries follow.

The norm of lyric versus the norm of *"Encyclopedic Poem"*

In her recent *Lyric Time,* Sharon Cameron distinguishes lyric from narrative and drama as follows: "Unlike the drama, whose province is conflict, and unlike the novel or narrative, which connects isolated moments of time to create a story multiply peopled and framed by a social context, the lyric voice is solitary and generally speaks out of a single moment in time. . . . its propensity [is] to interiorize as ambiguity or outright contradiction those conflicts that other mimetic forms conspicuously exteriorize and then allocate to discrete characters who enact them in the manifest pull of opposite points of view."[46] According to this distinction, even a long sequence like *Notes toward a Supreme Fiction* is a lyric poem: a solitary voice speaks out of a single moment in time, interiorizing as ambiguity conflicts that would, in fiction or drama, be allocated to discrete characters. In the Canon Aspirin poems, for example, there are slight gestures toward narrative: "We drank Meursault, ate Lobster Bombay with mango / Chutney. Then the Canon Aspirin declaimed / Of his sister," and so on. But of course the Canon's sister has no life of her own, any more than do Nanzia Nunzio or the maiden form Catawba. "Characters," when they do appear in a lyric sequence like *Notes,* serve as projections of particular personal fantasies. Thus the Canon Aspirin represents a certain reckless element in the poet's personality: his urge is to move on "ascending wings" into the "orbits' outer stars." As one who "imposes orders as he thinks of them, / As the fox and snake do," the Canon must finally be surpassed by the poet himself, who comes to see that "to impose is not / To discover." Yet Stevens knows that he can never separate the "angel in his cloud / Serenely gazing at the violent abyss" from himself; indeed, in canto 8 he wonders: "Is it he or is it I that experience this?"

Not surprisingly, then, Sharon Cameron's chapter on modern poetry in *Lyric Time* makes much of Stevens. Pound's name, on the other hand, does not even appear in her index, and for good reason. For a text like Canto LXXXI does not fit into Cameron's generic framework: it is both "narrative" and "lyric," with, for that matter, bits of "drama" interspersed. Indeed, it is not particularly helpful to define *Cantos* as a "lyric-plus" or "epic-minus" genre, for surely, as Northrop Frye says, "The paradoxical technique of the poetry which is encyclopedic and yet discontinuous, the technique of *The Waste Land* and of Ezra Pound's *Cantos,* is, like its direct opposite in Wordsworth, a technical innovation heralding a new mode."[47] That new mode has been called, quite rightly I think, *collage* – the juxtaposition without explicit syntactic connection of disparate items[48] – in this case, references to Greek mythology, the conversation of Padre Elizondo, the image of "George Santayana arriving in the port of Boston," and so on. It is interesting to note that despite the temporality inherent in any verbal structure, Pound's way of relating word groups is essentially spatial. The words of John Adams, for example, could precede those of André Spire instead of following them with no appreciable difference, or again, it would be possible to interlard a passage from, say, Canto LXXIX somewhere between the references to Possum and the Crédit Agricole without altering the basic movement or momentum of his discontinuous encyclopedic form. In his challenging book, *The Tale of the Tribe,* Michael Bernstein puts it this way: "The seemingly unobtrusive moment in Canto VIII [the first Malatesta Canto] when the first series of historical letters is introduced into the *Cantos* and the personality of Sigismundo is shown by juxtaposing his prose instruction concerning a painter he wishes to engage with a lyric poem he writes for Isotta degli Atti without privileging either medium, represents one of the decisive turning-points in modern poetics, opening for verse the capacity to include domains of experience long since considered alien territory."[49] *Without privileging either medium* – this is the distinctive feature of "canto structure" as Pound devises it. Despite its great lyric coda, Canto LXXXI is not essentially a lyric poem; its collage surface bears the traces of any number of diverse genres: epic, romance, satire, tall tale, travelogue, song, and so forth. By contrast, Stevens's lyric poems, ambiguous as their meanings may be, exhibit what the Romantics and New Critics called organic form. Thus Kermode can say quite rightly that in *Notes* "there is . . . a genuine beginning and end, an early candour and a late plural. . . . A good deal of the doctrine is contained in the opening poems; and in the final part of the fables are used to achieve a deliberate intensity of feeling. The complex and majestic Canon Aspirin poems . . . justify not only the sober ecstasies of the conclusion but the immense and beautiful claims for poetry made in III. viii." And he quotes the whole canto "What am I to believe?"[50] Similarly, Helen Vendler writes of the final "Fat girl" canto, "In the suavity of the last five lines, the poet is already, even before the stability to come, in control of his images . . . and the final civilized calling-by-name will take place not under a tree but framed in crystal in a gildered street, as the green primitive is at last seen for what it is – a beginning leading to the crystal, not an end in itself."[51]

Which is to say that there *is* closure in *Notes toward a Supreme Fiction,* however much the ending speaks to us of new beginnings. What Vendler calls the "massively solid structure" of the lyric sequence has little in common with the serial mode of the *Cantos,* a form which is, in Kenner's words, "a gestalt of what it can assimilate,"[52] or, as I have put it elsewhere, a running transformer, constantly ingesting incoming unprocessed data.[53] Stevens's rage for order, his need to make analogies ("It is only *au pays de la métaphore qu'on est poète"* – *OP,* p. 179), is at odds with Pound's deployment of metonymic linkages, his creation of Cubist surfaces or aerial maps where images jostle one another

Accordingly, when critics complain, as does Frank Kermode, of the ultimate incoherence of the *Cantos,* what they really mean is that Pound violates the norms of the lyric, specifically the Romantic lyric. In cutting out the discursive base of the Romantic ode, Kermode argues, a base still present in Yeats and revived by Stevens, whose "solution to the image-and-discourse problem is to make the problem itself the subject of the poems," Pound creates a vast ideogram that has "no intellectual content whatever."[54] Conversely, when Donald Davie calls Stevens's "Le Monocle de Mon Oncle" a "strikingly old-fashioned poem," his argument is that "Stevens' poem, like an ode by Keats, is still *discursive;* it moves from point to point, always forward from first to last. Lose the thread, and you may go back and look for it." Such discursiveness, Davie suggests, goes hand in hand with Stevens's "metrical conservatism": " 'To break the pentameter,' said Pound, 'that was the first heave.' Stevens has never made the break." And he concludes: "If I am right in thinking that a Keatsian allegiance is the clue to Stevens, then his metres are accounted for – his conservatism in this department is part and parcel with his conservatism in structure and in rhetoric . . . His novelty is all on the surface."[55] Which is to say that for Davie the ratio of meter to meter-making argument first put forward by Emerson is exactly reversed.

The loss of history and the mythology of self versus history and mythology as other

"Life," remarks Stevens in one of the *Adagia,* "is an affair of people not of places. But for me life is an affair of places and that is the trouble" (*OP,* p. 158). The absence of others in Stevens's poetry has been remarked upon by many critics, most notably by Hugh Kenner, who writes:

> You will search Stevens' canon in vain for human actions with agents good and bad. . . . There is a great deal of language in

these poems with no one speaking it except the grave impersonal voice of poetry, and there is little variety of feeling. . . .
That grave equable voice, as dispassionate as *things,* weaves its
whimsical monologue: Crispin and Mrs. Pappadopoulos and
Mrs. Alfred Uruguay and other improbable folk are nodes in
the monologue. . . . The Stevens world is empty of people.
This is because he is in the Wordsworth line, a Nature poet,
confronting an emptied Nature, but a Nature without Presences, no longer speaking.[56]

The same point is made, but with less hostility, by Denis Donoghue,
one of the few participants in the Modernist debate who has written
sympathetically of both Stevens and Pound, although he clearly prefers
the former.[57] In *Connoisseurs of Chaos,* Donoghue uses "The Idea of
Order and Key West" as exhibit and argues that for the Stevens of this
poem, "There is no authority but the poet himself, no structures of
belief but the structures he makes for his own appeasement. The poet's
own act of faith is: I believe in the inventions of my own productive
imagination." "Where there is nothing, you put yourself and your
inventions, thereby raising desires and appeasing them. Life becomes a
rhetorical situation in which you are your own audience. History becomes mythology. . . . There are some poets whose consciousness is
historical. For these, tradition is a great drama of people and institutions, conflicts of values in their full temporal idiom. . . . But for Stevens the past is not only dead but deadly."[58] "Poets whose consciousness is historical," for whom "tradition is a great drama of people and
institutions" – here, of course, is Pound, though Donoghue does not
mention him in this context. His main text is Stevens's discussion, in
The Necessary Angel, of the futility of paying visits to historic shrines –
in this case the old Zeller house in Tulpehocken, Pennsylvania, once
inhabited by Lutheran refugees. "The vast mausoleum of human memory," Stevens comments, "is emptier than one had supposed. . . . there
could not be any effective diversion from the reality that time and
experience had created here, the desolation that penetrated one like
something final" (*NA,* p. 101). By contrast, an exhibition of illustrated
books from foreign countries, inspected shortly after the Tulpehocken
visit, excites the poet's imagination: "[It was] as if the barren reality
that I had just experienced had suddenly taken color, become alive"
(*NA,* p. 102). Donoghue remarks: "This is Stevens in one of his most
revealing aspects: he will entertain reality only when it has been refracted through the idiom of art, when the artist has certified it by
giving it the seal of his authority. This is the 'mythology of self' that
replaces history" (p. 194).

The mythology of self, the faith in the autonomy of the redemptive imagination, depends upon the ruthless elimination of the past, whether that past is that of the whole culture or merely one's own. Surely Stevens is the least "confessional" of poets. As Marie Borroff puts it: "Our veneration for the past is the object of Stevens' constant and endlessly resourceful attack. It is labelled 'history,' 'doctrine,' 'definitions,' 'the rotted names'; it is a garbage dump, a junk shop, a theatre beaten in by a tempest in which the audience continues to sit; it is the second-rate statuary on savings banks, the equestrian statues in public squares, the vested interests of the academies and the museums. To rid one's mind of it is 'freedom,' a redeeming 'ignorance,' 'salvation,' 'health.' "[59]

But the paradox is that Stevens's denial of the past as not only dead but deadly goes hand in hand with an inability to escape it. However much he may dislike the "barren reality" of old country houses, his literary and philosophical roots are, as everyone remarked, squarely in the Romantic tradition. Pound's case is precisely the opposite. I quote again from Denis Donoghue, this time from his comments at the Commemorative Pound Symposium held at Queens College, Belfast, in 1973: "In Canto 54 . . . Pound writes: 'history is a school book for princes'. . . . this is the central concern of the entire *Cantos*. . . . they are designed as a primer, a school-book for an ideal prince. . . . They are an attempt not to impose one man's will upon a reading of time but to enter into such intimate liaison with fact, with time, with history, with the luminous details which history offers, that the result is a rhythm, a profound sense of life which surely constitutes meaning." Donoghue now goes on to contrast Pound's respect for the given, for the form of the object, to Yeats's symbolist transformation of objects, and conludes: "Pound's . . . acknowledgement of history, his acknowlegement of other minds, his recognition that there have been other times and other places . . . isn't this what all the quotations, all the allusions to other cultures are doing in *The Cantos*? Are they not saying: there have been other times, other places, other people, other attempts to find significance and value in human life? I take these allusions in *The Cantos* partly as gestures toward different civilizations, but more fundamentally as Pound's assertion that we have not invented meaning."[60] *That we have not invented meaning* – here is the opposite pole from Stevens's strenuous effort to reimagine what he calls the First Idea. As opposed to the solitary and central consciousness of an expanded self in *Notes toward a Supreme Fiction*, we find in Canto LXXXI a galaxy of time frames that coexist: John Adams speaking to "his volatile friend Mr. Jefferson ('You the one, I the few')" exists on the same plane as George Santayana "arriving in the port of Boston" and with Basil Bunting telling tales of the village fiestas in the Canaries. *Dove sta memoria:* the prisoner in the cage at Pisa ("hot wind came from the marshes / and death-chill from the mountains") is *there,* as recording center ("thank Benin for this table ex packing box"), but he refuses to make distinctions between his present and the events, whether from the near or the mythological past, that impinge upon his consciousness. Stevens's "vast mausoleum of human memory" thus gives way to a shallow screen upon which any number of actions can unfold. Time, in other words, becomes space.

Here again *The Cantos* defy Romantic paradigms. As Guy Davenport observes: "The placing of events in time is a romantic act; the *tremendum* is in the distance. There are no dates in the myths; from when to when did Heracles stride the earth? In a century obsessed with time, with archeological dating, with the psychological recovery of time (Proust, Freud), Pound has written as if time were unreal, has, in fact, treated it as if it were space. . . . In Pound's spatial sense of time the past is here now; its invisibility is our blindness, not its absence."[61] Stevens, we might say, tries to obliterate time by rejecting history and myth (even the Christian myth) and equating consciousness with vision, which is the imagination's sanctity. Pound takes the opposite line: he treats all time and epochs as potential sources of wisdom to be tapped; "consciousness," in this case, is no more than the selection and synthesis of the input – a synthesis that, as critics often complain, often remains partial.[62] Stevens rejects the past as deadly but paradoxically dwells in it; Pound plays the role of historian but paradoxically treats the past as if it were here and now.

A similar opposition may be found in the poets' sense of geography. "For me," says Stevens, "life is an affair of places," but Stevens's locales, whether called Pascagoula or Montrachet-le-Jardin or Ceylon, are always shadow worlds, symbolic embodiments of the poet's creation of "so many selves, so many sensuous worlds" (*CP,* p. 326). Pound's geography is, by contrast, characterized by a painstaking exactitude. In an essay called "The *Cantos:* Towards a Pedestrian Reading," Donald Davie demonstrates that the best guide to such poems as "Provincia Deserta" and "Near Perigord" is a Carte Michelin No. 75; indeed, "the first requirement for a study of Pound is a set of maps (preferably ½ inch to the mile) of at any rate certain regions of France, Italy and England."[63] No one, to my knowledge, has made a similar case for, say, "An Ordinary Evening in New Haven"; no city map could tell us much about the ghostly contours of what Stevens calls "These houses, these difficult objects, dilapidate / Appearances of what appearances" (*CP,* p. 465). Poetry, for Stevens, must finally resist "the vulgate of experience," the pressure of reality. And presumably Michelin maps would merely add to that pressure.

V

Let me now return to my original questions: What do we mean when we talk of Modernism in poetry? And, more important, what are our present norms for the "great poem"?

To posit that ours is, in Harold Bloom's words, the Age of Stevens is to believe that, as he puts it, "Modernism in literature has not passed; rather it has been exposed as never having been there." The best twentieth-century poetry, in other words, carries on the great tradition of Romantic visionary humanism, a tradition Anglo-American to its roots, with a slight influx of French Symbolisme to add piquancy. Such poetry takes the lyric paradigm for granted; it answers to the demand for organic unity and symbolic structure, avoiding all contact with the language of ordinary prose and therefore with the prose discourses of the novel and of historical writing. Despite this emphasis on the poem as a special kind of discourse, as sacred text whose language is inherently different from, say, such texts as Stevens's own letters and diaries,[64] the Stevens text subordinates such traditional lyric features as meter and qualitative sound repetition to the articulation of complex and ambiguous meanings. In keeping with the Romantic model, the "I" of Stevens is a Solitary Singer; his voice, even at its most whimsical or ironic, is never less than serious about the truths for which it searches; the tone is meditative and subdued; the addressee is always the poet himself. For Stevens, "Poetry and materia poetica are interchangeable terms," and so the emphasis, both of the poet and his critics, is on the creation of the Supreme Fiction, the poet's evolving consciousness as it comes to terms with what Bloom calls the "three crossings" central to the Romantic "crisis-poem" – the loss of the creative gift (am I still a poet?), the loss of love (am I still capable of loving another beside myself?), and the loss of life itself (am I capable of resisting the death instinct?).[65] These are "crossings" that, according to Bloom as well as to Helen Vendler and other Stevensians, all intelligent and receptive human creatures experience. In this sense, poetry clearly *matters;* it teaches us "how to talk to ourselves."

Poundians, of course, also believe that poetry *matters,* but in a very different sense. They regard Modernism less as a continuation of Romanticism than as a very real rupture with it. "Keatsian," an honorific word for Bloom or Kermode or Hartman or Vendler, is, as we have seen in the case of Davie's essay on Stevens, a derogatory term.

Instead–and perhaps curiously–we meet in Pound criticism such words as "Augustan" and "Enlightenment." Thus Kenner compares Pound's Confucian sense of history, with its "reconciliation of a loving feeling for detail with a search for eternal, archetypal situations," to that of the Augustans,[66] and Davie argues that Pound's America is "the America of the Founding Fathers, Jefferson and John Adams. . . . specifically an Enlightenment product, a transplanting to American soil of the noblest values of that French eighteenth century which had also as a matter of historical record first introduced Europe to the experience of Confucian and pre-Confucian China."[67]

The point, in any case, is to bypass Romanticism, to get back to something *prior* in time even as one is MAKING IT NEW. Surely it is no coincidence that Pound scholars have so often been classicists–D. S. Carne-Ross, J. P. Sullivan, Guy Davenport–or trained in medieval studies like Eva Hesse and Christine Brooke-Rose, or in Augustan literature like Davie and Kenner in their different ways.[68] For all these critics, the Pound Era is the era when the norms of the Romantic crisis poem as of the Symbolist lyric were exploded, when poetry found that it could once again incorporate the seemingly alien discourses of prose without losing its identity. It is curious, in this regard, to compare Pound's prose to that of Stevens. From *Gaudier-Brzeska* (1916) to *Guide to Kulchur* (1938) and beyond, Pound's critical prose is closely allied to his poetry by its structural properties: collage, fragmentation, parataxis. Again, the letters of the later years adopt all the stylistic oddities of *The Cantos:* phonetic spelling, the insertion of foreign phrases, documentary evidence, puns and other jokes, the juxtaposition of disjunctive images. The Romantic and Symbolist distinction between literary and ordinary language is thus blurred: the rule is that anything goes as long as the poet knows, in Charles Olson's words, how to "keep it moving," how to make the poem an energy discharge, a field of action. The *how,* for Poundians, thus becomes more interesting than the *what:* if poetry teaches us how to talk to ourselves, it is not because it provides us with a vision of Reality but because its processes imitate the processes of the external world as we have come to know it.

The Pound critics do not, then, equate poetry with lyric; rather, they return to the Aristotelian definition of *poiesis* as *mimesis praxeos,* the imitation of an action. The eclectic nature of *The Cantos,* their capacity to assimilate all kinds of material and to incorporate many voices, makes more sense when we read Pound's text against, say, the *Satyricon* or *Le Neveu de Rameau* than when Pound's "poem including history" is compared to *The Prelude* or *Song of Myself.* Again, with respect to Pound's contemporaries, *The Cantos* are closer to the poetry of Apollinaire or the Merz pictures of Kurt Schwitters than they are to the poetry of Yeats or Frost or even Eliot. Yeats, we remember, was convinced that Pound had not got "all the wine into the bowl."[69]

Read synchronically, against the backdrop of the avant-garde arts of Europe in the period *entre deux guerres,* Pound's structures seem quintessentially modern. Read diachronically, against the paradigm of the Anglo-American lyric from Blake to Emerson to Emily Dickinson, Pound will seem, as he did to Stevens, "an eccentric person." A "Last Romantic" and a "First Modern" – William Carlos Williams, who was able to appreciate Stevens's "discipline" even as he admired Pound's experimentation and invention,[70] bridged the gap between the two by finding a third party to vilify. That party was, of course, T. S. Eliot, a bloke whose work both Pound and Stevens had been reading since its inception. But then no one today, whether we look to critics like Bloom or Kenner or Vendler or to poets like John Ashbery or James Merrill or Adrienne Rich or Allen Ginsberg, seems eager to call the first half of the twentieth century the Eliot Era. Perhaps this is the case because Eliot's poetry does not as fully pose the problem that came to obsess Modernism: whether poetry should be lyric or collage, meditation or encyclopedia, the still moment or the jagged fragment. It is, as Gregory Ulmer points out,[71] the larger aesthetic dichotomy at the heart of Modernism, the dichotomy between what Kandinsky called the "two poles" – the expressionist and the constructionist. Not until the sixties did the balance begin to tip in favor of the latter.

NOTES

1 Pound to Williams, 27 October 1955. Previously unpublished letter by Ezra Pound, copyright © 1982 by the Trustees of the Ezra Pound Literary Property Trust. Reprinted by permission of the Collection of American Literature, Beinecke Rare Book and Manuscript Library, Yale University. The obituary essay appeared in *Poetry,* 87, No. 4 (January 1956), 234–39.

2 *Letters of Wallace Stevens,* ed. Holly Stevens (New York, 1966), p. 565.

3 For an evenhanded account that is representative of the literary histories of the period, see David Perkins, *A History of Modern Poetry (from the 1890s to the High Modernist Mode)* (Cambridge, Mass., 1976). In this first of a projected two volumes, Perkins naturally gives Pound more space than he does Stevens, the volume ending with the early twenties, when Stevens's first book of poems, *Harmonium,* appeared. Even so, it is clear that Perkins takes Stevens to be one of the major figures.

For a listing and summary of the various essays by the New Critics on Pound and Stevens, see the bibliographical essays by John Espey (on

Pound) and Joseph N. Riddel (on Stevens), in *Sixteen Modern American Authors,* ed. Jackson R. Bryer (New York, 1973). Blackmur's essays are especially interesting: see "Masks of Ezra Pound" (1933), "An Adjunct to the Muses' Diadem, A Note on E.P." (1946), "Examples of Wallace Stevens" (1931), and "Wallace Stevens: An Abstraction Blooded" (review of *Notes toward a Supreme Fiction,* 1943), all collected in *Form & Value in Modern Poetry* (New York, 1957).

4   In *Forms of Discovery* (Denver, 1967), Winters criticized Pound's "associational" method but declared that "eccentric for eccentric, I would rather read the Pound of the early *Cantos* than the Spenser of *The Faerie Queene.*" As for Stevens, Winters argued (in *Primitivism and Decadence* [New York, 1937] and in *The Anatomy of Nonsense* [Norfolk, Conn., 1943]) that "Sunday Morning" is one of the great poems written in English, but that after "Sunday Morning" Stevens's style declined into obscurantism and the emotional confusions of Romantic irony. See Bryer, pp. 452, 543.

5   *The Pound Era* (Berkeley and Los Angeles, 1971), pp. 516–17, 554.

6   *A Map of Misreading* (New York, 1975), p. 28.

7   *Wallace Stevens: The Poems of Our Climate* (Ithaca and London, 1977), p. 152.

8   Lucy Beckett, *Wallace Stevens* (Cambridge, 1974), pp. 62–64.

9   Beckett, p. 64; italics mine.

10   "Toward Literary History," in *Beyond Formalism: Literary Essays 1958–1970* (New Haven and London, 1970), p. 358, and "Spectral Symbolism," in *The Fate of Reading and Other Essays* (Chicago and London, 1975), p. 59.

11   *On Extended Wings: Wallace Stevens' Longer Poems* (Cambridge, Mass., 1969), p. 314.

12   *Introspective Voyager: The Poetic Development of Wallace Stevens* (New York, 1972), p. vi.

13   *Poems of Our Climate,* p. 168.

14   The texts used are *The Collected Poems of Wallace Stevens* (New York, 1954), pp. 401–5, subsequently cited as *CP,* and *The Cantos of Ezra Pound* (New York, 1971), pp. 517–19.

15   *Wallace Stevens* (Edinburgh and London, 1967), pp. 117–19.

16   "*Notes toward a Supreme Fiction:* A Commentary," in *Wallace Stevens: A Collection of Critical Essays,* ed. Marie Borroff (Englewood Cliffs, N.J., 1963), p. 19.

17   "*Notes toward a Supreme Fiction,*" Borroff, p. 19.

18   *On Extended Wings,* p. 197.

19   *Poets of Reality: Six Twentieth-Century Writers* (1965; rpt. New York, 1969), p. 283. Such distrust of thematics has become more marked in Miller's more recent deconstructionist essays on Stevens. See, e.g., "Stevens' *Rock* and Criticism as Cure," *Georgia Review,* 30 (1976), 330–48.

20   *On Extended Wings,* p. 205.

21   "Apollo's Harsher Songs" (1979), in her *Part of Nature, Part of Us: Modern American Poets* (Cambridge, Mass., 1980), pp. 41–42.

22   *The Necessary Angel: Essays on Reality and the Imagination* (1951; rpt. New York, 1965), p. 40, subsequently cited as *NA*.

23   *ABC of Reading* (1934; rpt. New York, 1960), p. 46, subsequently cited as *ABC*.

24   *Adagia,* in *Opus Posthumous* (New York, 1957), p. 169, subsequently cited as *OP*.

25   *Letters of Wallace Stevens,* p. 544.

26   *A Homemade World* (New York, 1975), p. 55.

27   In *Wallace Stevens: The Making of Harmonium* (Princeton, 1967), Buttel writes: "Stevens' style arises out of his deeply felt need to discover valid ideas of order in an age of cultural change and confusion." He is the "direct descendant of the Romantic poets in his unceasing exploration of the relationship between the inner, subjective human point of view, and outer, objective reality" (p. x). This line of reasoning is carried on by Adelaide Kirby Morris in *Wallace Stevens: Imagination and Faith* (Princeton, 1974). See also *Wallace Stevens: A Celebration,* ed. Frank Doggett and Robert Buttel (Princeton, 1980), esp. Frank Kermode, "Dwelling Poetically in Connecticut," and Roy Harvey Pearce, "Toward Decreation: Stevens and the Theory of Poetry."

28   "The Music of a Lost Dynasty: Pound in the Classroom," *Boston University Journal,* 21 (Winter 1973), 26–27.

29   "Music of a Lost Dynasty," pp. 38–39; italics are Carne-Ross's.

30   "Persephone's Ezra," in *New Approaches to Ezra Pound,* ed. Eva Hesse (Berkeley and Los Angeles, 1969), pp. 157, 161.

31   *Ezra Pound: Poet as Sculptor* (New York, 1964), pp. 176–77, 181.

32   See *The Pound Era,* pp. 133, 136.

33   *The Poetry of Ezra Pound* (New York, 1951), p. 105.

34   See George Kearns, *Guide to Ezra Pound's Selected Cantos* (New Brunswick, N.J., 1980), p. 168.

35   *Paideuma,* 6, No. 1 (Spring 1977), 3–4.

36   Introd., *New Approaches,* p. 23; cf. Albert Cook, "Rhythm and Person in *The Cantos,*" in *New Approaches,* pp. 349–64.

37   *Guide to Ezra Pound's Selected Cantos,* p. 161.

38   "Wisdom Past Metaphor: Another View of Pound, Fenollosa, and Objective Verse," *Paideuma,* 5, No. 1 (Spring 1976), 21–22. Cf. Bloom's dismissal of the "Pound-Williams machine made out of words," in "The New Transcendentalism: The Visionary Strain in Merwin, Ashbery, and Ammons," *Figures of Capable Imagination* (New York, 1976), p. 145.

39   Ezra Pound, "A Retrospect," in *The Literary Essays of Ezra Pound,* ed. T. S. Eliot (London, 1954), p. 3, subsequently cited as *LE*.

40   See esp. Davie, *Ezra Pound: Poet as Sculptor,* pp. 41–46, 60–63, and *Pound* (London, 1975), ch. 5, "Rhythm in the Cantos"; D. S. Carne-Ross, "New Metres for Old: A Note on Pound's Metric," *Arion,* 6, No. 2 (Summer 1967), 216–32; James A. Powell, "The Light of Vers Libre," *Paideuma,* 8, No. 1 (Spring 1979), 3–34; Sally M. Gall, "Pound and the Modern Melic

Tradition: Towards a Demystification of 'Absolute Rhythm,' " *Paideuma*, 8, No. 1 (Spring 1979), 35–47.

41   *On Extended Wings*, pp. 9–10.

42   See, e.g., Maria Corti, *An Introduction to Literary Semiotics*, tr. Margherita Bogat and Allen Mandelbaum (Bloomington and London, 1978), pp. 115–43.

43   *A ZBC of Ezra Pound* (London, 1971), p. 177.

44   Davie, *Pound*, p. 43.

45   *Gaudier-Brzeska, A Memoir* (1916; rpt. New York, 1970), p. 92.

46   *Lyric Time: Dickinson and the Limits of Genre* (Baltimore and London, 1979), p. 23.

47   *Anatomy of Criticism* (Princeton, 1957), p. 61.

48   See esp. David Antin, "Some Questions about Modernism," *Occident*, 8 (Spring 1974), 19–21. Antin writes: "The reason the collage elements are more or less free is that the strategy of collage involves suppression of the ordering signs that would specify the 'stronger logical relations' among the presented elements. By 'stronger logical relations' I mean relations of implication, entailment, negation, subordination and so on" (p. 21).

49   *The Tale of the Tribe: Pound and the Modern Verse Epic* (Princeton and London, 1980), p. 40.

50   *Wallace Stevens*, p. 118.

51   *On Extended Wings*, pp. 204–5.

52   *The Pound Era*, p. 185.

53   *The Poetics of Indeterminacy: Rimbaud to Cage* (Princeton, 1981), p. 197.

54   *Romantic Image* (New York, 1957), pp. 153, 136.

55   "Essential Gaudiness: The Poems of Wallace Stevens," *The Twentieth Century*, 153 (June 1953), 458–59; rpt. in *The Poet in the Imaginary Museum: Essays of Two Decades*, ed. Barry Alpert (Manchester, 1977), pp. 12–14. Davie's 1977 Postscript is illuminating: "This reads oddly now, because it was addressed to a public that thought 'the modern,' whatever else it was, was 'unromantic.' For many years now on the contrary American critics like Harold Bloom have contended that the (American) 'modern' is continuous with the (American, i.e. Emersonian) 'romantic'; and so they find Stevens much less in need of excuses than for instance Eliot. Accordingly I should now probably be more captious about Stevens than I was when I wrote this" (p. 17).

56   *A Homemade World*, pp. 74–75.

57   Donoghue has written frequently on Stevens, from "Wallace Stevens and the Abstract," *Studies*, 49 (1969), 389–406, to *The Sovereign Ghost* (Berkeley and Los Angeles, 1976). In the latter, Donoghue expounds a theory of the poetic imagination that draws heavily on Stevens and, behind Stevens, on Coleridge.

58   *Connoisseurs of Chaos: Ideas of Order in Modern American Poetry* (New York, 1965), pp. 191, 193–94.

59   "Wallace Stevens: The World and the Poet," in *Wallace Stevens: Critical Essays*, ed. Borroff, p. 3.

60 Cited by G. Singh in "Ezra Pound: A Commemorative Symposium," *Paideuma*, 3, No. 2 (Fall 1974), 158–61.

61 "Persephone's Ezra," pp. 156–57.

62 In *The Tale of the Tribe*, Michael A. Bernstein makes a strong case for the difficulty Pound had in reconciling two codes, "the historically analytic and explanatory elements (the 'prose traditions' of the great novels recaptured for verse) and the mythological intuitive insights, the religious revelations of universal truths (traditionally the rightful domain of verse). If either code begins to displace the other, the poem as a whole risks fragmentation or intellectual incoherence" (p. 24). The contrary position is argued very persuasively in Jean-Michel Rabaté's recent Lacanian essay, "Pound's Art of Naming: Between Reference and Reverence" *South Atlantic Quarterly*, 83 (Winter 1984).

63 *The Poet in the Imaginary Museum*, p. 239. The essay first appeared in *Paideuma*, 1, No. 1 (Spring-Summer 1972), 55–62.

64 It is illuminating to compare Stevens's letters and diaries to his poems; the former are just as straightforward and expository as the latter are self-reflexive and ambiguous. Moreover, Stevens's endless, patient explications of his poems testify to his consuming interest in interpretation. He wants his reader to understand the meaning *behind* the words on the page.

65 *Poems of Our Climate*, pp. 375–406.

66 *The Pound Era*, p. 434.

67 *Ezra Pound: Poet as Sculptor*, p. 72.

68 Denis Donoghue, in most respects the proponent of the Stevensian "august imagination," is also able to find value in that "school-book for Princes," *The Cantos*. Perhaps – and this is a point to ponder long and hard – the catholicity of taste that allows Donoghue to appreciate both Stevens and Pound represents a critical position less firmly articulated and therefore finally less authoritative than that of a Harold Bloom or a Hugh Kenner.

69 Introd., *The Oxford Book of Modern Verse, 1892–1935*, chosen by W. B. Yeats (1936; rpt. Oxford, 1966), p. xxvi.

70 See Williams, "Wallace Stevens," *Poetry*, 87, No. 4 (January 1956), 234–39.

71 "Of a Parodic Tone Recently Adopted in Criticism," *New Literary History*, 13 (Spring 1982), 552.

APPENDIX

Wallace Stevens, *Notes toward a Supreme Fiction* Part III: *It Must Give Pleasure*

v

We drank Meursault, ate Lobster Bombay with mango
Chutney. Then the Canon Aspirin declaimed

Of his sister, in what sensible ecstasy

She lived in her house. She had two daughters, one
Of four, and one of seven, whom she dressed
The way a painter of pauvred colors paints.

But still she painted them appropriate to
Their poverty, a gray-blue yellowed out
With ribbon, a rigid statement of them, white,

With Sunday pearls, her widow's gayety.
She hid them under simple names. She held
Them closelier to her by rejecting dreams.

The words they spoke were voices that she heard.
She looked at them and saw them as they were
And what she felt fought off the barest phrase.

The Canon Aspirin, having said these things,
Reflected, humming an outline of a fugue
Of praise, a conjugation done by choirs.

Yet when her children slept, his sister herself
Demanded of sleep, in the excitements of silence
Only the unmuddled self of sleep for them.

vi

When at long midnight the Canon came to sleep
And normal things had yawned themselves away,
The nothingness was a nakedness, a point,

Beyond which fact could not progress as fact.
Thereon the learning of the man conceived
Once more night's pale illuminations, gold

Beneath, far underneath, the surface of
His eye and audible in the mountain of
His ear, the very material of his mind.

So that he was the ascending wings he saw
And moved on them in orbits' outer stars
Descending to the children's bed, on which

They lay. Forth then with huge pathetic force
Straight to the utmost crown of night he flew.
The nothingness was a nakedness, a point

Beyond which thought could not progress as thought.
He had to choose. But it was not a choice
Between excluding things. It was not a choice

Between, but of. He chose to include things
That in each other are included, the whole,
The complicate, the amassing harmony.

vii

He imposes orders as he thinks of them,
As the fox and snake do. It is a brave affair.
Next he builds capitols and in their corridors,

Whiter than wax, sonorous, fame as it is,
He establishes statues of reasonable men,
Who surpassed the most literate owl, the most erudite

Of elephants. But to impose is not
To discover. To discover an order as of
A season, to discover summer and know it,

To discover winter and know it well, to find,
Not to impose, not to have reasoned at all,
Out of nothing to have come on major weather,

It is possible, possible, possible. It must
Be possible. It must be that in time
The real will from its crude compoundings come,

Seeming, at first, a beast disgorged, unlike,
Warmed by a desperate milk. To find the real,
To be stripped of every fiction except one,

The fiction of an absolute – Angel,
Be silent in your luminous cloud and hear
The luminous melody of proper sound.

viii

What am I to believe? If the angel in his cloud,
Serenely gazing at the violent abyss,
Plucks on his strings to pluck abysmal glory,

Leaps downward through evening's revelations, and
On his spredden wings, needs nothing but deep space,
Forgets the gold centre, the golden destiny,

Grows warm in the motionless motion of his flight,
Am I that imagine this angel less satisfied?
Are the wings his, the lapis-haunted air?

Is it he or is it I that experience this?
Is it I then that keep saying there is an hour
Filled with expressible bliss, in which I have

No need, am happy, forget need's golden hand,
Am satisfied without solacing majesty,
And if there is an hour there is a day,

There is a month, a year, there is a time
In which majesty is a mirror of the self:
I have not but I am and as I am, I am.

These external regions, what do we fill them with
Except reflections, the escapades of death,
Cinderella fulfilling herself beneath the roof?

Ezra Pound, From Canto LXXXI

Zeus lies in Ceres' bosom
    Taishan is attended of loves
                under Cythera, before sunrise
        and he said: "Hay aquí mucho catolicismo – (sounded
                            catolithismo)
      y muy poco reliHion"
and he said: "Yo creo que los reyes desaparecen"
(Kings will, I think, disappear)
That was Padre José Elizondo
              in 1906 and in 1917
or about 1917
      and Dolores said: "Come pan, niño," eat bread,
                        me lad
Sargent had painted her
        before he descended
(i.e. if he descended
      but in those days he did thumb sketches,
impressions of the Velázquez in the Museo del Prado
and books cost a peseta,
        brass candlesticks in proportion,
hot wind came from the marshes
    and death-chill from the mountains.

And later Bowers wrote: "but such hatred,
    I had never conceived such"
and the London reds wouldn't show up his friends
                (i.e. friends of Franco
working in London) and in Alcázar
forty years gone, they said: go back to the station to eat
you can sleep here for a peseta"
         goat bells tinkled all night
           and the hostess grinned: Eso es luto, *haw!*
mi marido es muerto
         (it is mourning, my husband is dead)
when she gave me paper to write on
with a black border half an inch or more deep,
      say 5/8ths, of the locanda
"We call *all* foreigners frenchies"
and the egg broke in Cabranez' pocket,
          thus making history. Basil says
they beat drums for three days
till all the drumheads were busted
        (simple village fiesta)
and as for his life in the Canaries . . .
Possum observed that the local portagoose folk dance
was danced by the same dancers in divers localities
        in political welcome . . .
the technique of demonstration
         Cole studied that (not G. D. H., Horace)
"You will find" said old André Spire,
that every man on that board (Crédit Agricole)
has a brother-in-law
           "You the one, I the few"
         said John Adams
speaking of fears in the abstract
    to his volatile friend Mr Jefferson.
(To break the pentameter, that was the first heave)
or as Jo Bard says: they never speak to each other,
if it is baker and concierge visibly
        it is La Rouchefoucauld and de Maintenon
                      audibly.
"Te cavero le budella"
        "La corata a te"
In less than a geological epoch
        said Henry Mencken

"Some cook, some do not cook
   some things cannot be altered"
Ἰυγξ. . . . 'εμὸν ποτί δβμα τὸν 'άνδρα
What counts is the cultural level,
    thank Benin for this table ex packing box
      "doan yu tell no one I made it"
         from a mask fine as any in Frankfurt
"It'll get you offn th' groun"
        Light as the branch of Kuanon
And at first disappointed with shoddy
the bare ram-shackle quais, but then saw the
high buggy wheels
      and was reconciled,
George Santayana arriving in the port of Boston
and kept to the end of his life that faint *thethear*
of the Spaniard
      as a grace quasi imperceptible
as did Muss the *v* for *u* of Romagna
and said the grief was a full act
    repeated for each new condoleress
working up to a climax.
and George Horace said he wd/"get Beveridge" (Senator)
Beveridge wouldn't talk and he wouldn't write for the
   papers
but George got him by campin' in his hotel
and assailin' him at lunch breakfast an' dinner
     three articles
and my ole man went on hoein'·corn
    while George was a-tellin' him,
come across a vacant lot
     where you'd occasionally see a wild rabbit
or mebbe only a loose one
  AOI!
   a leaf in the current
       at my grates no Althea

2 The portrait of the artist as collage-text: Pound's *Gaudier-Brzeska* and the "italic" texts of John Cage

Pound's "memoir" of the sculptor Henri Gaudier-Brzeska, "MORT POUR LA PATRIE . . . after months of fighting and two promotions for gallantry . . . in a charge at Neuville St. Vaast on June 5, 1915" at the age of twenty-three,[1] was published in 1916 by Bodley Head in London in a limited edition containing thirty-eight plates and bearing Gaudier's Vorticist emblem on the cover (Figure 2.1). It did not have a good press. The reviewer for the *New York Times* complained:

> Mr. Pound diminishes the value of his memoir by including a number of his own pronouncements on the subject of sculpture and of art in general. There is indeed too much Pound in the book and too little Gaudier-Brzeska.[2]

More recently, Pound scholars have tended to see it the other way around: too little Pound, except in the Vorticist manifestos that begin with Chapter XI, and too much Gaudier: too many of the sculptor's own writings – manifestos, art reviews, letters from the front – as well as tributes by fellow artists, personal vignettes, and biographical accounts. "Pound's most explicit attempt to distinguish his poetry, which he calls 'imagiste,' from symboliste poetry," says Donald Davie, "is to be found in what is unfortunately the most incoherent though also one of the most important of his prose works."[3]

But the "incoherence" of *Gaudier-Brzeska* is not without motivation; indeed, the seemingly random form of Pound's memoir-manifesto can be related to *The Cantos,* whose structural principles it oddly anticipates. Pound himself provides us with some helpful hints on how to read his text when he remarks, right at the start, "I am not particularly anxious to make this 'my book' about Gaudier-Brzeska" (GB, 18), and again, "I am writing it very much as I should have written it if he had

33

Figure 2.1. Gaudier-Brzeska, *Charm,* 1914. Green stone. Six casts in bronze. 4 by 3½ in. Courtesy of Mary de Rachewiltz.

lived. . . . For I should in any case have written some sort of book upon vorticism, and in that book he would have filled certain chapters" (GB, 19). And he warns the reader that the discussion of Gaudier's art in relation to his own Vorticist poetic will "entail a certain formal and almost dreary documentation at the very outset" (GB, 20).

Documentation is a key word here. For *Gaudier-Brzeska,* I shall argue in this essay, is best understood in the context of the "documentary" collages, Futurist as well as Cubist, that were its exact contemporaries. The principle of construction in collage or *assemblage,* as it is now more broadly called,[4] is that of *juxtaposition,* the "setting of one thing beside the other without connective."[5] From the first *papiers-collés* of Braque and Picasso in 1912 down to the present, collage juxtaposes objects, object fragments, and materials drawn from disparate contexts, a process that inevitably alters their individual appearance and signification. In the artworks of the sixties – say, in Robert Rauschenberg's "flatbed" paintings or in John Cage's "italic" texts, which I shall discuss later, assemblage has been reinvented, the Cubist transformation of collage elements now giving way to simple transfer in that the object calls attention to itself as being unabashedly material (wood, cloth, newspaper, etc.). In such collage, images, to quote Leo Steinberg, "each in itself illusionistic – keep interfering with one another" on a flat documentary surface or aerial map, a map that stands, in Steinberg's words, "for the mind itself . . . as running transformer of the external world, constantly ingesting incoming unprocessed data to be mapped in an overcharged field."[6]

This last sentence recalls Pound's famous definition of the "VORTEX" as "a radiant node or cluster . . . from which, and through which, and into which, ideas are constantly rushing" (GB, 92). And indeed the Vortex must be understood, so Hugh Kenner tells us, as a "self-interfering pattern."[7] But this is not to say that the form of Pound's book on Gaudier resembles the so-called Vorticist form of Gaudier's sculptures discussed in its pages. To understand the radical decentering characteristic of Poundian collage, I want to begin by distinguishing the mode of his Vorticist memoir-manifesto from the painting and sculpture with which it is usually associated.

II

What was the peculiar attraction Gaudier's art held for Pound? In his 1914 essay "Vorticism," reprinted in *Gaudier-Brzeska,* Pound remarks: "We are all futurists to the extent of believing with Guillaume Appollonaire [*sic*] that 'On ne peut pas porter *partout* avec soi le cadavre de son père' " (GB, 82). "Le cadavre de son père," was, in Pound's case, the Symbolism he inherited from Yeats and the Pre-Raphaelites, which he equates in *Gaudier-Brzeska* with "mushy technique" (85), "images as ornaments" (88), and "*an ascribed or intended meaning*" (86). As such, this "cadavre" corresponds neatly to Gaudier's early allegiance to Rodin.[8] "The Rodin admixture," says Pound, "[Gaudier] had purged from his system when he quit doing representative busts of Frank Harris and Col. Smithers" (GB, 79). This is rather wishful thinking: *The Dancer* of 1913 (Figure 2.2) is a recognizably Rodinesque study of "tran-

Figure 2.2. Gaudier-Brzeska, *The Dancer,* 1913. Plaster. Seven bronze casts. 31 by 7¼ in. Courtesy of the Tate Gallery, London.

Figure 2.3. Gaudier-Brzeska, *Stags,* 1914. Veined alabaster. 13 ¾ in. Courtesy of The Art Institute of Chicago.

sition" or potential movement, and even the semi-abstract *Stags* of 1914 (Figure 2.3) looks curiously like *The Burghers of Calais* (Figure 2.4).

But from Pound's perspective, what mattered was that Gaudier was turning away from mimetic art, a turn made much clearer in the sculptor's theory, as spelled out in his two Vortex pieces for *BLAST,* than in his practice. Indeed, their statements of aesthetic correspond so closely that one wonders whether Gaudier wasn't writing, at least in part, to please the poet who had become both friend and patron. Thus Gaudier's rejection of representational conventions in art is stated aggressively as follows: "I SHALL DERIVE MY EMOTIONS SOLELY FROM THE ARRANGEMENT OF SURFACES, I shall present my emotions by the ARRANGEMENT OF MY SUR-FACES, THE PLANES AND LINES BY WHICH THEY ARE DEFINED" (GB, 28). In this context, even a Mauser rifle becomes, so Gaudier insists, the occasion for an abstract carving; he makes of the butt end "A VERY SIMPLE COMPOSITION OF LINES AND PLANES." These formulations were made in

Figure 2.4. Auguste Rodin, *The Burghers of Calais,* 1884–1886. Bronze, cast no. 10. 82½ by 93½ by 70¾ in. Courtesy of Norton Simon Art Foundation, Norton Simon, Inc. Museum of Art, Pasadena.

the trenches in the fall of 1914; they follow closely Pound's own Vorticist credo, represented the preceding spring at the Rebel Art Centre in Ormond Street in a lecture that Gaudier attended: "It is no more ridiculous that a person should receive or convey an emotion by means of an arrangement of shapes, or planes, or colours, than that they should receive or convey such emotion by an arrangement of musical notes" (GB, 81). Pound, in turn, follows Gaudier when he rejects, again and again, the "Symbolist" habit of "defin[ing] things in terms of something else" (GB, 117) and praises those works of ancient art that, unlike the "caressable" work of the Greeks, "depend upon an arrangement of forms" (GB, 97). "If I were a painter," he exclaims, ". . . I might found a new school . . . of 'non-representative' painting, a painting that would speak only by arrangements in colour" (GB, 87). In its advocacy of such "non-representative" art, Gaudier's "Vortex," so Pound believes, "will be undoubtedly the first textbook of sculpture in many academies before our generation has passed from this earth" (GB, 107).

Pound's anti-Symbolist stance, both in *Gaudier-Brzeska* and else-where, has been discussed often enough,[9] and I don't wish to labor the point here. There have also been excellent discussions – most notably by William Wees, Richard Cork, Timothy Materer, and Douglas Mes-serli – of the slipperiness of the term "Vorticism" and its complicated derivation and differentiation from the Futurism of Marinetti and the Cubism of Picasso.[10] It is always helpful to remember that the manifes-tos appearing in the first issue of *BLAST* (June 1914) preceded the naming of the movement. On 1 April of that year Pound wrote to Joyce: "Lewis starting a new Futurist, Cubist, Imagiste Quarterly . . . it is mostly a painter's magazine with me to do the poems."[11] And the advertisements of 1 April and 15 April in *The Egoist,* which promise discussions of "Cubism, Futurism, Imagisme and All Vital Forms of Modern Art," say nothing of a Vorticist movement.[12] Perhaps Pound explains the naming of the movement most sensibly when he remarks in *Gaudier-Brzeska* that Vorticism came into being "when we wished a designation that would be equally applicable to a certain basis for all the arts. Obviously you cannot have 'cubist' poetry or 'imagiste' painting" (GB, 81). Or, as Hugh Kenner puts it succinctly, "Vorticism was the English, not the French or the Russian, version of abstract art."[13]

But what about the meaning of *Vortex?* Here designation becomes more precise and the differences between Pound and Gaudier, like those between Pound and Lewis, can be located. Here is the definition in the NED: 1.a. "In older theories of the universe (esp. that of Descartes), a supposed rotary movement of cosmic matter round a centre or axis, regarded as accounting for the origin or phenomena of the terrestrial and other systems"; and l.c. "In modern scientific use: A rapid move-ment of particles of matter round an axis; a whirl of atoms, fluid, or vapour." The word *vortex* turns up in Pound's writing as early as 1908 in the poem "Plotinus":

> As one that would draw thru the node of things,
> Back sweeping to the vortex of the cone. . . .
>
> Obliviate of cycles' wanderings
> I was an atom on creation's throne. . . .[14]

Timothy Materer comments:

> The poem draws on Plotinus' description of the soul's inher-ently circular motion "about the source of its own existence." The word *vortex,* however, comes not from Plotinus but from the pre-Socratic doctrine that the four elements were formed as they rotated in a vortex or *dine.* From Allen Upward's *New World* (1908), Pound learned that the double vortex of a water-

> spout expresses "the true beat of strength, the first beat . . .
> which we feel in all things that come within our measure, in
> ourselves, and in our starry world."[15]

At the heart of all these formulations, we find the same paradox: the circulation occurs around a still center; energy is arrested at what Gaudier calls "THE POINT ONE AND INDIVISIBLE" (GB, 22). It is in this sense, as a system of energies drawing in whatever comes near, that Pound and his friends referred to the London Vortex, the Vortex Lewis, and so on. Thus Pound in London writes to William Carlos Williams in Rutherford, New Jersey: "You may get something slogging away by yourself that you would miss in The Vortex."[16]

But of course, given the basic polarity of motion and rest, whirlpool and center, one may choose to emphasize one or the other. For Lewis, the stress is always on centering, on the process whereby energy is transformed into stasis:

> We think at once of a whirlpool. At the heart of the whirlpool
> is a great silent place where all energy is concentrated. And
> there, at the point of concentration, is the Vorticist.[17]

Or, as he puts it more polemically in *BLAST* 1:

> The Vorticist is at his maximum point of energy when
>   stillest.
> The Vorticist is not the Slave of Commotion, but its Master.
> The Vorticist does not suck up to Life.
> He lets Life know its place in a Vorticist Universe![18]

These are not aphorisms one is likely to meet in *Gaudier-Brzeska*. For although Pound defines the vortex as "the point of maximum energy" (GB, 81), he is much less interested in the "point" or axis of the whirlpool than in its energy, its rhythmic vitality. Indeed, the original typescript of "Plotinus" notes: "The 'cone' is I presume the "Vritta' whirl-pool, vortex-ring of the Yogi's cosmogony," a designation, so Eva Hesse tells us, roughly translatable as "mental activity," "eddy of consciousness," or, as Pound was to put it in a letter to John Quinn of 10 March 1916, "every kind of whirlwind force and emotion."[19]

Vortex as whirlwind, as "radiant node or cluster . . . from which, and through which, and into which, ideas are constantly rushing" (GB, 92) – the formulation is in fact much closer to Italian Futurist doctrine than to the mechanist aesthetic that governs Lewis' static and stylized hard-edged abstractions (see Figure 2.5). In 1913, Giacomo Balla made a series of charcoal drawings called *Vortice,* and Carlo Carrà published

Figure 2.5. Wyndham Lewis, *Timon of Athens,* plate 100, 1913. Offset lithograph. Courtesy of the Herbert F. Johnson Museum, Cornell University.

his manifesto "The Painting of Sounds, Noises and Smells," which contains the following passage:

> This bubbling and whirling of forms and light, composed of sounds, noises and smells has been partly achieved by me in my *Anarchical Funeral* and in my *Jolts of a Taxi-cab* by Boccioni in *States of Mind* and *Forces of a Street* by Russolo in *Revolt* and Severini in *Bang Bang,* paintings which were violently discussed at our first Paris Exhibition in 1912. This kind of bubbling over requires a great emotive effort, even delirium, on the part of the artist, who in order to achieve a *vortex,* must be a *vortex of sensation* himself, a *pictorial force* and not a cold multiple intellect.[20]

Here, and in related Futurist documents, are the immediate sources of Pound's Vortex. Indeed, his frequent testy remarks about the Futurists (in Chapter XI of *Gaudier-Brzeska* he calls Futurism "a sort of accelerated impressionism") must be understood for what they were: defensive gestures appropriate for the Vorticist fervor on the eve of the Great War, and largely motivated by Pound's close association with Lewis, whose break with Marinetti in 1913 was both ideological and irreparable.[21] After the war when he was living in Italy, Pound acknowledged his debt much more openly:

> Marinetti and Futurism gave the whole of European Literature a great push forward. The movement that Eliot, Joyce, I myself and others began in London, would not have taken place without futurism.[22]

It is in this context that we must consider Pound's sometimes misleading account of Gaudier's move toward "Vorticist" abstraction. Here is his commentary on one of Gaudier's first proto-Cubist compositions, the *Red Stone Dancer* of 1914 (Figure 2.6):

> This . . . is almost a thesis of [Gaudier's] ideas upon the use of pure form. We have the triangle and circle, asserted, *labled* [*sic*] almost, upon the face and right breast. Into these so-called "abstractions" life flows, the circle moves and elongates into the oval, it increases and takes volume in the sphere or hemisphere of the breast. The triangle moves toward organism it becomes a spherical triangle (the central life-form common to both Brzeska and Lewis). These two developed motifs work as themes in a fugue. We have the whole series of spherical triangles, as in the arm over the head, all combining and culminating in the great

Figure 2.6. Gaudier-Brzeska, *Red Stone Dancer*, 1914. Red Mansfield stone. One bronze cast. 17 by 9 in. Courtesy of the Tate Gallery, London.

43

sweep of the back of the shoulders, as fine as any surface in all sculpture. The "abstract" or mathematical bareness of the triangle and circle are fully incarnate, made flesh, full of vitality and of energy. The whole form-series ends, passes into stasis with the circular base or platform.   (GB, 137–38)

Here, in his role of art critic, Pound does apply the classic Vorticist formula: energy arrested in stasis, the parts resolved into a coherent whole. In his catalogue of Gaudier's drawings and sculpture, written half a century later (1965), Mervyn Levy provides a watered-down version of Pound's critique:

The exposition of movement as a dynamic but subtly arrested phase of strength, arising from the vortex of an inward energy, is the quintessence of the artist's application of the Vorticist idea. . . . It is the *arresting* of the circular ripple of energy (motion) spreading outward from the core of an activity which distinguishes the objectives of Vorticism from those of Futurism. The arresting of this energy is the single image.[23]

When we compare *Red Stone Dancer* to sculptures of the same period by, say, Brancusi or Arp, Levy's enthusiasm, like Pound's own, may strike us as somewhat excessive. It is debatable, for example, whether the cubist forms (the triangle of the face and circle of the breast) are fully integrated into the form of the whole, or whether they are, to use Pound's own word, "labeled" or superimposed on what is basically a stylized nude figure carved in the African manner. But the point is that, whether or not Gaudier succeeds in this instance, his intent, as Pound and Levy both see, is to present the arresting of energy in "the single image." Whether Pound's own verbal structures are similarly dependent upon a generative ideational center is another matter.

A sculpture that succeeds more fully in fusing organic form and geometrical stylization is *Birds Erect* of 1914 (Figure 2.7). Pound calls this one of Gaudier's "most important pieces" and remarks that "The representative element is very slight" (GB, 130). This is quite so: the freestanding forms made of limestone cannot be clearly identified as birds, the main referential clue being their "erect" quality, recalling, so says Richard Cork, "a group of birds thrusting out of a nest in readiness for the arrival of food."[24] Gaudier's semi-abstract shapes are perched on top of a tall, uneven, sloping base, shaped into four main planes, the asymmetry acting to punctuate the continuous movement of the figures. Indeed, so crowded are the forms that they seem to be on the verge of falling over the edge of the "ramp." The instability of

Figure 2.7. Gaudier-Brzeska, *Birds Erect*, 1914. Limestone. 26⅜ by 10¼ by 12⅜ in. Collection, The Museum of Modern Art, New York. Gift of Mrs. W. Murray Crane.

planes thus creates tension; each swaying upright is, moreover, broken by the incision of diagonal and zigzag planes. The effect is that Gaudier's forms, with their broken surfaces, seem to collide with their neighbors or else to contradict their own directional movement.[25]

Birds Erect, with its conflicting planes and strong diagonals, is probably Gaudier's most thorough-going experiment in non-representational art. "As a composition of masses," Pound declares, "I do not think I have seen any modern sculpture to match it" (GB, 130). But even here, we should note, Gaudier is by no means creating purely abstract forms. His sculptor friend Horace Brodsky insisted that the initial inspiration for the sculpture came from some cactus plants Gaudier had in his studio.[26] The forms also recall, as Timothy Materer notes and as the title suggests, the erect phallus.[27] Such reference to nature sets Gaudier apart from Wyndham Lewis and explains why the latter was to remark, many years later, "I must confess that even Gaudier seemed a little too naturalistic and not starkly XX-century enough."[28]

But if *Birds Erect* has little in common with Lewis' own fantastic machine forms, neither does its fusion of geometric Cubism and bimorphic forms – a fusion called *Vitalist* by the art historian Jack Burnham, who relates Gaudier to Moore and Brancusi[29] – have any meaningful analogue in Pound's verbal structures, in which individual items do not (and are not meant to) build up to such concentricity. The difference will become clearer if we look at another sculpture, made in the same year as Gaudier's *Birds Erect:* Picasso's painted lead relief called *Violin* (Figure 2.8).

Here the fragments of descriptive language fail to integrate the separate planes of the construction into a single coherent object. As Rosalind Krauss puts it in her important study of the problematic of modern sculpture:

> Picasso constructs his reliefs from two types of perceptual fact which interlock across the surface of the work. The first of these is a combination of planes and shadow-filled gaps between planes. Through this treatment . . . the shape of the object . . . is utterly dispersed. And what we encounter instead is something like a corrugated plane – a surface that has become dense with the cues of tactile experience: shadow and texture. Interwoven through this array of tactile cues is a second visual element, which one might characterize as decorative pieces drawn from a language of description. For the musical instruments and still-life objects from which Picasso's reliefs are built carry on their surface the fragments of a pictorial language.[30]

In the case of *Violin,* these fragments of descriptive language include the mesh of lines decorating four of the planes, and the two shallow troughs on either side of the work's center, one slightly smaller and lower than the other. In two-dimensional representation, crosshatching

Figure 2.8. Picasso, *Violin*, 1914. Painted lead. 38 by 26¼ in. Estate of the artist.

(here the characteristic of the mesh) is used to shade or model surfaces, giving them the illusion of volume. Similarly, the troughs, representing the sound holes of the real instrument, are elements taken over from the language of painting to indicate depth on what is really a flat surface. But since *Violin* is already three-dimensional, both these pictorial items have what Krauss calls a "functional redundancy"; they act as "ref- ugee[s] from the descriptive language of another medium" (48). And she concludes:

> Picasso's reliefs do not present a moment of organization that lies *beyond* the surface of the object – an ideational center which we can intellectually occupy to give the object a significance that transcends our perception of it. He insists that there is a logic immanent *in* that surface and that conception arises with experience rather than prior to or apart from it.   (48)

Such "logic immanent *in* the surface" is, I think, also Pound's logic, and his move beyond the Vorticist concept of an energy arrested and centered can be taken as emblematic of his ability to grow beyond the more limited achievements of a Gaudier or a Lewis. Let us recall, in this connection, Lewis' sharp criticism of Picasso's collages of 1911–1913, which he saw in London. "[Picasso]," he declared, "has become a miniature naturalistic sculptor of the vast natures-mortes of modern life."[31] Lewis' dismissal of these collages as "lacking invention" sug- gests a basic misunderstanding on his part of what were, in fact, the beginnings of Synthetic Cubism. For Picasso was not, of course, re- turning to Naturalism or, as Lewis believed, to an easy Impressionism. In incorporating "real" objects into their pictures, thus lifting them out of their "normal" contexts, the Cubists were creating a visual space that, in David Antin's words, "no longer yielded an iconic representa- tion, even of a fractured sort, though bristling with significations."[32]

It is a curious anomaly that of all the art movements of the War period – Cubism, Futurism, Dada, the beginnings of Surrealism – Vor- ticism was the only one that engaged in no experiment with collage.[33] For all their talk of a new non-representational art, neither the painters like Lewis nor the sculptors like Gaudier seem to have called into ques- tion the integrity of their medium. Pound, on the other hand, was already moving, in poems like "Near Perigord" and the first Cantos, toward an art of quotation that closely resembles the collagiste's appro- priation of "real" objects – bits of cardboard, wood, string, newspaper cuttings – into the picture plane. If he displayed little of Lewis' rancor against the Cubists, it is probably because he never quite shared Lewis' demand for an absolute dichotomy between nature and art. Thus he writes in "Affirmations" (1915):

> The Image can be of two sorts. It can arise within the mind. It is then "subjective." External causes play upon the mind, perhaps; if so, they are drawn into the mind, fused, transmitted, and emerge in an Image unlike themselves. Secondly, the Image can be objective. Emotion seizing upon some external scene or action carries it intact in the mind; and that vortex purges it of all save the essential or dominant or dramatic qualities, and it emerges like the external original.[34]

The "external original" – an image from the "real world" – can thus coexist with the mental or "subjective" image just as the "little splotches of colour" (GB, 89) can coexist with bits of newspaper and iron nails in Cubist collage. So, in *BLAST,* Pound names Picasso as the father of the Vortex and Kandinsky as its mother.[35] This is not as foolish a parentage as it sounds. His own collage, one assumes, will be more eclectic than Picasso's, drawing upon a wider range of references; it will, moreover, emphasize the need for an abstract "language of form and colour" (GB, 86), expressive of what Kandinsky called "inner resonance."[36]

III

We are now in a better position to understand the structure of *Gaudier-Brzeska.* Pound's "incoherent" portrait of the artist is an assemblage of fragments that we must piece together, rather as we do when we look at Cubist or Futurist portraits. The story (what there is of it) has little chronological order, and Pound's poetic is presented neither logically nor sequentially. Rather, we are given bits and pieces: snatches of newspaper articles about Gaudier; his own Vortex manifestos from *BLAST* as well as Letters to the Editor and a long review he wrote of the Holland Park sculpture show of 1914; his letters from the front, both to Pound and to his friends, Olivia Shakespear and Edward Wadsworth; his youthful journal entries in French and his later account of his enlistment, given partly in French, partly in English ("The caption: 'It's a very good thing you did [volunteer], otherwise you'd have got twenty years in Africa. What! Non! la patrie n'est pas en danger!! 'MÈNE MOI C'T HOMME LA!!!' "). Again, Pound inserts into the text a hostile article in Italian from the Trieste "Il Piccolo della Sera," and Gaudier's artist friends, Horace Brodsky and Alfred Wolmark, are informally questioned about the sculptor's work in two passages that prefigure the contemporary *Paris Review*-style interview. Embedded in such documentation, we find intermittent verbal still shots of the artist: Gaudier at the *BLAST* celebratory dinner, speculating on the nude planes likely to exist beneath the dress of a certain guest; Gaudier appearing suddenly like a wolf behind Pound at the Albert Hall show and correcting his pronunciation; Gaudier in the studio, sculpting the Great Head of Ezra. Snatches of Gaudier's conversation are set off in quotation marks; later, extracts from Pound's own poetry and criticism (e.g. "In the Station of the Metro," the Vorticism essay of 1914 published in the *Fortnightly Review,* and the *Egoist* essay of 1915 called "Affirmations") are set side by side with quotations from Stendhal's *De L'Amour,* Laurence Binyon's *Flight from the Dragon,* or the comments of a Russian correspondent on Pound's poem "Heather." Every ten pages or so, we meet a set of illustrations – reproductions of Gaudier's sculpture and drawings as well as photographs of the artist at work. In this sense, *Gaudier-Brzeska* is the precursor of the contemporary artist's book.

How the montage I have been describing is actually spliced may be demonstrated by taking a look at Pound's first two chapters. The book begins with a series of cut-ups: (1) the *BLAST* obituary of July 1915; (2) a brief statement of Pound's own grief ("It is part of the war waste. . . . A great spirit has been among us, and a great spirit is gone"); (3) Ford Madox Ford's rather florid memorial piece from *The Outlook* of 31 July, which provides us with a "frame" for two further images: that of the nameless critic who cruelly "pours ridicule" on Gaudier, even as the young man is dying on the front; and that of Gaudier's last public appearance in London:

> I think of poor Gaudier as I last saw him, at a public dinner, standing sideways, with his fine sanguine features, his radiant and tolerant smile, his delicate movements of the hands, answering objection after objection of stimulated, after-dinner objectors to his aesthetic ideas with such a gentleness, with such humour, with such good humour. At that date there was no thought of war; we were just all separating at the end of the London season.

Ford's epiphany gives way, in turn, to (4) Pound's own first manifesto: to wit, "I do not believe that there is any important art criticism . . . which does not come *originally* from a master of that art. If a man spend all his life, all his intensest life, putting sweet sounds together, he will know more about music than a man who is merely pleased by an occasional tune *en passant.*" The man in question is, of course, not only Gaudier but Pound himself, and thus Pound's words here justify the pronouncements that will come in the second half of the book. More immediately, they lay the groundwork for (5) the reprinting, in its entirety, of the "VORTEX GAUDIER BRZESKA" from *BLAST* 1. This apocalyptic essay, of which I shall say more in a moment, is followed by an aside (6), in which Pound wryly admits that Vorticism, as Gaudier conceived of it, was not necessarily the same thing as Lewis' Vorticism or his own, and that, in any case, Gaudier was next planning to write an essay called "The Need of Organic Forms in Sculpture," thus diverging openly from Lewis' aesthetic. But this essay was left unwritten; instead, Gaudier, now in the trenches, wrote another "VORTEX GAUDIER BRZESKA" for the second *BLAST;* it is again reproduced in its entirety (7), prefaced by a kind of program note in which Pound summarizes Gaudier's military actions up to the time of writing. Immediately following this second "VORTEX," we find (8) reproductions, both front and rear views, of the *Red Stone Dancer* and *The Boy with a Coney.*

Both these sculptures date, not from the beginning of Gaudier's career, but from 1914; they are purposely placed out of sequence (a juxtaposition that unfortunately disappears in the New Directions text, in which all the plates come at the end) so as to illustrate certain key items in Gaudier's manifestos:

> The PALEOLITHIC VORTEX resulted in the decoration of the Dordogne caverns. . . .
> The HAMITE VORTEX of Egypt, the land of plenty –
> Man succeeded in his far reaching speculations – Honour to the divinity!
> Religion pushed him to the use of the VERTICAL which inspires awe. His gods were self made, he built them in his image, and RETAINED AS MUCH OF THE SPHERE AS COULD ROUND THE SHARPNESS OF THE PARALLELOGRAM.

And again:

> . . . I shall present my emotions by the ARRANGEMENT OF MY SURFACES, THE PLANES AND LINES BY WHICH THEY ARE DEFINED.

The first time that we read these grand assertions about the "PALEOLITHIC" and the "HAMITE" vortices, we are likely to conclude that Gaudier's texts are merely silly and pretentious. Who is this young man who pronounced, in five pages here and another three pages there, on the history of art from the Dordogne caverns to the present? But Pound's collage structure creates a way of understanding Gaudier's el-

liptical statements. For one thing, the manifestos are framed by contradictory elements: the aside about the slipperiness of all "isms," and the
program note about the trenches, which gives us some sense of the real
desperation behind Gaudier's energetic phrase making. More important, the plates themselves act as interpretive guides. I have already
referred to Pound's own commentary on the *Red Stone Dancer,* in which
Gaudier retains, to paraphrase his own words on the "HAMITE VORTEX,"
as much of the sphere as could round the sharpness of the triangle. As
for *The Boy with a Coney* (Figure 2.9), Pound cites, immediately after
Gaudier's second Vortex and another fragment from Ford's *Outlook*
article, his own remarks on this sculpture, which appeared in the *Egoist*
in March 1914:

> . . . it is no use saying that Epstein is Egyptian and Brzeska is
> Chinese. . . . They approach life in different manners. . . .
> "The Boy with the Coney" is "Chou" or suggests slightly the
> bronze animals of the period. Brzeska is as much concerned
> with representing certain phases of animal life as is Epstein with
> presenting some austere permanence. . . .

And Pound recalls: "Brzeska takes up my mild allusion with considerable vigour in his critique entitled, 'The Allied Artists' Association Ltd,'
which appeared in the *Egoist* three months later."

That critique itself is now immediately reproduced: in the midst of
much irrelevant talk about other artists from Zadkin and Kandinsky to
an "A de Souza Cardoso," a "Miss Rowley Leggett," and a "Mme.
Karlowska," who has contributed "a happy composition of figures in a
half circle," we find the following:

> I have on show "a boy with a coney" which has been referred
> to in these columns as an echo of the bronze animals of the
> Chow dynasty. It is better than they. They had, it is true, a
> maturity brought by continuous rotundities – my statuette has
> more monumental concentration – a result of the use of flat and
> round surfaces. To be appreciated is the relation between the
> mass of the rabbit and the right arm with that of the rest.

Now we begin to see the point of Pound's juxtapositions. For what
Gaudier's remarks make clear is that all the arrogant talk in the manifesto about the "HAMITE VORTEX" and the later dispersion of its
"HAMITO-SEMITIC energies through Roman traditions" at the same time
that the Chinese Vortex (of the "Shang and Chow dynasties") was still
at a point of "INTENSE MATURITY," is meant, not as a history lesson, but
as a way of making the reader see that Gaudier's own aesthetic, based

Figure 2.9. Gaudier-Brzeska, *The Boy with a Coney*, 1914. Red-veined alabaster. No casts. 11 in. high. Brunnenburg Collection, property of S. W. de Rachewiltz.

on certain principles learned from archaic and non-Western sculpture, is concerned with "the relation between the mass of the rabbit and the right arm with that of the rest [of the sculpture]," which is to say, in the words of the "VORTEX GAUDIER BRZESKA," "Sculptural feeling is the appreciation of masses in relation," and again, "I shall present my emotions by the ARRANGEMENT OF MY SURFACES." The juxtaposition of fragments from Pound's, Ford's, and Gaudier's essays on art make this point more vividly, and with much greater immediacy than could a chronological exposition of Gaudier's evolving aesthetic. Ideas in action, Pound would say. Or, the VORTEX is a "radiant node or cluster . . . from which, and through which, and into which, ideas are constantly rushing."

And indeed, from this starting point in the first two chapters, vortices radiate in all sorts of directions. Gaudier, rushing to serve the French army and being first detained as a technical deserter: the anecdote is told by Ford in the *Outlook* piece; it is repeated, this time by Gaudier himself, in conversation with Pound, in Chapter VI (53), and referred to again in the letters Gaudier writes from the front, reproduced in the next chapter. Or again, Gaudier's early life is pieced together from accounts of Sophie Brzeska (41), Horace Brodsky (75–76), and Alfred Wolmark (77–79), but the stories don't quite fit. Compare the following passages:

> Piecing together Gaudier's early biography from Miss Brzeska's data, I find that he was born at St. Jean de Braye, Loiret, on October 4, 1891. He was the son of Joseph Gaudier, a joiner. Henri respected his father because he was a good workman with some pride in his craft and because le père Gaudier had made a fine door or doorway for some place or other in Loiret.   (41)

> Gaudier's ancestors had been masons and stone carvers for generations and had worked on the cathedral of Chartres. Brodsky himself had discovered an almost exact portrait of Gaudier, carved on some French cathedral facade. This gave piquancy to an, of course, unverifiable fancy.   (76)

The second story repeats the first but the tone is quite different: less factual, more genial, turning Gaudier into a kind of legend. In between these two sketches of Gaudier's past, Pound places the portrait of the artist as seen for the first time by the poet himself:

> I was with O. S. [Olivia Shakespear] at a picture show in the Albert Hall ("International," "Allied Artists," or something). We wandered about the upper galleries hunting for new work

and trying to find some good amid much bad, and a young man came after us, like a well-made young wolf or some soft-moving, bright-eyed wild thing. I noted him carefully because he reminded me a little of my friend Carlos Williams.

He also took note of us, partly because we paused only before new work, and partly because there were few people in the gallery, and partly because I was playing the fool and he was willing to be amused by the performance. It was a warm, lazy day, there was a little serious criticism mixed in with our nonsense. On the ground floor we stopped before a figure with bunchy muscles done in clay painted green. It was one of a group of interesting things. I turned to the catalogue and began to take liberties with the appalling assemblage of consonants: "Brzxjk – " I began. I tried again, "Burrrzisskzk – " I drew back, breathed deeply and took another run at the hurdle, sneezed, coughed, rumbled, got as far as "Burdidis – " when there was a dart from behind the pedestal and I heard a voice speaking with the gentlest fury in the world: "Cela s'appelle tout simplement Jaersh-ka. C'est moi qui les ai sculptés."

And he disappeared like a Greek god in a vision. I wrote at once inviting him to dinner, having found his address in the catalogue. (44–45)

The placement of this anecdote is of central importance because, up to this point, we have seen Gaudier only as a sort of newspaper item, the young sculptor whose tragic death in the trenches is recorded, the author of manifestos and reviews, the subject of gossip and encomia. In the chapters that follow, such documentation continues to predominate, so that only here in Chapter V are we permitted to see the artist as an actual young man, a little bit like another very real "soft-moving," "bright-eyed," "wild" young man named William Carlos Williams. The conundrum of his last name is played with, although never in *Gaudier-Brzeska* are the real reasons for the assumption of that name so much as mentioned; we are told only that "At this time (1911) he calls himself definitely Henri Gaudier-Brzeska" (42). No personal information, in other words, is divulged; for the love story we have to turn to H. S. Ede's *The Savage Messiah* or to Sophie Brzeska's own diaries.[37] Rather, Pound presents Gaudier as his own charming alter ego, a figure at once foolishly real (with his "appalling assemblage of consonants" of a name) and mythic: a wolf, a "Greek god in a vision." As such, Gaudier is regarded as "certainly the best company in the world, and some of my best days, the happiest and most interesting, were spent in his uncomfortable mud-floored studio when he was doing my bust" (47). Ironically, the bust itself is remote from life: abstract, stylized, gigantic, phallic: an Easter Island idol made of white marble (Figure 2.10).

We thus come to "see" Gaudier from any number of different angles; Pound's portrait has fewer similarities to Gaudier's *Hieratic Head* than to such Futurist collages as Severini's *Portrait of Marinetti* (Figure 2.11), which Pound must have seen at the Marlborough Gallery in 1913.[38]

Marinetti, who was always photographed wearing a correct black suit with stiff white shirtfront, black bow tie, and bowler hat, is presented by Severini in a stylized composition of spheres and geometric planes, with strong diagonal movement. One eye is closed (painted as an outlined egg shape); the other is hollowed out and surrounded by the heavy black shadowing of the exaggerated brow; a real moustache, moreover, is pasted in above the mouth. Marinetti's receding hairline is presented as an isosceles triangle; it is balanced against another such triangle to its left, this one of actual black velvet, representing the lapel of the suit. The ovoid head becomes one of a rhythmical series of cylinders, giant versions of Marinetti's proverbial cigarette, crossing and recrossing the canvas. And above and behind these cylinders, Severini places the cut up French titles, as they appeared in *Le Figaro*, of Marinetti's most important works, the *Manifeste du Futurisme* (1909) and *L'Imagination sans fil – Les mots en liberté* (1913).[39] Placed diagonally, these broken titles have behind them and around them the texts of the manifestos themselves, reduced to what looks like a series of pointillist dots arranged in lines. Everything seems to be in motion in keeping with Severini's insistence that "Today, in this epoch of dynamism and simultaneity, one cannot separate any event or object from the memories, the plastic preferences or aversions, which its *expansive action* calls up *simultaneously* in us."[40] Indeed, Severini's definition of *Form* in his own Futurist Manifesto of 1913, could just as easily be Pound's:

1. Simultaneous contrast of lines, planes and volumes, and of groups of analogous forms disposed in spherical expansion. – Constructive interpenetration.
2. Rhythmic arabesque-like construction. . . . *The subject-matter, when its effect is considered, sacrifices its integrity, and therefore its integral qualities, in order to develop to the utmost its qualitative continuities.*
3. Dynamic composition open in all directions. . . .
4. Suppression of the straight line which is as static and formless as a colour without tonal gradations, and of parallel lines.[41]

Figure 2.10. Gaudier-Brzeska. *Hieratic Head of Ezra Pound*, 1914. Marble. No casts. 36 by 24 in. Privately owned.

57

Figure 2.11. Gino Severini, *Portrait of Marinetti*, 1913. Collage with mustache and velvet. 25⅝ by 21¼ in. Benedetta Marinetti Collection, Rome.

The "suppression of the straight line" is certainly a central figure of *Gaudier-Brzeska*. When Pound says, again and again, that he can give only "diminished memories of past speech and action" (38), that "This is the way memory serves us, details return ill assorted, pell mell, in confusion" (40), or that "My memory of that order of events from then on is rather confused" (51), he is being disingenuous. For it is no coincidence that the account of Pound's first meeting with Gaudier is delayed until Chapter V or that Pound's own poetic, which most readers take to be the real heart of the book, is introduced only in Chapter XI. The Vorticist credo, this arrangement implies, can be understood only after it has been *lived;* we see it in action in Gaudier's life and art before we meet its abstract formulations. And even in these later chapters, Pound always interrupts his own statements of theory in order to introduce documentary bits from Stendhal and Whistler, anecdotes about his own poems, and further discussions about Gaudier's sculpture. Thus, when he says of Gaudier's first "Vortex" for *BLAST:* "I confess that I read it two or three times with nothing but a gaiety and exhilaration arising from the author's vigour of speech" (106), he might be telling us how to read his own "remarkable arrangement of thought." It takes a few readings before we understand the significance of these *papiers-collés.*

"Speed," says Severini, "has given us a new conception of space and time, and consequently of life itself; and so it is perfectly reasonable for our Futurist works to *characterize* the art of our epoch with the *stylization of movement* which is one of the most immediate manifestations of life."[42] It is precisely as such "stylization of movement" that we can understand the function of Pound's three additions to the 1916 text, introduced into the New Directions edition.

In the original text, the final chapter is XIX, which follows the catalogues of Gaudier's sculptures and drawings. "I might do worse," says Pound, "than close with the following citations from so conservative a work as Mr. Binyon's 'Flight from the Dragon.' They bear on much of Gaudier's work, not merely upon the cut brass" (134). As an Orientalist, Pound felt, Binyon made the right discriminations; he understood, for instance, that "the waves of Korin's famous screen are not like real waves: but they move, they have force and volume" (135). The gist of Binyon's definition of art is contained in the following passage:

> Art is not an adjunct to existence, a reproduction of the actual.
> "FOR INDEED IT IS NOT ESSENTIAL THAT THE SUBJECT-MATTER SHOULD REPRESENT OR BE LIKE ANYTHING IN NATURE: ONLY IT MUST BE ALIVE WITH A RHYTHMIC VITALITY OF ITS OWN." (134)

Having quoted this and related passages, Pound modestly affixes his initials in the right-hand corner.

Such closure is singularly un-Poundian. As he says of the *Hieratic Head,* "The bust of me was most striking, perhaps, two weeks before it was finished. I do not mean to say that it was better, it was perhaps a *kinesis,* whereas it is now a *stasis;* but before the back was cut out, and before the middle lock was cut down, there was in the marble a titanic energy. . . . [Gaudier] himself, I think, preferred a small sketch made later, to the actual statue, but in sculpture there is no turning back" (49).

In a verbal construct like *Gaudier-Brzeska,* however, a "turning back" was perfectly possible. So Pound replaced the "stasis" of the original ending with a new "kinesis." He added three sections: (1) the "Preface to the Memorial Exhibition 1918," which provides another survey of Gaudier's sculpture and alludes, once again, to his two manifestos; (2) "Gaudier: A Postscript 1934," which takes the larger, retrospective view of Gaudier's art, now that that art has receded into history; and (3) "Peregrinations, 1960," a witty account of how the "big bust" of Pound got from Violet Hunt's front garden on Camden Hill to Schloss Brunnenburg in the Tyrol, via the Albergo Rapallo where it stood by the poet's lunch table, and then No. 12 Via Marsala, where "the stone eyes gazed seaward."

This account of how the statue was saved is not a trivial anecdote. For "After [the] wars and permutations" survived by the *Hieratic Head,* Gaudier had finally become famous. Pound now alludes to the Milan memorial show and a second exhibit in Merano, recalling with some bemusement that the Italians came to these shows "hoping to meet the new sculptor and writing to say so" (146). And Pound concludes:

> The remarkable Scheiwiller issued a booklet and, I suppose, guided the two excellent catalogues, though those of the London and French shows were in larger format. (147)

An end and a beginning: as in *The Cantos,* which refused to terminate with a round number like 100, the text insists that VORTEX IS ENERGY! Pound rejoices in Gaudier's "arrival," but the "London and French shows" are part of a larger process whose end cannot be foreseen. Nor does Pound try to foresee it. He has made his memoir-manifesto a remarkable "first text-book" of the doctrine succinctly expressed in the 1934 Postscript: "The key word of vorticist art was Objectivity in the sense that we insisted that the value of a piece of sculpture was dependent on its shape" (142). The shape of *Gaudier-Brzeska,* best described as a collage in motion, was to have widespread repercussions.

IV

The collage manifesto, as we have seen it take shape in *Gaudier-Brzeska,* clearly owes more to Continental texts, especially to Marinetti's early Futurist manifestos, than to any English or American model. As a genre, it came into its own in the Dada period; Williams' Prologue to *Kora in Hell* (1920) is an interesting conflation of the Dada model, with its playful imagery and absurdist humor, and the Poundian "documentary" mode: like *Gaudier-Brzeska*, Williams' Prologue juxtaposes aphorism and anecdote, lyric interlude and actual letters received by the poet – in this case from Stevens, H. D., and Pound himself.

One can trace a line from *Gaudier-Brzeska* and *Kora* to Olson's "Projective Verse" or "Apollonius of Tyana," and further to the series of "Assemblings," as Richard Kostelanetz calls his remarkable annual anthologies of the seventies. But the particular blend of manifesto, memoir, autobiography, and art criticism found in Pound's "first text-book" is reinvented, perhaps most notably, by John Cage in the "lecture poems" or "texts" collected in *Silence* (1961), *A Year from Monday* (1967), *M* (1973), and *Empty Words* (1979).[43] Cage's verbal collages probably owe more to Dada than to any British or American model (with the notable exception of *Finnegans Wake*), and I do not wish to imply that they were directly influenced by Pound. Indeed, a recent Cage mesostic pays what is at best a back-handed compliment to the author of *The Cantos*:[44]

> *For William McN. who studied with Ezra Pound*
> in ten Minutes
> Come back: you will
> have taught me chiNese
> (sAtie).
> shall i retUrn the favor?
> Give you
> otHer lessons
> (Ting!)?
> Or would you prefer
> sileNce?

Cage, who disliked the fuss Pound had made over George Antheil,[45] may well have preferred "otHer lessons" to those of the *Cantos*. Nevertheless, the collage form first found in Cage's "Erik Satie" (1958), in which statements by the artist-subject (whether made in books, articles, letters, interviews, or simply conversation) are fragmented and "cut" into a larger text, their presence being signalled by some change in typographic format, is a technique anticipated in *Gaudier-Brzeska*. Witness the following:

> After which they put Gaudier into what he called a "swank automobile" with a lieutenant and four men with (I think he said) "fixed bayonettes." (GB, 53)

Take away the phrases "what he called" and "I think he said" and the
method is identical to Cage's. In fact, a page later, Pound gives us a
pure Cagean example:

> The bombardment of Rheims was too much for him, his dis-
> gust with the boches was too great to let him stay "idle."

Here the subject's speech is and is not incorporated into the narrative.
As in Cage's pieces on Robert Rauschenberg and Jasper Johns, quotation becomes a way of merging the identities of two artists. The writer
submits to his subject's speech patterns, inflections, and idioms; he
allows the other's voice to take over.

Consider the opening of "On Robert Rauschenberg, Artist, and His
Work" (1961):

> Conversation was difficult and correspondence virtually ceased.
> (Not because of the mails, which continued.) People spoke of
> messages, perhaps because they'd not heard from one another
> for a long time. Art flourished.   (S, 98)

Whose idea is it that the new art is no longer based on "normal"
channels of communication, that art flourishes just when "correspondence" virtually ceases? Is this Rauschenberg's thinking or Cage's? Or,
as Cage puts it a few lines further down: "I know he put the paint on
the tires. And he unrolled the paper on the city street. But which one of
us drove the car?"

A provisional answer to this question is given in the italicized passage
that follows, signalling Rauschenberg's own words:

> *As the paintings changed the printed material became as much of a*
> *subject as the paint (I began using newsprint in my work) causing*
> *changes of focus. A third palette. There is no poor subject. (Any*
> *incentive to paint is as good as any other.)*

But this formulation is not final either. The text now gives us a series of
"shots" of Rauschenberg: (1) his own speech, as in the passage just
cited; (2) Cage's extrapolation of what he takes to be Rauschenberg's
thoughts ("Would we have preferred a pig with an apple in its mouth:
That too, on occasion, is a message and requires a blessing"); (3) Cage's
description and analysis of the art works themselves ("There are three
panels taller than they are wide fixed together to make a single rectangle
wider than it is tall. Across the whole thing is a series of colored
photos. . . ."); and (4) asides in which Cage steps out of the frame
("Left to myself, I would be perfectly contented with black pictures,
provided Rauschenberg had painted them"). So the angle of vision

shifts continually, and it is only after we have read Cage's text a number of times that we realize to how many of Rauschenberg's paintings he manages to refer and how deeply familiar he is with the work.[46]

Rauschenberg's own collage, as Rosalind Krauss suggests in an essay for *Artforum,* differs from the Cubist or Futurist model in its treatment of the image:

> [In Cubist collage] a bit of newspaper absorbed into the shape of a wine glass can identify itself as a piece of the real world only from within the depths of a whole network of ambiguity. Caught up in the process of mapping, it is on the way to being absorbed, it has already been absorbed, into the transformational mesh of the image.[47]

In Rauschenberg's work, on the other hand, the objects to be collaged are not transformed by their absorption into the pictorial design or tone; they are simply transferred, "taken out of the space of the world and embedded into the surface of a painting, never at the sacrifice of their density as material. . . . By never transcending the material world, the image is unambiguously identified with that material world" (40). A work like *Fossil for Bob Morris, N.Y.* (Figure 2.12) resembles Cubist collage in that it juxtaposes disparate types of images – street and traffic signs, photographic negatives, newspaper and magazine clippings, an ornamental grate, steel bars and chains that are silk-screened or mounted onto the canvas. Yet, as Krauss points out, "because each image is given the same level of density as object, one is struck not by their multivalence as signs, but rather by their sameness as things" (40). The space of the collage thus becomes a kind of memory-space, for only in memory does such levelling occur: an image of a scene from a film or from a novel may be just as vivid as the image of something that has really happened to us.

Cage's "italic method" works in similar ways. The poet's own words and the words of his artist-subject are not transformed by their juxtaposition; rather the layering of verbal elements creates the impression that what one says or when one says it is finally no more or less important than what others say about that person. The masterpiece in this vein is the text called "Mosaic" (1966), Cage's homage to his first great teacher and model, Arnold Schoenberg. It was written, Cage tells us in the headnote in *A Year from Monday,* in response to an assignment from the *Kenyon Review,* inviting him to review Schoenberg's *Letters,* selected and edited by Erwin Stein and translated from the German by Eithne Wilkins and Ernst Kaiser (New York: St. Martin's Press, 1965). Cage's wholly unorthodox "review" of the Schoenberg letters is a collage that

Figure 2.12. Robert Rauschenberg, *Fossil for Bob Morris, N.Y.,* 1965. Paper, metal, plastic, rubber, and fabric on canvas, 84⅞ by 60⅝ in. Hirshhorn Museum and Sculpture Garden, Smithsonian Institution.

juxtaposes extracts from the letters (in italics) with remarks Schoenberg made when Cage was studying with him (in quotation marks), and Cage's own commentary. The result of such splicing is a seven-page text that creates what seems to be a simultaneous portrait of the artist as younger and older man, a contradictory voice and presence: alternately lovable and unbearable, self-centered and generous, brilliant and fool-ish – a pompous Germanic type who is also a cynical Austrian.

Consider the complexity generated by the juxtaposition of first and third-person reference. Here is the opening of "Mosaic":

> He became a Jew loyal to Jews. *I don't know whether such at-tempts to make things easier don't merely increase the difficulties.* Berg, Schoenberg, Webern. Another punctuation clarifies the matter: Berg, Schoenberg; Webern. *Now seriously . . . I . . . (. . . have only contempt for anyone who finds the slightest fault with anything I publish. One God.* The questions he asked his pupils had answers he already knew. Answers his pupils gave didn't tally with him.   (YFM, 43–44)

Here the first sentence appears to be an impartial summary of what Schoenberg regularly said in letters and conversation. But as soon as the first person is introduced, it creates a discordant, comic note. For one thing, we have no idea to what "*attempts*" and "*difficulties*" Schoenberg is alluding. For another, the formality of Schoenberg's epistolary style appears almost bombastic when juxtaposed to Cage's own flat, laconic narrative. Then, after some rapid sorting out of Schoenberg's musical affiliations (is he closer to Berg or to Webern?), a sudden cut introduces another quotation which is itself cut up. Here the effect of the internal ellipses and the hesitant repetition of "I" is to poke gentle fun at Schoen-berg's self-importance; we hardly need a "*Now seriously . . .*" to tell us how *serious* this man is. Even more comic is the splicing of the long clause expressing Schoenberg's contempt for his critics, a clause whose subject pronoun is missing, with the fragment "*One God.*" The jux-taposition implies that the One God is right before us, a hint confirmed by the very next statement, "The questions he asked his pupils had answers he already knew."

The interpolation of Schoenberg's earnest and slightly foreign inflec-tions into the purposely bland expository discourse points up the absur-dity of the composer's situation:

> Troubled by asthma and needing 5000 marks *quickly,* he lists three unpublished works, praises two, and discusses in connec-

tion with the third, his feelings regarding praise, finding self-praise, though *malodorous,* preferable to that bestowed by others.

Or again:

Two years before he died, Vienna honored Schoenberg right and left, granting him free entry into the city. This gave him *pride and joy, singular pleasure,* but reminded him too of his opponents, diminished though they were in number and power.

Or:

Becoming an American citizen didn't remove his *distaste for democracy and that sort of thing.*

These are fairly simple cases of binary opposition between narration and quotation; a phrase is taken out of its original context in a given letter and made to serve the purpose of the narrator. More frequently, however, a third term that acts as mediator or leveller is introduced: a statement seemingly made by Cage as narrator takes on the tone and inflections of Schoenberg without being a direct quote. For example:

What became evident (and we knew it anyway) is that unless one is a comedian (and Schoenberg wasn't, though he played tennis at least once with the Marx brothers) all's lost. One's intentions make life nearly unendurable. *A glass of brandy and . . . enjoyed it.* Righteous indignation. *It would be possible to establish a unified terminology and . . . relevant descriptions and definitions if one could begin by getting doctors to describe their own pains.* . . . He wouldn't enter a house because Strang, who lived there, had a cold. His students worshipped him.

Here we move from Cage speaking directly to us ("we knew it anyway") to Cage slyly mimicking the master's tone ("one is a comedian"; "One's intentions make life nearly unendurable"), to an actual quote, cut up to look foolishly solemn (what else can one do with a glass of brandy but enjoy it?), to an interpretation ("Righteous indignation"), to another quote, this time absurd in its pseudo-scientific pretensions, and finally to the narrator's matter-of-fact expository discourse, punctuating the preceding statement: "He wouldn't enter a house because Strang, who lived there, had a cold." The final sentence, in keeping with the collage principle that disparate materials are juxtaposed "without commitment to explicit syntactical relations between elements,"[48] is a non sequitur that makes sense only in terms of the total assemblage.

In the following passage, the transitions are even more complicated:

Though U.C.L.A. could no longer use him (he was too old),
others called upon him. The Burgomaster of Vienna sum-
moned him back to Austria; Israel would have had him shape
its Academy of Music. Too late. The great man was – it is
true – on his last legs . . . *face to face with the difficulties, problems, and inherent terms of the given material. Schoenberg.* Having
heard of a *"cutting conspiracy,"* Schoenberg explained that that
would not shorten a work: it would still be a long piece that
was *too short in various places (where it had been cut).*

The first two sentences provide straightforward narrative. But how do
we take "Too late"? Is this Cage's commentary or Schoenberg's response to the invitation? Or both? The next sentence could be characterized as *oratio obliqua* – the narrator giving a third-person rendition of a
character's speech: "The great man was – it is true – on his last legs."
The citation that follows leaves the reader hanging: the noun phrase is
left suspended and we never know what being *"face to face with the
difficulties, problems, and inherent terms of the given material"* leads to. The
phrase may not even refer to the invitations to Austria and Israel; Cage
may have picked it up from another context. But it hardly matters.
Schoenberg seems to regard all these things as part of a *"cutting conspiracy,"* and *"cutting"* now becomes a play on words as the composer
refuses to make any "cuts" at all.

A painted portrait is, by definition, a spatial construct, allowing us no
opportunity to "see" its subject at different temporal stages. Collage
makes it possible to introduce more than one time frame: in "Mosaic,"
Schoenberg's voice speaks at different moments of the twentieth century and in different places. Interestingly, the aspiring young composer
shares with the old exile an almost irritating self-confidence:

Musical conventions, complexity, yes – but let no objects and
settings for operas puzzle his audience. . . . *it is much more interesting to have one's portrait painted by some mere practitioner of
painting whose name will be forgotten in 20 years, whereas even now*
(he was thirty-five) *my name belongs to history. Our values.*

By appending the fragment *"Our values"* to the first sentence, Cage
makes it appear that Schoenberg takes his values to be the only values;
his immodesty knows no bounds. Yet in old age, as in youth, conceit is
tempered by a note of laissez-faire: "Before acting, he examined all the
possibilities; aged seventy-six, he left the decisions to others. *Think it
over, and if you find it works, then do it.*"

Cage claims to have chosen his extracts from the *Letters* at random by

I Ching operations,[49] but the fact is that, once chosen, a particular motif reappears again and again, just as certain motifs like the *BLAST* dinner and the image of the trenches come back at odd junctures in *Gaudier-Brzeska*. Thus, early in "Mosaic" we learn, in the course of a parenthesis, that Schoenberg played tennis at least once with the Marx brothers. Tennis, here regarded as a serious challenge, is an important concern for Schoenberg. A bit later we read:

> He asked Dehmel to write the text for an oratorio, giving him the subject in detail and *only one limitation: . . . 60 printed pages. As for living-quarters and tennis, the fact is these two problems are for us very closely connected.* He wanted to get home easily after playing. *It costs money, having to take a taxi: unless of course one buys oneself a car!* He considered using marble as a wall covering.

Here the contradictions in Schoenberg's personality are nicely brought out: the oratorio and the tennis game – both must be meticulously planned and executed. And in characteristic refugee fashion, Schoenberg takes the ownership of a car to be the wildest of extravagances (not to mention the price of taxis), whereas the acquisition of elegant home furnishings – say marble wall coverings – is held to be *de rigueur*. What such details tell us is that, in his private life, Schoenberg was entirely bourgeois, a good family man although a very bad provider ("The twelve-note system, the U.C.L.A. Retirement System are different. How? The Schoenbergs [wife, three children] received $29.60 monthly"). Family life, in any case, must be preserved:

> At the age of seventy-two he wrote a charming letter to Dr. Perry Jones, president of the Los Angeles Tennis Organization, asking for advice about how to proceed with tennis experience for his daughter, fifteen, and his son, ten. Lessons, membership in a club? Invited as a guest of honor to a party to be given two weeks thence, he refused (honored guests should be invited at least a month or six weeks in advance).

The longing to have proper tennis matches set up for his daughters, to live decently in the "South," as he referred to Los Angeles, is shown, in the course of Cage's collage text, to have caused the composer much grief. The separation of art from life, a Modernist credo that Schoenberg, as we see from his words and actions, firmly believes in, is mocked throughout: "His view (music's not something we experience, but rather an idea we can have, the expression of which can never be perfect though we ought – for artistic and moral reasons – to bring it as close to perfection as possible) is former and foreign" (YFM, 47). And again, "Though his experience was space-time, his idea of unity was two-dimensional: vertical and horizontal. On paper. The twelve-note system" (YFM, 49). Indeed, like *Gaudier-Brzeska,* though much more obliquely, "Mosaic" is a veiled manifesto. The very form of Cage's "book review" challenges the notion that art can be distinguished from life, that there is a natural separation between, say, Schoenberg's vulgar green and yellow striped T-shirts and his belief in "priests of art, approaching art in the same spirit of consecration as the priest approaches God's altar" (YFM, 46). On the contrary, in the verbal collage Cage has assembled, there can be no such dichotomy because the whirl of atoms has no center; Schoenberg's music simply becomes a part of everything else, a piece in the "material" mosaic of Cage's own education as an artist. In this context, Schoenberg's most irritating qualities – his absurd vanity and his supreme self-confidence – can become his most endearing, for in our teachers it is conviction and enthusiasm that win us over:

> Studying English late in life, Schoenberg made a few mistakes, later becoming fluent. We'd all written fugues. He said he was pleased with what we'd done. We couldn't believe our ears, divided up his pleasure between us. First afraid (*each new person might be a Nazi*), later delighted and grateful; someone was interested in his art.

With this modulated understatement – a layering of external commentary, direct quotation, and the final oratio obliqua – "Mosaic" ends. The juxtaposition of such collage elements produces a portrait of the artist that is oddly impersonal. As in Rauschenberg's painting, the field of memory becomes collective – a profusion of facts and impressions drawn from different sources that leave their imprint on the mind in the course of ordinary experience. Not, Cage seems to be saying, what Schoenberg meant to me as particular individual but how Schoenberg has taken his place in the collective imagination.

There is no indication that Pound read this or related Cage pieces, written within the decade prior to his own death. But I think he would have approved of what we might call Cage's Schoenberg Vortex, a text that fulfills Pound's own demand for "rhythmic vitality," a collage in which images, themselves quite literal, interfere with one another on a shallow screen. The art of quotation, as Richard Sieburth notes in his study of Pound and Gourmont, "involves shifting the emphasis from language as a means of representation to language as the very object of representation. To quote is thus to adduce words as facts, as exhibits, as documents, to lift them out of context, to isolate them, to make them self-evident."[50]

As "self-evidencing" works, the collage-portraits or collage-manifestos of John Cage, like Pound's *Gaudier-Brzeska*, refuse to remain quietly in the critical corner, detached from the "art works" they ostensibly talk about. On the contrary, these critical assemblings become art constructs in their own right. Indeed, *Gaudier-Brzeska* has less in common with such seemingly comparable works as Pater's portraits in *Appreciations* or Ford's *Portraits from Life* than it does with *Homage to Sextus Propertius* or the *Cantos*. These are connections we must explore more fully if we wish to come to terms with the hybrid texts of our own time – with, say, the "criticism" of Roland Barthes or the "fiction" of Gilbert Sorrentino or the "poetry" of Edmond Jabès or the "anthologies" of Jerome Rothenberg. Read against *Le Livre des questions* or *The Big Jewish Book*, Pound's Gaudier Vortex, his tribute to the young sculptor's last works and days, becomes an exemplary "first text-book" for the eighties.

NOTES

1 *Gaudier-Brzeska, A Memoir* (London: John Lane. The Bodley Head, 1916). All page references in this essay, unless otherwise noted, refer to the New Directions edition (New York, 1970), subsequently cited as GB. Where this text is discussed at length, the acronym is omitted before the page number. Pound's title needs a note of explanation: Gaudier took on the name of his mistress, Sophie Brzeska, when he came with her to London in 1911.

2 *The New York Times Review of Books,* 13 August 1916, p. 314.

3 *Ezra Pound: Poet as Sculptor* (New York: Oxford, 1962), p. 54.

4 See William C. Seitz, *The Art of Assemblage* (New York: The Museum of Modern Art, 1968), p. 10.

5 Roger Shattuck, *The Banquet Years,* rev. ed. (New York: Vintage Books, 1968), p. 332. Cf. Seitz, *The Art of Assemblage,* pp. 15–25; David Antin, "Modernism and Postmodernism: Approaching the Present in American Poetry," *Boundary 2,* 1 (Fall 1972), 106–107; and "Some Questions about Modernism," *Occident,* 7 (Spring 1974), 19–24. The most comprehensive general treatment of collage in the visual art is Herta Wescher's *Collage,* trans. Robert E. Wolf (New York: Harry N. Abrams, 1971). A more sophisticated analysis of Cubist collage is found in Robert Rosenblum, *Cubism and Twentieth-Century Art,* rev. ed. (New York: Harry N. Abrams, 1976), pp. 67–107.

6 *Other Criteria: Confrontations with Twentieth Century Art* (New York: Oxford, 1972), pp. 87–88.

7 *The Pound Era* (Berkeley and Los Angeles: University of California Press, 1971), p. 71.

8   See Richard Cork, *Vorticism and Abstract Art in the First Machine Age,* 2 vols. (Berkeley and Los Angeles: University of California Press, 1976 and 1977), Vol. 1: *Origins and Development,* pp. 166–167; Roger Cole, *Burning to Speak: The Life and Art of Henri Gaudier-Brzeska* (New York: E. P. Dutton, 1978), p. 81; Timothy Materer, *Vortex: Pound, Eliot, and Lewis* (Ithaca and London: Cornell University Press, 1979), p. 77.

9   See esp. Donald Davie, *Ezra Pound: Poet as Sculptor,* pp. 54–57; 177–181; Davie, *Pound* (London: Fontana / Collins, 1975), pp. 42–44; Kenner, *Pound Era,* pp. 128–133; Herbert N. Schneidau, *Ezra Pound: The Image and the Real* (Baton Rouge: Louisiana State University Press, 1969), Chapter 1 passim. I take up the problem at some length in *The Poetics of Indeterminacy: Rimbaud to Cage.*

10 See William C. Wees, *Vorticism and the English Avant-Garde* (Toronto: University of Toronto Press, 1972), esp. Chapters 7 and 8; Cork, *Vorticism,* Vol. 1, Chapters 2, 9, and 10; Materer, *Vortex,* Chapter 1; and especially Giovanni Cianci, "Futurismo e avanguardia inglese: il primo Pound tra Imagismo et Vorticismo," in *Quaderno,* 9 (May 1979), 7–66. (Cianci's essay has been translated into English in *Arbeiten aus Anglistik und Amerikanistik,* 1 [1981], 3–39.) The *Quaderno* special issue *Futurismo / Vorticismo* contains other important essays as well as a useful bibliography by Patrizia Ardizzone.

The distinction between the aesthetic of Lewis and that of Pound is discussed in a short but seminal essay by Douglas Messerli, "Vorticist Lewis / Vorticist Pound," *Art Quarterly,* I, 4 (Autumn 1978), 397–402.

11 *Pound / Joyce: The Letters of Ezra Pound to James Joyce,* ed. Forrest Read (New York: New Directions, 1967), p. 26.

12 See Kenner, *Pound Era,* pp. 236–237; Messerli, 398.

13 *Pound Era,* p. 238.

14 *Collected Early Poems of Ezra Pound,* ed. Michael John King (New York: New Directions, 1976), p. 36.

15 *Vortex,* pp. 15–16.

16 *The Selected Letters of Ezra Pound, 1907–1941,* ed. D. D. Paige (New York: New Directions, 1971), p. 28.

17 As quoted by Violet Hunt, *I Have This To Say* (New York: Boni and Liveright, 1926), p. 211. Cited by Wees in *Vorticism,* p. 161.

18 *BLAST* 1 (June 1914), 148. The second and final number appeared in July 1915. See Cork, *Vorticism,* Vol. 1, pp. 239–296 for the publication history of *BLAST.*

19 See Eva Hesse, "On the Source of Pound's 'Vortex,' " *Paideuma,* 9 (Fall 1980), 329–331; Pound, *Selected Letters,* p. 74.

20 *Futurist Manifestos,* ed. Umbro Apollonio (New York: The Viking Press, 1973), p. 115. The Balla *Vortice* drawings are reproduced in *Archivi del Futurismo,* ed. Maria Drudi Gambillo and Teresa Fiori (Rome: De Luca Editore, 1958), Vol. 2, pp. 111–112.

21 For a helpful, succinct discussion of the rupture between Lewis and Marinetti in late 1913, see Caroline Tisdall and Angelo Bozzola, *Futurism* (Lon-

don: Thames and Hudson, 1977), pp. 102–104. The difference in aesthetic
is summarized nicely by Richard Cork:

> Where Marinetti was a diehard Romantic, who revelled in the flux of
> modern life, its speed, uproar and confusion, the sympathies of his
> English opponent resided in Classical control, preferring to stand back
> and appraise twentieth-century phenomena with a cold, aggressive
> passion. And while Futurism expressed itself in terms of multiform
> images, Lewis clung instead to the viability of separate, precisely de-
> fined objects. (*Vorticism*, Vol. 1, p. 227)

William Wees makes a similar point in his discussion of the Timon of
Athens series: "Instead of multiple images and blurred merging forms . . .
the Vorticists' machine aesthetic produced static, rigidly geometrical, and
nearly or completely abstract designs" (p. 115).

22 This statement, which appeared in the Torino newspaper *La Stampa* in
1931, is reproduced by Giovanni Cianci, *Quaderno*, 66 or, in English in
Arbeiten, 26.

23 *Gaudier-Brzeska: Drawings and Sculpture* (London: Cory, Adams and
MacKay, 1965), p. 17.

24 *Vorticism*, Vol. 2: *Synthesis and Decline*, p. 440; but cf. Materer, *Vortex:*
"Birds Erect shows a mother bird with a swelling breast perched above her
two fledglings who turn and stretch their necks toward her with open
beaks" (p. 97).

25 See Cork, *Vorticism*, Vol. 2, p. 442; Materer, pp. 97–99.

26 *Henri Gaudier-Brzeska*, 1891–1915 (London: Faber and Faber, 1933), p. 92.

27 Materer, *Vortex*, p. 97.

28 Letter to *Partisan Review*, 1949, cited by Barry S. Alpert in "Permanence
and Violence: Ezra Pound, The English Review, and *BLAST*," *Occident*, 8
(Spring 1974), p. 86.

29 *Beyond Modern Sculpture* (New York: George Braziller, 1969), pp. 80–83,
and cf. Albert E. Elsen, *Origins of Modern Sculpture: Pioneers and Premises*
(New York: George Braziller, 1974), p. 49.

30 *Passages in Modern Sculpture* (New York: The Viking Press, 1977), pp. 47–48.

31 *BLAST* 1, 139. For a fuller discussion of Lewis' attack on Cubism, see
Messerli, 399–400; Cork, *Vorticism*, Vol. 1, pp. 281–284. Messerli traces
the difference between Lewis and Pound's view of Cubism back to the
latter's Bergsonism; see pp. 400–401. See also Hugh Kenner, "Introduction," to Walter Michel, *Wyndham Lewis, Paintings and Drawings* (Berkeley
and Los Angeles: University of California Press, 1971), p. 18. Kenner
adopts Lewis' own perspective and argues for the superiority of Vorticism
over Cubism.

32 "Some Questions about Modernism," *Occident*, 19.

33 In her monumental history of collage, Herta Wescher has chapters on all
these movements; her illustrations and discussion make clear just how
ubiquitous collage was in the various "isms" of the 1910s and 1920s. The
absence of any mention of Vorticism in *Collage* is thus quite striking.

34 *The New Age* (28 January, 1915), p. 61.

35 *BLAST* 1, 154; cf. GB, 82: "There is another artistic descent *via* Picasso and Kandinsky; *via* cubism and expressionism." Kandinsky's *Ueber das Geistige in der Kunst* is cited on p. 86 as support for Pound's belief that "The image is the poet's pigment."

36 See Wassily Kandinsky, "On the Problem of Form" (1912), in Hershel B. Chipp, *Theories of Modern Art, A Source Book by Artists and Critics* (Berkeley, Los Angeles, and London: University of California Press, 1968), p. 163. On Pound's view of Kandinsky in this period, see Ronald Bush, *The Genesis of Ezra Pound's Cantos* (Princeton: Princeton University Press, 1976), pp. 38–39, 49–50.

37 Ede's *The Savage Messiah* (1931; rpt. Bedford: Gordon Fraser, 1971); Extensive quotations from Sophie Brzeska's diaries may be found in Materer, *Vortex,* pp. 68–77.

38 Severini's one-man show at the Marlborough Gallery in April of 1913 caused a great stir among future Vorticists; see Cork, *Vorticism,* Vol. 1, pp. 105, 108–109.

39 The first of these texts was published in *Le Figaro* on 20 February 1909; the second in *Lacerba* (Florence) on 11 May and 15 June 1913. By citing both in French rather than Italian, Severini creates a further irony in his collage, wittily suggesting that these texts can be read only in French. For the texts, see *Futurist Manifestos,* ed. Umbro Apollonio, trans. Robert Brain et al. (New York: The Viking Press, 1970), pp. 19–24, 95–106.

40 Apollonio, *Futurist Manifestos,* p. 121.

41 *Futurist Manifestos,* p. 123.

42 *Futurist Manifestos,* p. 125.

43 All four texts are published by Wesleyan University Press, Middletown, Connecticut. *Silence* is subsequently cited as S, *A Year from Monday* as YFM.

44 *Empty Words,* p. 78. "William McN." is the poet and Orientalist William McNaughton. In the foreword to *M*, Cage explains that a *mesostic* is simply an acrostic whose row of letters runs down the middle rather than the left margin. The rule of making mesostics is that "A given letter capitalized does not occur between it and the preceding capitalized letter." Such observance of rule is itself a questioning of Pound's verse forms.

45 See Cage, "The Dreams and Dedications of George Antheil," *Modern Music* (January 1946); rpt. in *John Cage,* ed. Richard Kostelanetz, Documentary Monographs in Modern Art (New York: Praeger, 1970), pp. 73–74.

46 When this piece was first published in *Metro,* a Milan art journal, in February 1961, reproductions of Rauschenberg paintings were interspersed in the text. It is a pity that *Silence* does not provide us with the illustrated text.

47 "Rauschenberg and the Materialized Image," *Artforum,* 13, no. 4 (December 1974), 40.

48 David Antin, "Modernism and Post-Modernism," *Boundary 2,* 36.

49 See *A Year from Monday,* p. 43.

50 *Instigations, Ezra Pound and Remy de Gourmont* (Cambridge and London: Harvard University Press, 1978), p. 121.

3 "Letter, penstroke, paperspace": Pound and Joyce as co-respondents

Ezra Pound in Rapallo, writing to T. S. Eliot in London on 25 April 1936 on the occasion of the latter's invitation to contribute an article on Robert Bridges to *The Criterion:*

Why dunt you NEVER talk TURKEY

I don't mind earning the rent, but whazz use of a letter all full of irrelevance. If I interrupt the flow of soul, life of reason, luminous effulgence of internal mediatation, stop playin tennis against Palmieri and in general lower the TONE of the tenor of my life, I gotter be PAID.

Why don't you say / will you do IO quid worth of hack work?

I mean if that's what you do mean.
and say how many pages of typescript is necessary to keep the goddam M. 1 Econome from shaving off the last 8/ and 3d.
I take it all I gotter do is to talk about Britches, not necessarily read the ol petrification?

so DO be specific / Rabbit Britches indeed!!!

whaaar he git the plagazization of Rabbit aza name ANYHOW//
and as it wd. stop my doing an article already begun on three blokes that aren't yet mortician's, I spose I cd. be aloud to make an occasional confronto between Britches' dulness and the serious unreadability of a few blokes that would write if they could, but at any rate don't pretend, like the buzzardly
[lacuna]

74

proposed title of the article
<blockquote>
Testicles versus Testament
an embalmsamation of the Late Robert's Britches.
</blockquote>

all the pseudo rabbits / Rabbit Brooks, Rabbit Britches / whotter hell / your own hare or a wig sir ???

I spose I can cite the what I once said of Britches?

I managed to dig about IO lines of Worse Libre out of one of his leetle bookies. ONCT.

and then there iz the side line of Hupkins / couldn't you send and / or loan. In fact the pooplishers OUGHT to donate a Hupkins, and the Pubkins LETTERS so az to treat Britches properly.

bak ground for an articl that wdn't be as DULL oh bloodily as merely trying to yatter about wot be WROTE

Something ought certaintly to be done to prevent the sale of Oxford Press publications / thaaaar I AM wiff yuh.

and now getting to BIZNIZ / whatter bout that vullum of ez/? who iza sleepink in THAT.

and PUTSCH to the last degree. . . .[1]

Compare this to another letter Eliot received just a few years earlier (1 January 1932), this time from James Joyce in Paris. The original is handwritten:

> Dear Eliot:
> Excuse me if I am backward in my work and correspondence. I have been through a bad time telephoning and wiring to Dublin about my father. To my great grief he died on Tuesday. He had an intense love for me and it adds anew to my grief and remorse that I did not go to Dublin to see him for so many years. I kept him constantly under the illusion that I would come and was always in correspondence with him but an instinct which I believed in held me back from going, much as I longed to. *Dubliners* was banned there in 1912 on the advice of a person who was assuring me at the time of his great friendship. When my wife and children went there in 1922, against my wish, they had to flee for their lives, lying flat on the floor of a railway carriage while rival parties shot at each other across their heads and quite lately I have had experience of malignancy and treachery on the part of people to whom I had done nothing but friendly acts. I did not feel myself safe and my wife and son opposed my going.

I have been very broken down these last days and I feel that a poor heart which was true and faithful to me is no more.

I will prepare the end of Pt. I after a few days' rest.

I have heard about your Harvard appointment. I offer my congratulations if the appointment is pleasant for you and I hope Mrs. Eliot and yourself will have all luck and happiness this year.

Sincerely yours,
James Joyce[2]

Pound and Eliot were very old friends; Joyce and Eliot, literary colleagues rather than comrades, so that one expects Joyce's letter to be, as it is, more detached, more distant than Pound's. But it is less a matter of degrees of friendship than of basic attitude toward the letter-writing process. That attitude, in turn, reveals some important facets of their conflicting poetic, their very different sense of how *art* is to be related to *life*.

Consider, first, the format. Pound's letter, like almost every letter he wrote, is composed on the typewriter. The paper used is the blue-and-white Rapallo letterhead with the poet's profile by Gaudier-Brzeska sharply etched in the square at top center (Figure 3.1). Joyce, by contrast, uses here, as he regularly does, pen and ink, and he writes on ordinary thin notepaper. These are not unimportant details. Pound conceives of the page – whether it contains poem or prose text or letter – as a visual construct; increasingly, in the Rapallo years, he begins to embellish the page with various designs and to use phonetic spelling, capitals and underlinings for emphasis, unusual spacing and even lineation to create and to intensify his meanings. The process is, for that matter, not entirely different from what we find in *The Cantos*.

Joyce, on the other hand, takes a letter to be just that – a standard form to be used for the purposes of essential communication. Accordingly, his spelling, punctuation, syntax, and paragraphing are entirely orthodox. The letter begins conventionally with the salutation in the upper left; it ends with the signature in the lower right. Joyce's opening sentence is a standard formality: "Excuse me if I am backward in my work and correspondence." Then comes the news about his father's death: Joyce expresses his grief as well as his guilt for not having made the trip to Dublin; he explains his reasons for having stayed away in simple declarative sentences. The language is not only ordinary; it tends toward formula: "I feel that a poor heart which was true and faithful to me is no more." And, having made the promise to "prepare the end of Pt. I after a few days' rest," Joyce ends as he began with a polite convention: "I offer

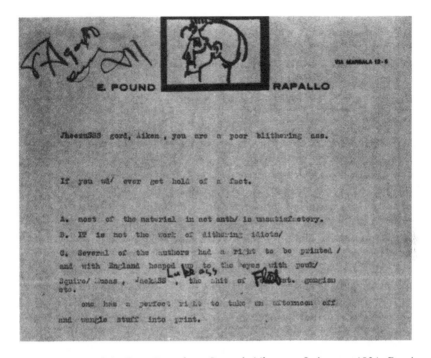

my congratulations. . . . I hope Mrs. Eliot and yourself will have all luck and happiness this year." There is not a word or locution here that any bereaved and slightly guilt-ridden son, living in exile from his native country, might not have written to a friend or acquaintance.

To turn from Joyce's letter to Pound's is to shift one's radius of discourse: where Joyce's writing is formal and conventionalized, Pound's looks at first like the simulation of direct speech. But not quite direct speech either: The text of the letter, like *The Cantos* themselves, occupies an equivocal space between speech and writing, one being played off against the other. We can, for example, hear the punning on Robert Bridges ("Rabbit Britches," "Robert's Britches"), and those other "pseudo rabits [*sic*]" like "Rabbit Brooke," as well as on *vers libre* ("Worse Libre") and publishers ("pooplishers"). Other oral devices include the comic Western American slang ("Why dunt you NEVER talk

TURKEY"), the neologisms ("confronto," "embalmsamation"), the play on related sounds, as when Pound proposes to call his article "Testicles versus Testament," and the insistent questions, exclamations, and interpolations. On the other hand, the simulation of Western accent must be seen on the page for full effect: for instance, "I gotter be PAID," "whotter hell," "whaaar he git," "whazz use of," "aza name," "thaaaar I AM wiff yuh." A related form of visual play involves abbreviations ("wd.," "cd.," "wdn't") as well as archaisms like "Onct" ("once"). Beyond these verbal effects, Pound also plays games with syntax, cutting into clauses or breaking off sentences before completion as in "couldn't you send and/or loan." Ellipsis, tmesis, augmentation, echolalia – all these combine to create an energetic associative rhythm neither that of standard written English nor of actual conversation, a rhythm we have come to regard as *Poundspeech*. Poundspeech jumps easily and repeatedly from the twang of "Why dunt you NEVER talk TURKEY" to the voice of the aesthete, parodically inflated: "If I interrupt the flow of soul, life of reason, luminous effulgence of internal mediatation . . .," and then just as easily modulates back to the down-to-earth suggestion that the poet might have to "stop playin tennis against Palmieri."

For Pound, verbal composition was continuum rather than artifact. Increasingly as he wrote *The Cantos,* the question of genre was subordinated to the question of finding the appropriate phalanx of particulars. Unlike Joyce, for whom a work of art was one thing and a personal letter quite another, Pound was one of the initiators of the process, so central to our own time, of collapsing the boundaries, whether between Art and Life or between the various conventionally defined arts, or between poetry and prose, "the language of inspiration and the language of ordinary discourse."[3] Indeed, when Pound said that poetry must be at least as well written as prose, he meant it. In an obituary essay on Ford Madox Ford (1939), he declared:

> It [i.e., Ford's program] advocated the prose values of verse-writing, and it, along with his verse, had more in it for my generation than all the groping (most worthily) after "quantity" (i.e., quantitative metric) of the late Laureate Robert Bridges or the useful, but monotonous, in their day unduly neglected, as most recently unduly touted, metrical labours of G. Manley Hopkins.[4]

Accordingly, when we turn from the preceding letter to Eliot to the Cantos of the same period – which is to say, the Adams Cantos (LII–LXXL) – we find some curious parallels. Here is a passage from Canto LXII about the Boston Massacre of 1770:

(Boston about the size of Rapallo)
>scarce 16,000,
>>habits of freedom now formed
even among those who scarcely got so far as analysis
so about 9 o'c in the morning Lard Narf wuz bein' impassible
was a light fall of snow in Bastun, in King St.
and the 29th Styschire in Brattle St
Murray's barracks, and in this case was a
>>barber's boy ragging the sentinel
so Capn Preston etc/
lower order with billets of wood and 'just roving'
force in fact of a right sez Chawles Fwancis
>>at same time, and in Louses of Parleymoot . . .
so fatal a precision of aim,
>>>sojers aiming??
Gent standing in his doorway got 2 balls in the arm
and five deaders 'never Cadmus . . . ' etc
>>was more pregnant
patriots need legal advisor
>>measures involvin' pro-fessional knowl-edge
BE IT ENACTED / guv-nor council an' house of assembly
>>(Blaydon objectin' to form ov these doggymints)
Encourage arts commerce an' farming'. . . .[5]

The narrative is a patchwork of documents and interpolations, its principal source being *The Works of John Adams,* edited by his grandson Charles Francis Adams (Boston, 1850).[6] To give just two examples, the lines:

>so about 9 o'c in the morning Lard Narf wuz bein' impassible
>was a light fall of snow in Bastun, in King St.

are based on Adams' account:

>At about nine o'clock of the night on which Lord North declared himself impassible to menace, a single sentry was slowly pacing his walk . . . in King St. . . . It was moonlight, and a light coating of fresh snow had just been added to the surface of the ground. (CC, p. 261)

Or again, the lines:

>Gent standing in his doorway got 2 balls in the arm
>and five deaders 'never Cadmus . . . ' etc

telescope two passages from Adams:

> [1] Five men fell mortally wounded, two of them receiving two balls each. Six more were wounded, one of whom, a gentleman, standing at his own door, observing the scene, received two balls in his arm.
>
> [2] The drops of blood then shed in Boston were like the dragon's teeth of ancient fable – the seeds, from which sprung up the multitudes who would recognize no arbitration but the deadly one of the battle-field.   (CC, pp. 261–62)

Pound condenses, modernizes, interjects, juxtaposes unlike elements as in the case of the "five deaders" and Cadmus, all the while foregrounding the same rhetorical devices that characterize his letters. For example:

1. Phonetic spelling, this time in imitation of the Boston accent as well as the more usual Western twang, as in "Lard Narf wuz bein' impassible," "was a light fall of snow in Bastun," "Capn Preston," "Chawles Fwancis," "sojers aiming," "commerce an' farmin'."
2. Pun and word play as in "Louses of Parleymoot" ("Houses of Parliament"), "doggymints" ("documents"), "five deaders."
3. Coinage, as in "Styschire" on the model of British regiments like Wiltshire or Hampshire, to imply that soldiers were pigs living in a sty (see CC, p. 261).
4. Digression, as in "(Boston about the size of Rapallo)."
5. Ellipsis, as in "was a light fall of snow in Bastun," "so Capn Preston etc/," "lower order with billets of wood" (i.e., "lower order of men"), "Encourage arts commerce an' farmin'."
6. Hyphenation, often coupled with ellipsis and phonetic spelling, as in "pro-fessional," "knowl-edge," "guv-nor."

The radical condensation, lineation, and consequent rhythmic groupings:

> (Boston about the size of Rapallo)
>   scarce 16,000,
>   habits of freedom now formed

distinguishes Canto LXII from the letter to Eliot discussed earlier, but the difference is perhaps one of degree rather than of kind: the forms of discourse, we might say, are on the same continuum. We could, in other words, take a line or two out of the Canto and insert it into the letter or vice versa without noticing the kind of radical shift that would occur if we made the same experiment in Joyce's case.

To return to that case and to some of its complexities, let us look at two more letters, this time from the Pound–Joyce correspondence itself. First, here is Pound to Joyce (21 December 1931):

> Dear Jhayzus Aloysius Chrysostum Greetin's of the season to you and to yr wives and descendents legitimate and illegitimate (*selon*).
>
> Blarney Castle, it come into me mind. Do you know anything, apart from the touchin' ballad; about it. I mean when did fat ladies from Schenekdety or Donegal first begin to be held by their tootsies with their hoopskirts falling over their priavtes [*sic*] to in public osculate: he [the] said stone
>
> and for what reason? fecundity? or the obverse?
> Whose stone, in short, was it?
>
> I regret not havin had the opporchunity to sing you my last ditty when in Paris, or rather the last before I went thither, composed for yr / special postprandial dilectation and then, domme, I forgot it. At least I think I forgot it, I can't remember having performed it.
>
> When you get an address send it on; or come down and watch the icicles forming on the edge of the mare Thyrenno.
> benedictions   E.P.[7]

And Pound appends his five-stanza parody ballad on Irish prudery and provinciality, entitled "Song for Informal Gatherings" and signed by one "On'Donal Hugh Red O'Donnel."

Joyce responded on 1 January 1932 by providing an extract from "The Groves of Blarney" by Richard Milliken (actually by Frances Sylvester Mahoney, as Richard Ellmann's note tells us) and then proceeding as follows:

> Extract from Work in Progress, Part I, section 6
> (it is the second of the four masters ,who here represents Munster, answering. He has been asked a riddle .What Irish capital city of six letters ,beginning with D and endung with N etc etc[1] but he answers)
>
> Dorhqk. and, sure, where can you have such good old chimes anywhere , and leave you, as on the Mash and how 'tis I would be engaging you with my plovery soft accents and descanting upover the scene beunder me of your loose vines in theirafall with them two loving loofs braceletting the slims of your ankles and your mouth's flower rose and sinking ofter the soapstone of silvry speech'

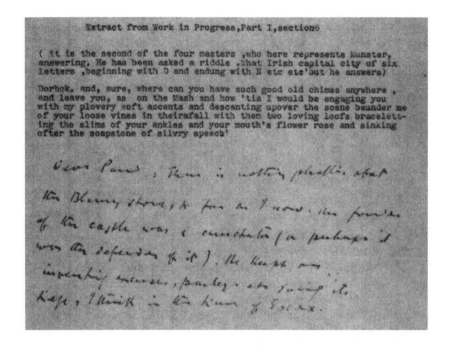

Figure 3.2. James Joyce to Ezra Pound, 1 January 1932. Reprinted by permission of the Collection of American Literature, Beinecke Rare Book and Manuscript Library, Yale University.

This portion of the letter is typed as is the extract from "The Groves of Blarney." Now Joyce shifts to the pen (see Figure 3.2):

> Dear Pound: There is nothing phallic about the Blarney stone, so far as I know. The founder of the castle was a cunctator (or perhaps it was the defender of it). He kept on inventing excuses, parleys etc. during its siege, I think in the time of Essex. The stone is flat and so far as I can remember let into the wall a few feet below a window. I never understood why it could not have been kissed from a ladder. I heard there were double bands of elastic to fasten the women's dresses. I did not kiss the stone myself.   (*Letters*, III, p. 239)

Having answered Pound's question, Joyce shifts, as in the earlier letter to Eliot, to the subject of his father's death, and he concludes with the usual politeness: "We send you and Mrs Pound our best wishes for the New Year, sincerely yours" (III, p. 240).

Pound's letter has his typical stylistic signature: oral inflections played off against stilted formalities, as when "Blarney Castle, it come into me mind" is followed, three lines later, by talk of fat ladies "with their hoopskirts falling over their priavtes [*sic*] to in public osculate." Again, we meet playful namecalling ("Jhayzus Aloysius Chrysostum"), Western American twang ("Greetin's of the season," "touchin' ballad"), phonetic spelling ("opporchunity," "Schenekdety"), slang ("tootsies"), and interpolation of foreign words ("*selon*," "domme"). By contrast, Joyce is wholly chaste: the explanation of the myth of the Blarney stone, the news of his father's death, the polite good wishes for the New Year–all are expressed in complete sentences in normal paragraphs with justified left and right margins.

But–and here is a fine irony–Pound's epistolary style does have its analogue in Joyce's text, not in the body of the letter itself but in the inserted passage from *Work in Progress*, as *Finnegans Wake* was then called,[8] typed into the handwritten script (see Figure 3.2) as if to say to the reader that the fictional text is in no way coterminous with the nonfictional one. Pound's punning and echolalia, his ellipses and telescoping of words, his insertion of foreign phrases and interpolations– these turn up in more extreme and complex form in the *Wake,* the book Pound had dismissed, when he first read a fragment of it ("The Book of Shaun," FW, pp. 403–590) on 15 November 1926, as follows:

> Dear Jim:
> Ms. arrived this A.M. All I can do is to wish you every possible success.
>
> I will have another go at it, but up to the present I make nothing of it whatever. Nothing so far as I can make out, nothing short of divine vision or a new cure for the clapp can possibly be worth all the circumambient peripherization. (III, p. 145; PJ, p. 228)

Pound was never to change his mind about *Finnegans Wake* even though Joyce's great work is in certain ways a mirror of *The Cantos*. The linguistic play in the inserted passage surely recalls the Pound extracts we have looked at, whether the letters or Canto LXII. The imitation Irish, for instance, "sure, where can you hear such good old chimes anywhere," with the pun on "chimes" ("times"). Or the phonetic spelling of "Dorhqk" ("Cork") and the telescoping of words ("upover," "beunder," "theirafall"). Like Pound, Joyce is fond of neologisms ("two loving loofs," "my plovery soft accents"), and he is likely to place an adjective in a noun slot as in "the slims of your ankles." The construction "beginning with D and endung with N" is one that must have tickled Pound: "endung" on the model of "ending" and sounding appropriately Germanic (although the correct word is "das Ende"), gives us a play on *end* plus *dung*.

But on closer inspection, Joyce's use of these rhetorical devices is really quite unlike Pound's. The language of *Finnegans Wake* is multi-layered, complex, ambiguous; it demands to be interpreted, to be, as it were, translated into an English we can understand. Here, for example, is still another letter, this time embedded in the narrative originally called "The Hen" (FW, I, v) that introduces Anna Livia Plurabelle:

> The bird in the case was Belinda of the Dorans, a more than quinquegintarian (Terziis prize with Serni medal, Cheepa-lizzy's Hane Exposition) and what she was scratching at the hour of klokking twelve looked for all this zogsag world like a goodish-sized sheet of letterpaper originating by tranship from Boston (Mass.) of the last of the first to Dear whom it proceded to mention Maggy well & allathome's health well only the hate turned the mild on the *van* Houtens and the general's elections with a *lovely* face of some born gentleman with a beautiful present of wedding cakes for dear thankyou Chriesty and with grand funferall of poor Father Michael don't forget unto life's & Muggy well how are you Maggy & hopes soon to hear well & must now close with fondest to the twoinns with four crosskisses for holy paul holey corner ho-lipoli wholly island pee ess from (locust may eat all but this sign shall they never) affectionate largelooking tache of tch. The stain, and that a teastain (the overcautelousness of the masterbilker here, as usual, signing the page away), marked it off on the spout of the moment as a genuine relique of ancient Irish pleasant pottery of that lydialike languishing class known as hurry-me-o'er-the-hazy.   (FW, p. 111)

Here the formulaic style of Joyce's own letters ("well & allathome's health well," "well how are you and Maggy & hopes soon to hear well & must now close with fondest to the twoinns") is exploded by such teasing ambiguities as:

> "bird" = the hen of the previous page but possible also "poule" (prostitute) named Biddy Doran, here Belinda in a parodic allusion to Pope's *Rape of the Lock*.[9]
> "Cheepalizzy" = "Chapelizod," the Dublin suburb but also "cheap" + "Lizzy" or again the "cheep" of the hen, finding the torn letter on the dung heap.

"transhipt from Boston" = transported from Boston (trans + ship or train + ship) but also "transcript."
"funferall" = "fun for all" but also "funeral."

And so on.

When words and phrases have such multiple meanings, the passage that contains them is obviously open to a wide variety of interpretations. Here, for example, is Anthony Burgess:

> . . . we are told how a clever little hen called Belinda scratched up "a goodish-sized sheet of letterpaper originating by transhipt from Boston (Mass.)" from a mud-mound flavoured with bits of orange-peel. The letter mentions wedding cakes and the "grand funferall of poor Father Michael" (Michael Finnegan?) and sends love to the twins. It is tea-stained and unsigned. (Think of the Boston Tea Party, the release from ancient bondage and the start of a new epoch in history. Marriage, family life have replaced the old theocratic but unfruitful paternalism. And the Orange shall decay, says the Shan Van Vocht).[10]

In Canto LXII, Pound similarly refers to tea:

> produced not in Britain:
>   *tcha*
> tax falls on the colonists   (*Cantos,* p. 341)

and he gives the Chinese ideogram for tea. But here the reference does not have multiple meanings, even though the structural links *between* references may be highly obscure. Pound's meanings, once we have identified his sources, are right on the surface: when he says "so about 9 o'c in the morning Lard Narf wuz bein' impassible," he is saying just that, although the condensation of the line is radical, the source reading "At about nine o'clock of the night on which Lord North declared himself impassible to menace . . . " (CC, p. 261). But "Lard Narf" is *not* also a reference to, say, "Love Nest" or to "North Pole." Which is to say that the "overcautelousness" of Joyce's "masterbilker" has no parallel in Pound's parody narrative; indeed, the polysemy of Joyce's language struck Pound as just so much "circumambient peripherization."

It is not, of course, a matter of right or wrong. Pound and Joyce are emblematic of two major strains of Modernism: the constructivist and the aesthetic. For Joyce, art was never to be confused with mere life; it was to be treated reverently, religiously, and it had to be as perfect as possible, every rift loaded with ore. Pound's art is less set apart and worked over, intentionally more "imperfect"; his texts, far from being self-contained artifacts, constitute a poetic mode continuous from Canto to manifesto to letter to critical essay, a mode that provides us with a paradigm of what *writing* can be (and has more or less turned out to be) in a time when established boundaries are undergoing erasure. Joyce inserts the typed text, the "artwork," into the "ordinary prose" of his handwritten letter. Pound subverts the conventions of "ordinary prose" and typographical format so as to make the letter itself the artwork.

NOTES

1 My source for this letter is a carbon copy in the Ezra Pound Collection at Yale. Copyright © 1983 by the Trustees of the Ezra Pound Literary Property Trust. Reprinted by permission of the Collection of American Literature, Beinecke Rare Book and Manuscript Library, Yale University. I reproduce the letter exactly as is except for an occasional word moved, due to lack of space, from one line to the next. All spacings, spellings, and punctuation forms are Pound's.

   The letter appears with some normalization in *The Selected Letters of Ezra Pound 1907–1941*, ed. D. D. Paige (New York: New Directions, 1971), p. 280.

2 According both to Richard Ellmann (letter to the author, 27 November 1982) and Mary Maturo of the Beinecke Rare Book and Manuscript Library, the original of this letter cannot be located. However, the format would obviously resemble that shown in Figure 3.2 and other examples of his handwriting may be found in the three-volume edition of the collected letters. For the printed version used here, see *Letters of James Joyce*, Vol. I, ed. Stuart Gilbert (London: Faber and Faber, 1957), p. 311.

3 The phrase is Jerome Rothenberg's; see "New Models, New Visions: Some Notes toward a Poetics of Performance" (1977), in *Pre-Faces & Other Writings* (New York: New Directions, 1981), p. 168.

4 "Ford Madox (Hueffer) Ford; obit," in *Selected Prose 1909–1965*, ed. William Cookson (New York: New Directions, 1973), p. 461.

5 *The Cantos of Ezra Pound* (New York: New Directions, 1971), p. 342.

6 My source is Carroll F. Terrell, *A Comparison to the Cantos of Ezra Pound*, vol. I (Berkeley and Los Angeles: University of California Press, 1980), pp. 259ff. Subsequently cited as CC.

7 I have not been able to locate the original of this letter; see no. 2, this chapter. Richard Ellmann writes: "I think Mrs Eliot still has JJ's letters to Eliot and presumably Pound's as well, but this is speculation."

   The text cited here is found in *Letters of James Joyce*, vol. 3, ed. Richard Ellmann (New York: The Viking Press, 1966), pp. 237–38. All further page references are to this volume. Pound's letter and Joyce's response are also included in Forrest Read's collection *Pound/Joyce: The Letters of Ezra Pound to James Joyce* (New York: New Directions, 1967), pp. 241–44. Subsequently cited as PJ. Ellmann and Read give a slightly normalized version of the original; presumably its appearance would resemble Pound's letter of 25 April 1936.

8   The passage in question was published as the sixth installment of "Work in Progress" in *transition* in September 1927. It appears in *Finnegans Wake* (New York: Viking Press, 1968), p. 140. Subsequently cited as FW.

9   See Adaline Glasheen, *Third Census of Finnegans Wake* (Berkeley and Los Angeles: University of California Press, 1977), p. 76.

10   *Re Joyce* (New York: Norton, 1965), p. 210.

4 "To give a design": Williams and the visualization of poetry

William Carlos Williams, aged 73, in conversation with Edith Heal about his characteristic verse forms:

> Free verse wasn't verse at all to me. All art is orderly. . . . From the beginning I knew that the American language must shape the pattern; later I rejected the word language and spoke of the American idiom – this was a better word than language, less academic, more identified with speech. As I went through the poems I noticed many brief poems, always arranged in couplet or quatrain form. I noticed also that I was peculiarly fascinated by another pattern: the dividing of the little paragraphs in lines of three. I remembered writing several poems as quatrains at first, then in the normal process of concentrating the poem, getting rid of redundancies in the line – and in the attempt to make it go faster – the quatrain changed into a three line stanza, or a five line stanza became a quatrain, as in:

The Nightingales

Original version	*Revised version*
My shoes as I lean	My shoes as I lean
unlacing them	unlacing them
stand out upon	stand out upon
flat worsted flowers	flat worsted flowers.
under my feet.	
Nimbly the shadows	Nimbly the shadows
of my fingers play	of my fingers play
unlacing	unlacing
over shoes and flowers.	over shoes and flowers.

See how much better it conforms to the page, how much better it looks?[1]

Like most of Williams' attempts to account for his own prosodic inventions, to theorize about verse, this one is confusing and contradictory. "Free verse isn't verse to me" – over and over again, Williams made this declaration,[2] and yet the fact is that "The Nightingales" is written in "free verse," there being no measurable recurrence of phonic elements – the stress count ranges from 1 ("unlácing") to 3 ("flát wórsted flówers"); the syllable count from 3 to 6 – no definable pattern of word repetition or even of syntactic parallelism. Again, Williams' repeated insistence that his poetry is written in "the American idiom" – "the language as spoken"[3] – belies what is actually on the page, for what conceivable voice speaks this way?

> My shoes as I lean unlacing them stand out upon flat worsted flowers under my feet. Nimbly the shadows of my fingers play unlacing over shoes and flowers.

From the "as" clause, awkwardly embedded between subject and verb, to the gratuitous repetition of "unlacing" and especially that final curious locution "unlacing over" where we would expect a direct object, this surely is *not* the natural American idiom. Nor does Williams' reference to tempo make much sense: the elimination of a single short line, "under my feet," from a nine-line poem cannot make it appreciably "go faster"; indeed, when we listen to the second version read aloud, we may well distinguish the absence of meter and rhyme, the brevity of the line-units, the preponderance of monosyllables, and so on, but the overall sound structure remains almost the same.

What, then, is the difference that so excites Williams? The *look,* of course.[4] ("See how much better it conforms to the page, how much better it looks?") The verse of "The Nightingales" is not, Williams would have it, "free" because its look on the page is that of two symmetrical units; indeed, in the revised version, we see two quatrains, almost square in shape. This symmetrical form provides stability against which the words of the little poem push and jostle, just as in, say, an Elizabethan sonnet, the actual rhythm is played off against the chosen metrical base and rhyme scheme. The visual shape also directs our attention to particular words and the relationships between them. "My shoes," for example, does not get a line to itself because it is not, in fact, the subject of the poem; rather, the emphasis is on what happens when something – "unlacing" – is done to them as the poet "leans" in their direction. "Lean" and "unlacing" share the letters *l* and *n:* the act "stands out" visually as well as semantically in juxtaposition to the longer line "flat worsted flowers," with its repetition of *fl* and *t* and the chiasmus of *wo – ow*. In the second stanza, expectation is again raised and deferred. "Nimbly the shadows" must wait for the second line and in turn the third and fourth before we understand what it is that is happening. "Unlacing" gets a line all to itself because it is the key word, and the unlacing now takes on a different meaning as the play of shadows takes precedence over the act. Indeed, the "shoes" previously "stand[ing] out upon / flat worsted flowers" now become equated with them. In the imaginative metamorphosis of the poem, the shadows of the poet's fingers have become birds – the nightingales of the title – flying through space. Accordingly, the second reference to "flowers," which corresponds visually to the first, no longer means the same thing. The look of the poem on the page thus creates a play of sameness and difference, identity and change.

I do not mean to imply that sound plays no part in this pattern or that the poem is to be perceived instantaneously as a "spatial form."[5] Clearly, the words must be perceived in time as our eye moves from line to line; just as clearly, the visual arrangement foregrounds certain sounds – for example, the voiced spirant endings in shoe*s*, a*s*, flower*s*, finger*s*, shoe*s*, flower*s* (7 of the 25 words or almost one-third); or the three nasals in a vertical row at line endings in the first quatrain: lea*n*, the*m*, upo*n*. All the same, these are, in Hugh Kenner's words, "stanzas you can't quite *hear*,"[6] in that sentence rhythm (one declarative sentence per stanza) overrides all line endings and that there is no marked rhythm to oppose its forward push. Rather, "The Nightingales" is written in what Kenner calls "stanzas to see": indeed, they could not have existed prior to the invention of the typewriter, an invention that made it possible for the poet to compose directly for the printed page with no intermediary process of transposition.

Stanzas to see – it is interesting that Williams himself never quite understood the workings of his own prosody. Thus when, in an interview of 1950, John W. Gerber asked the poet what it is that makes "This Is Just To Say" a poem, Williams replied, "In the first place, it's metrically absolutely regular. . . . So, dogmatically speaking, it has to be a poem because it goes that way, don't you see!"[7] But the poem actually goes like this:

> Í have éaten
> the plúms
> that were ín
> the ícebôx

and whích
yôu were próbably
sáving
for bréakfast

Forgíve me
they were delícious
sô swéet
and sô cóld[8]

The stanzas exhibit no regularity of stress or of syllable count; indeed, except for lines 2 and 5 (each an iamb) and lines 8 and 9 (each an amphibrach), no two lines have the same metrical form. What then can Williams mean when he says, "It's metrically absolutely regular"? Again, he mistakes sight for sound: on the page, the three little quatrains look alike; they have roughly the same physical shape. It is typography rather than any kind of phonemic recurrence that provides directions for the speaking voice (or for the eye that reads the lines silently) and that teases out the poem's meanings.

Williams did not hit upon this visual mode without a good bit of struggle, although in his later years, he wanted his readers to think otherwise. By 1950, he was telling the following story about his poetic beginnings:

> My first poem was born like a bolt out of the blue. It came unsolicited and broke a spell of disillusion and suicidal despondency. Here it is:
>
> A black, black cloud
> flew over the sun
> driven by fierce flying
> rain.
>
> The joy I felt, the mysterious, soul-satisfying joy that swept over me at that moment was only mitigated by the critical comment which immediately followed it: How could the clouds be driven by the rain? Stupid.
> But the joy remained. From that moment I was a poet.[9]

The spell of "disillusion and suicidal despondency" to which Williams refers was evidently brought on by an episode of heart strain that ended his adolescent dreams of becoming a track star. He was eighteen at the time. Appreciative biographers and critics have repeatedly cited Williams' little story as an instance of the poet's early premonition of his future poetic power.[10] I hope, therefore, that I shall not be thought too irreverent if I suggest that, like so much of the self-invention that characterizes the *Autobiography*,[11] this charming account may well be apocryphal. It provides a myth of origins for what was in fact a confusing trial-and-error process; I say "myth" because, judging from the poems Williams was to publish a full decade later in *Poems* (1909) and *The Tempers* (1913), it is doubtful that he would have known of a convention according to which the four short lines in question could possibly qualify as a "poem," and therefore equally doubtful that the young Williams would have preserved them as such.[12] Indeed, his wholly distinctive visual prosody came into being only gradually as he put first conventional metrics and then Imagist free verse behind him and began to place poetry in the context of the visual arts, as those arts were practiced by his great French contemporaries. How this process took place and how the resulting visualization of the "poetic page" has changed our concept of the lyric – this is my subject.

II

Surely few first volumes give as little indication of a poet's future direction as does *Poems* (1909), published when Williams was twenty-six. Of its twenty-six (is the number a coincidence?) poems, fourteen are sonnets, all but three Petrarchan. Here is a representative octave:

> Sweet Lady, sure it seems a thousand years
> Since last you honored me with gentle speech.
> Yet, when, forsaking fantasy, I reach
> With memory's index o'er the stretching tiers
>
> Of minutes wasted, counting, (as who fears
> Strict-chiding reason, lest it should impeach
> All utterance, must) a mighty, gaping breach
> 'Twixt truth and seeming verity appears.[13]

Williams was to recall five decades later that the early poems were much "preoccupied with the studied elegance of Keats" (IWWP, p. 8), but the fact is that the sonnets, quatrains, ballad stanzas, heroic couplets, and hexameters of *Poems* are not appreciably different from hundreds of other lyrics published in this period: for example, Madison Cawein's "The Yellow Puccoon" or Percy MacKaye's "In the Bohemian Redwoods," both of which appeared side by side with seven of Williams' poems in the special American Poetry number of *The Poetry*

Review (October 1912).[14] It is as if the poet had not yet been born; indeed, Williams did not reprint a single poem from his first volume.

Williams' second book, *The Tempers* (1913), replaces the Poetic Diction and mechanical verse forms of the genteel poets of the 1900s with the Ezra Pound of *Personae* (1909) and *Ripostes* (1912), the latter dedicated to Williams. The results are curious. Here is the first stanza of "Postlude," a poem H. D. called "a Nike, supreme among your poems," and Pound, "splendid":[15]

> Nów that Î have coóled to yóu
> Lét there be góld of tárnished másonrỳ,
> Témples sóothed by the sún to rúin
> That sléep útterlỳ.
> Gíve me hánd for the dánces,
> Rípples at Phílae, | ín and oút,
> And líps, ‖ my Lésbiàn,
> Wáll flôwers | that ónce were fláme.   (CEP, p. 16)

Williams' earliest free verse is distinguished by its slow phrasal rhythm, its end-stopping and frequent mid-line pauses ("And líps, ‖ mŷ Lésbiàn"), its conjunction of syntactic and line units, its alliteration, assonance, and open vowel sounds. All these are features found in Pound's early free verse, for example:

Williams:	Lét there be góld of tárnished másonrỳ
Pound:	Lét us búild hêre an éxquisìte fríendshîp
Williams:	Témples sóothed by the sún to rúin
Pound:	Góds of the wíngèd shóe
Williams:	Rípples at Phílae, ín and óut
Pound:	Álgae reach úp and óut, beneáth
Williams:	And líps ‖ mŷ Lésbiàn
Pound:	Mŷ Cíty, ‖ mŷ belóved. . . .[16]

For Pound, the line as unit, composed "in the sequence of the musical phrase, not in the sequence of the metronome," was to remain the basic building block of poetry; his are, moreover, lines to be *heard* as well as seen, their rhythm being highly pronounced and frequently repeated with delicate variations in successive lines:

> Eár, eár for the séa-sûrge;
>   ráttle of óld mên's vóices.
> And thén the phántom Róme,
>   márble nárrow for séats. . . .   (Canto VII)[17]

Williams' free verse is of a different order. Having begun with Poundian line units:

> O crímson sálamánder,
> Becáuse of lóve's whím
> > sácred!   (CEP, p. 23)

he soon shifts to a syntax that purposely goes *against* the line, blocking
its integrity. The single line heard as musical phrase is replaced by the
set of lines as "suspension system,"[18] whose guiding principle is the
syntactic opening or *cut* that decomposes sentences and recombines
words into new structures.

In *The Egoist* of 15 August 1914, for example, Williams published
nine poems, only three of which ("My townspeople, beyond in the
great world" later titled "Gulls," "In Harbour" and "The Revelation")
he later chose to reprint. Most of the rejected poems are again written
in imitation of Pound: for example, "Rendezvous," which begins:

> My song! It is time!
> Wilder! Bolder! Spread the arms!
> Have done with finger pointing.[19]

Others bring to mind the Imagist lyrics of Richard Aldington or John
Gould Fletcher:

> Slowly rising, slowly strengthening moon,
> Pardon us our fear in pride:
> Pardon us our troubled quietnesses!

But the final poem in the selection, "The Revelation," which Williams
was to reprint in *Collected Poems 1921–1931,* contains what are probably
the first intimations of Williams' own prosody:

> I awoke happy, the house
> Was strange, voices
> Were across a gap
> Through which a girl
> Came and paused,
> Reaching out to me
> With never a word.

Here the last four lines follow the free verse conventions of the period. In line 4, the subject noun ("girl") is separated from its predicate,
but the compound verb "Came and paused" is preceded by a natural
speech pause so that this particular cut seems quite normal. Lines 6 and

7 each contain a complete syntactic unit: participial phrase and prepositional phrase respectively.

The cuts in the first two lines are quite different. The separation of
subject noun ("the house") from copula, where the syntax allows for
no pause, and the suspension of the noun in a short line that already
contains one independent clause, creates a tone of hesitation:

> I awóke háppy, ‖ the house →

Does "house" look ahead to the next line so that the sentence can be completed or back toward the alliterating word "happy"? The same ambiguity
occurs in the case of "voices" / "Were" in the next line. Williams wants, of
course, to convey the confusion one feels at the moment of awakening
from a particularly absorbing dream; indeed in the revised version (CEP,
p. 39), he removed the last line and added a dash:

> Reaching out to me –

which underscores the sense of tentativeness, of equivocation.

The rest of the poem, both in the *Egoist* and *Sour Grapes* versions, is
unremarkable:

> Then I remembered
> What I had dreamed. . . .

and so on. But the prosodic "revelation" of Williams' poem by that
title is that when lineation goes *against* rather than *with* the syntax – a
phenomenon for the eye rather than the ear – a semantic shift takes
place. To put it another way, the linear pull can remove words from
their natural habitat in the sentence and create new configurations:

> Was stránge ‖ voíces
> Were . . .

becomes

> Was stránge, voíces . . .

By 1916, a vintage year in which Williams published twenty-two
poems in *Others* and six in *Poetry,* he had mastered this cutting technique. It is interesting, in this connection, to compare Williams' own
poems of 1916 to the free-verse poems included in the July issue of
Others, which Williams edited. The issue opens with Marianne Moore's
"Critics and Connoisseurs," a poem designed, like those of Williams,
to be seen rather than heard, its intricate symmetrical stanzas created
by complex typographical and syllable-counting rules. The volume
ends with Pound's Fenollosa poem "To-Em-Mei's 'The Unmoving

Cloud,' " in which almost every line is a subject–verb–object unit, complete in itself, rhythmic units recurring with delicate variation:

> I stóp in my róom toward the Eást, quíet, quíet,
> I pát my nêw cásk of wíne.
> My fríends are estránged, or fár dístant. . . .[20]

Pound and Moore have obviously devised ways of structuring the poem that Williams admires, but their ways are not his, any more than is Wallace Stevens', whose "The Worms at Heaven's Gate," written in blank verse, is included in Williams' selection for *Others*. Rather, we must look at the free verse of such poets as Skipwith Cannell, Alfred Kreymborg, Maxwell Bodenheim, Helen Hoyt, Mina Loy, and Conrad Aiken, free verse that superficially does look like Williams' own and which the audience of 1916 would not have distinguished from his. Consider the following examples:

(1) Helen Hoyt, "Damask"

> White blossoms,
> Frail tracery,
> Born of whiteness
> In a white world,
> You are more shadowy than frost flowers
> Growing in your smooth atmosphere,
> Vivid for a moment,
> Then palely
> Dimmed again:
> White lost in white.   (*Others*, p. 10)

(2) Conrad Aiken, "Illusions"

> Green fingers lifting a pebble,
> green fingers uncurling,
> the slant and splash of a waterdrop
> between eternities;
> earth slipping from old roots,
> and the stealth of white petals in the sun
> all day long;
> brown chimney pots
> descending against a cloud
> in silence;
> between walls
> the dry whir of a sparrow's wings . . .
> am I these, or more?   (*Others*, p. 16)

(3) Williams, "Love Song"

> the stain of love
> is upon the world!
> Yellow, yellow, yellow
> it eats into the leaves,
> smears with saffron
> the horned branches that lean
> heavily
> against a smooth purple sky!
> There is no light
> only a honey-thick stain
> that drips from leaf to leaf
> and limb to limb
> spoiling the colors
> of the whole world –
>
> you far off there under
> the wine-red selvage of the west![21]

All three poems are written in short free-verse lines, the stress count
ranging between 2 and 4; in all three, there is much trochaic or spondaic
rhythm ("Whíte blóssoms"; "gréen fíngers"; "sméars with sáffron"),
but not enough to establish a clear-cut metrical figure. But where Hoyt
and Aiken consistently use end-stopped lines and simple repetition of
syntactic and rhythmic units, Williams avoids the repeat, cuts in odd
places, and positions his words on the page so as to create an effect of
what might be called studied clumsiness. Aiken, for example, relies
heavily on the noun phrase –

> Gréen fingers lífting a pébble
> gréen fingers uncúrling . . .
>
> éarth slípping from óld róots . . .
> whíte pétals in the sún . . .
> brówn chímney póts – . . .

Hoyt, on participial modifiers:

> Bórn of whíteness
>
> Gró wing in your smóoth átmosphère
> Dímmed agáin. . . .

The result, in both cases, is a certain laxity as phrase is piled upon
phrase with little variety or tension.

Williams' three and four-stress lines are quite different. For one thing, he opens with an isolated line – a single, straightforward sentence, five of its six words monosyllables, its rhythm choppy and abrupt:

> I líe hêre | thínking of yóu: –

Then another simple sentence, but this time draped over two lines:

> the stáin of lóve
> is upón the wórld!

The first line here needs the second to complete it and even then we are left in a quandary. For unlike Hoyt's "white blossoms" (the damask) or Aiken's "green fingers" (tree branches), Williams' "stain of love" is less a metaphor than a surrealistic image of eroticism, the poet's semen becoming a mysterious flood that covers all, eating into the leaves and finally "spoiling the colors / of the whole world." In this context, the repetition "Yellow, yellow, yellow" is not a descriptive tag like Hoyt's "White blossoms . . . Born of whiteness / In a white world" or Aiken's "green fingers," but an exclamatory particle, the verbalization of the poet's frustrated desire.

Williams' strategy is to isolate words rather than to blend them in symmetrical rhythmic phrases: no two lines have the same stress pattern, and yet key words are carefully linked by alliteration – "*s*mears with *s*affron," "*h*orned *h*eavily," "*s*mooth *s*ky" – and assonance – "*ea*ts," "*lea*ves," "*sm*ears," "*lea*n" – as well as by what we might call, on the analogy to eye rhyme, "eye assonance" as in "*wo*rld!" / "*ye*llo*w*" and "*lea*n" / "*hea*vily." The word "heavily" gets a line all to itself in what is one of Williams' nicest effects in the poem:

> the hórned bránches that léan
> héavilỳ
> agáinst a smóoth púrple ský!

Thus isolated, "heavily" gets heavy stress, as if to suggest the weight of phallic power pressing against the "smooth purple sky." But "heavily," placed precisely at the mid-point of the stanza (the seventh of fourteen lines) refers, not only to the horned branches but to the "stain of love . . . upon the world" above it on the page as well as to the "honey-thick stain / that drips from leaf to leaf" a few lines below. "Love Song" thus becomes a design around a center, and yet the center is displaced as the narrative suddenly breaks off and gives way to the final exclamation:

> yóu fàr óff thêre únder
> the wíne-rêd sélvage of the wést!

Conrad Aiken, not surprisingly, was not keen on such asymmetries. Reviewing *Al Que Quiere* (1917) he remarks: "Beauty of sound [Williams] denies himself, beauty of prosodic arrangement too: the cadences are prose cadences, the line-lengths are more or less arbitrary, and only seldom, in a short-winded manner, are they effective."[22] These charges were echoed by other critics over the years: as late as 1950, Hayden Carruth complained that Williams' lines "are not run over, in the Elizabethan sense; nor are they rove over, in the Hopkinsian sense; they are hung over, like a Dali watch." The distinction is not incorrect, but for Carruth, the "hung over" quality of the lines must be a fault: "If this is done for typographical effect, as it sometimes appears, it is inexcusable, for it interferes with our reading."[23] A remarkable misunderstanding, implying, as it does, that typography is detachable from the poem, that lineation is just a nuisance, "interfer[ing] with our reading" of the poem for its substance.

But of course the typography *is* in many ways the poem's substance. Take a poem like "The Young Housewife," a short lyric often praised for what James Breslin has called its "tough colloquial flatness," its "matter-of-fact" verse,[24] but which, more precisely, uses that flatness for playful purposes:

> At ten A.M. the young housewife
> moves about in negligee behind
> the wooden walls of her husband's house.
> I pass solitary in my car.
>
> Then again she comes to the curb
> to call the ice-man, fish-man, and stands
> shy, uncorseted, tucking in
> stray ends of hair, and I compare her
> to a fallen leaf.
>
> The noiseless wheels of my car
> rush with a crackling sound over
> dried leaves as I bow and pass smiling.   (CEP, p. 136)[25]

Here the three stanzas are parody stanzas, the first, a neat-looking quatrain that has neither rhyme nor meter but slyly designates the young housewife by the same rhythmic group we find in "At ten A.M.":

> At tén Á. M̂.   the yóung hóusewîfe

The second line, with its odd construction "in negligee" on the model of "in furs" or "in silks," is cut after the word "behind," a word that thus gets construed as a noun (her "in negligee behind") rather than as a preposition. The same sexual innuendo occurs in line 7:

> shý, uncórseted |túcking ìn

where the separation of the verb from its object ("stray ends of hair") makes us expect a reference to what one usually tucks into a corset. The next line produces even greater surprise:

> stráy énds of *háir,* and Í compáre her

To what, we wonder?

> to a fállen léaf.

An absurd comparison, since surely the young housewife – she is constantly doing things, moving about, calling the ice-man or fish-man, tucking in stray ends of hair – is the very opposite of a fallen leaf. Or is she? Never mind the parody period after "leaf": the tercet now brings it all out into the open:

> The nóiseless whéels of my cár
> rúsh with a cráckling soúnd óver
> dríed léaves as I bów and páss smíling.

   In his erotic fantasy, the poet wants to make this attractive housewife a "fallen leaf" to the "noiseless wheels of his car," to "rush with a crackling sound over / her dried leaves." But it is, after all, only a daydream; normal life must continue and so "I bow and pass smiling." The tercet has lines of 7, 8, and 9 syllables (3, 4, and 5 stresses) respectively; the diagonal created by its line endings thus presents an image of one-step-at-a-time accretion, as if to say that, fantasize all we like, we must get on with it. Typography, in a case like this, is destiny.

III

How did the poet of *The Tempers* (1913) –

> Lady of dusk-wood fastnesses
>   Thou art my Lady –   (CEP, p. 17)

become, within three or four short years, the poet of "Love Song" and "The Young Housewife"? The Imagist movement clearly made a difference, but then, as we have seen, *The Tempers* is the book that pays the greatest homage to Pound; by 1917 when *Al Que Quiere* was published, Pound's imprint was no longer decisive; neither, for that matter, was that of H. D. or of Conrad Aiken or Carl Sandburg. Rather, the poems of the late teens represent Williams' first attempt to create verbal-visual counterparts to the paintings and drawings exhibited by the Photo-Secession (*291*) Gallery and reproduced in the pages of Alfred Stieglitz's *Camera Work* and later in *291* in the years preceding the entrance of the United States into the Great War. Williams' relationship to the visual artists of his time has been studied frequently, most notably by Bram Djikstra and Dikran Tashjian,[26] and I do not wish to rehearse the story of his reaction to the Armory Show and of his acquaintance with Stieglitz and the Arensberg Circle (Duchamp, Picabia, Man Ray, and others) again here. What I do want to suggest is that when we speak of the Cubist or Dada element in Williams' poetry, we must look, not only at the imagery and semantic patterning of the poems, as most critics, including myself, have done,[27] but also at the actual look of the poem on the page, the distribution of black letters in white space. The *mise en question* of the representability of the sign, raised by Picasso and Picabia as early as 1912–13, is not prominent in Williams' work before *Kora in Hell* (1920); but the visualization of the stanza, and the line cut comparable to the visual cut in Cubist or Dada collage – these begin to appear, as I noted earlier, in poems like "The Revelation" (1914); and *Al Que Quiere* is, among other things, an homage to the typewriter.

Picabia's "object-portraits" of 1915, a number of which were reproduced in *291*, present an interesting analogy to Williams' verse. These pen-and-ink drawings of isolated technological objects, many endowed with legends that identify them as particular personalities, look, at first glance, like the mail-order catalogue illustrations and newspaper ads on which they were, in fact, based.[28] Gabrielle Buffet-Picabia recalls:

> They drew inspiration from rudimentary, mechanical or geometric forms, and were executed with the dryness of blueprints. The colors are sober and few; Picabia sometimes added to his paintings strange substances, wood which created relief, gold and silver powders, and particularly poetic quotations which are integrated in the composition and indicate the title of the work. . . . The whole develops in an imaginary realm, where the relations between words and forms have no objective, representational intent, but recreate among themselves their own intrinsic relations.[29]

Consider *Ici, C'est Ici Stieglitz / Foi et Amour* (Figure 4.1), a drawing Williams surely knew since it appeared on the cover of *291* in 1915. The top and bottom of what seems to be Stieglitz's own folding camera are rendered realistically, as they might be in an illustrated catalogue. But

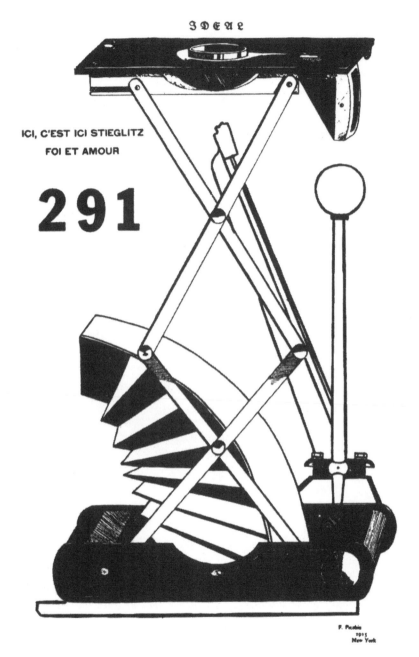

Figure 4.1. Francis Picabia, *Ici, C'est Ici Stieglitz. Foi et Amour*. Cover illustration, *291* (July 1915). Reprinted by permission of the Henry E. Huntington Memorial Library, San Marino, California.

what is inside this frame has a nice ambiguity. In one sense, Picabia gives us a drawing of magnified camera parts: the bellows, shutter, hinge, flashbulb. But the distortion by scale is such that we also seem to be looking at what is seen *by* the camera: a staircase on the left, a walking-stick and street lamp on the right. Or again, as in all of Picabia's drawings of the period, most obviously in the picture of a spark-plug called *Portrait D'Une Jeune Fille Américane Dans L'État De Nudité,* the "portrait" of Stieglitz has erotic overtones, reenforced by the words *FOI ET AMOUR* of the title and especially by the word *IDEAL,* placed over the hole which is also the lens.

In Picabia's drawings, as in a Picasso collage, the verbal is thus incorporated as a commentary on the visual: indeed, the picture must be "read" as well as seen. A similar attempt to fuse word and image is found in Gertrude Stein's verbal portraits, two of which – "Matisse" and "Picasso" – appeared in the special August 1912 issue of *Camera Work,* and a third, "Portrait of Mabel Dodge at the Villa Curonia," in the June 1913 issue. The latter also has a piece by Mabel Dodge herself called "Speculations," in which she observes that "In a large studio in Paris, hung with paintings by Renoir, Matisse and Picasso, Gertrude Stein is doing with words what Picasso is doing with paint." And again, "In Gertrude Stein's writing every word lives."[30]

Every word lives: Williams, who was to follow Stein in what he called her "unlink[ing]" of words "from their former relationships in the sentence,"[31] surely learned from an artist like Picabia that, if the visual work can also have a verbal dimension, why not the other way around? And so he began to experiment with the visual placement of words in lines: here is "Good Night," first published in *Others* in December 1916:

> In brilliant gas light
> I turn the kitchen spigot
> and watch the water plash
> into the clean white sink.
> On the grooved drain-board
> to one side is
> a glass filled with parsley –
> crisped green.
>
>   Waiting
> for the water to freshen –
> I glance at the spotless floor –
> a pair of rubber sandals
> lie side by side

> under the wall-table
> all is in order for the night. . . .   (CEP, p. 145)

Here it is lineation rather than the pattern of stresses that guides the reader's eye so that objects stand out, one by one, as in a series of film shots: first the gas light, then the spigot, then the plash of water, and finally the sink itself. The eye moves slowly so as to take in each monosyllable (all but 4 of the 19 words in the first lines, all but 12 of the 67 words in the whole verse paragraph): *in, gas, light, turn, the, and, watch.* . . . The sixth line, "to one side is," is what Hayden Carruth calls "hung over": it asks the question, what is it that is located "to one side"? The next line tells us: "A glass filled with parsley – ." But what does the parsley look like? Again a new line:

> Crísped gréen

Next there is a wait as the water runs from the tap, and so "Waiting" gets a line to itself and a prominent line at that because it is moved over toward the jagged right margin of the poem. Notice that the poem would *sound* exactly the same if "waiting" were aligned with "crisped" and "for" at the left margin; the effect, in other words, is entirely visual. And again, the ensuing lines are characterized by suspension: a "pair of rubber sandals" (line 12) do what? They "lie side by side" (line 13). But where?

> Únder the wáll-táble

As in Picabia's *Ici, C'est Ici Stieglitz,* ordinary objects are granted a curious sexual power.

If we look at the sound repetitions in Williams' poem, we immediately note the alliteration of *t*'s and *w*'s and assonance of *i*'s. But again, the visualization of these phonemes creates a stronger "echo structure" than does their sound. The first letter in the poem, for example, appears ten times in the 19 words of the first sentence: *in-brilliant-light-I-kitchen-spigot-int o-white-sink.* The first line-ending, "light," gets a near response from "spigot" in the slightly longer second line; it further chimes with "spotless" (line 11) and with the final word of the stanza, "night." From "light" to "night" – one would think that Williams had written a sonnet or Spenserian stanza. "A design in the poem," as he tells Walter Sutton, "and a design in the picture should make them more or less the same thing" (INTS, p. 53). Thus designed, "Good Night" provides us, quite literally, with the pleasure of the text. Each line waits for its fulfillment from the next, with "Waiting," coming, as it does, after "crisped green," exerting the central pull. Like "Love

Song," "Good Night" is a poem about desire, its "hung over" words reaching for the other even as the poet daydreams about the young girls he saw at the opera:

> full of smells and
> the resulting sounds of
> cloth rubbing on cloth and
> little slippers on carpet –

IV

I have been suggesting that *Al Que Quiere* is Williams' first significant tribute to the printed page as poetic unit; its poems embody the recognition, not shared by many of Williams' contemporaries, that a poem is "a small machine made of words" (SE, p. 256), a verbal text to be *seen* at least as much as to be heard. Stieglitz's photographs, *The Aeroplane* and *The Dirigible,* had appeared in *Camera Work* as early as 1911, and Picabia's machine drawings as well as Duchamp's ready-mades surely helped to bring the lesson home: the typographical lay-out of the page was not a sideline, some sort of secondary support structure, but a central fact of poetic discourse. Once this basic premise is understood, Williams' later prosodies become much easier to comprehend. Let me comment briefly on three developments in Williams' poetry.

1

From *Spring and All* (1923) through the thirties, the main thrust is to condense and to refine the principles of cut, displacement, and formal design adumbrated in the poems of the previous decade. Thus the long and slightly shaggy stanza of "Good Night" or of "Love Song" gives way to much smaller, disjunctive units – to very short lines, often no more than three syllables long, arranged in couplets ("At the Ball Game"), or tercets ("To Elsie"), or quatrains ("Death of the Barber").[32] This drive toward minimalism culminates in such poems of the mid-thirties as "Between Walls":

> the back wings
> of the
>
> hospital where
> nothing

```
will grow lie
cinders

in which shine
the broken

pieces of a green
bottle                                    (CEP, p. 343)
```

If we insert two small function words, "the" in the title and "of" at the beginning of the first line, and place a comma after "grow," we have here a perfectly normal sentence:

> Between the walls of the back wings of the hospital where nothing will grow, lie cinders in which shine the broken pieces of a green bottle.

An independent clause, its subject and verb inverted, embedded in multiple prepositional modifiers. Williams drapes this sentence across ten lines so that each and every word is taken out of its proper syntactic slot and hence defamiliarized:

```
of the . . .
will grow lie . . .
in which shine . . .
```

and so on. But there is something further. The visual pattern – five symmetrical couplets in which the long line is regularly followed by a short one – contradicts the aural one. Compare, for example, the first and third couplets:

```
the back wings          will grow lie
of the                  cinders
```

On the page, these are matching couplets, each having a syllable count of 3–2. The first two lines, moreover, each have three monosyllables almost identical in size. But when the words of the poem are spoken, "of the" (line 2) receives no stress at all whereas line 5 is scanned as follows

```
wíll grów ‖ líe
```

The result is that the first visual stanza has the stress pattern 2-0, the second, 3-1. What looks symmetrical is in fact disparate and other. The poem means, Williams tells Babette Deutsch, "that in a waste of cinders loveliness, in the form of color, stands up alive."[33] But, as so often, the poem Williams wrote is much better than the portentous meaning he ascribes to it. For what we admire in "Between Walls" is surely less the idea that beauty can be found even among trash, than the way this small observation is turned into a "field of action" in which line plays against syntax, visual against aural form, creating what Charles Olson was to call an energy-discharge, or projectile. Words are "unlink[ed] from their former relationships in the sentence" and recombined so that the poem becomes a kind of hymn to linguistic possibility.

2

The poems of Williams' last decade are written almost exclusively in what has been called the triadic stanza or three-step line:

> The smell of the heat is boxwood
> > when rousing us
> > > a movement of the air . . . [34]

Discussion of this triad has been confused by Williams' own claim that he is now using a unit called the "variable foot," which he defines as a foot "that has been expanded so that more syllables, words, or phrases can be admitted into its confines."[35] As such, the variable foot is, of course, a contradiction in terms, rather like an elastic inch.[36] It has been argued, most recently by Charles O. Hartman, that the three-line units of the triad are isochronous. Here Hartman is following Williams himself, who explained his "new measure" to Richard Eberhart with the following example:

> (count): – not that I ever count when writing but, at best, the lines must be capable of being counted, that is to say, *measured* – (believe it or not). – At that I may, half consciously, even count the measure under my breath as I write –

(approximate example)

> (1) The smell of the heat is boxwood
> > (2) when rousing us
> > > (3) a movement of the air
> (4) stirs our thoughts
> > (5) that had no life in them
> > > (6) to a life, a life in which

(or)

> (1) Mother of God! Our Lady!
> > (2) the heart
> > > (3) is an unruly master:

> (4) Forgive us our sins
>   (5) as we
>   (6) forgive
> (7) those who have sinned against
>
> Count a single beat to each numeral. You may not agree with my ear, but that is the way I count the line. Over the whole poem it gives a pattern to the meter that can be felt as a new measure.[37]

Hartman comments: "The prosody works for two reasons. First it builds on the convention of line division, essential to and recognized in all verse. Second, Williams became sufficiently well-known so that through letters and essays he could establish singlehandedly the convention that all lines take the same time – though only for his poems."[38]

Here Hartman bases his argument on the linguist Kenneth Pike's theorem that "the time-lapse between any two primary stresses tends to be the same irrespective of the number of syllables and the junctures between them" (p. 42). But the problem is that, in the example from "For Eleanor and Bill Monahan" that Williams gives Eberhart, the line "Mother of God! Our Lady!" has three primary stresses, whereas the next line, "the heart," has only one. If I insist on making these two lines isochronous, I have to make a wholly unnatural speech pause after "the heart":

> Móther of Gód! ‖ Oûr Lády!
>   the héart –
>   îs an unrúly máster . . .

The argument for isochrony thus seems to me to be no more satisfactory than an argument for a measure made up of "feet" that are somehow "variable." In the interview with Walter Sutton, Williams makes a more helpful comment about the triad. When Sutton asks him whether he thinks of feet in terms of stresses, Williams replies: "Not, as stresses, but as spaces in between the various spaces of the verse" (INTS, p. 39). This is, it seems to me, the point. Take the following passage from Book II of "Of Asphodel, That Greeny Flower":

> So to know, what I have to know
>   about my own death
>   if it be real
> I have to take it apart.
>   What does your generation think
>   Of Cézanne?

I asked a young artist.
          The abstractions of Hindu painting,
                    he replied,
is all at the moment which interests me.
          He liked my poem
                    about the parts
of a broken bottle,
          lying green in the cinders
                    of a hospital courtyard.
There was also, to his mind,
          the one on gay wallpaper
                    which he had heard about
but not read.
          I was grateful to him
                    for his interest.   (PB, pp. 162–163)

The line units here are related neither by stress count nor by isochrony: there is, for example, no way to equalize "What does your generation think" and the next line, "of Cézanne?". But on the page, the three-step line creates an attractive shape; it gives Williams a definite frame within which to lay out his sentences, a successor to such visual stanzas as the quatrains of "The Nightingales" and "This Is Just To Say."

My own sense, however, is that this particular frame does not have the complexity and tension of Williams' earlier visual forms; on the contrary, the three-step grid is an externally imposed geometric form, a kind of cookie cutter. For what happens is this. The locutions of prose ("There was also, to his mind, the one on gay wallpaper which he had heard about but not read") are forced into the triadic mold without sufficient attention to the relation between positioning and line-cut on the one hand and the structure of meanings on the other. Compare, for example, Williams' little poem "Between Walls," which I discussed earlier, to the reference to that poem in lines 11–15 above, and the difference will become clear. Syntactic units now break predictably enough at the point of natural juncture:

                    about the parts
          of a broken bottle,
                    lying green in the cinders
                              of a hospital courtyard.

In the case of "Between Walls," a change of word placement or the elimination of a single word would destroy the poet's mobile, the machine made of words which is the poem. In the case of "Asphodel," we read on pleasantly enough, but the sequence of words about the broken bottle or about the gay wallpaper has no inevitability, no sense of interacting force-field.

Such comparisons help us to understand that visual prosody is, after all, just as difficult as any other. In the wake of Williams, we have now lived through three decades of American poems that claim our attention by the sheer irregularity of pattern: words spread all over the page, words capitalized and in small letters and italics, lines that step up or down or go sideways. But just as a poem written in traditional meter – say, a Shakespeare sonnet – depends for its effectiveness on the relation of the phonemic to the semantic, so the visualization of the poem, the anchoring of its lines on the printed page, demands more than a typographical frame.

3

The premise that the poetic unit is no longer the metrical stanza or even the individual line but rather the printed page itself stands behind what is surely one of Williams' central contributions to American poetics: namely, the alteration and juxtaposition of "verse" to "prose." Williams began to experiment with the prose-verse page as early as *Spring and All* (1923) and *The Descent of Winter* (1928): in these works, lyrics are inserted into expository and narrative prose passages of some length. In *Paterson,* the opposite happens: the basic frame is the long free-verse stanza, and that frame is "cut," even as the line is cut in the earlier poems, by prose passages – documentary accounts of the history of Paterson, letters from friends like Allen Ginsberg, Edward Dahlberg and Marcia Nardi, case reports about patients, fictional narrative, and so on.

Critical speculation on the relation of prose to verse in *Paterson* has not been very helpful, the tendency being to assume that prose and verse must represent some sort of clear-cut dichotomy: for example, the dichotomy between the world of hard facts or "things" (prose) and the world of their imaginative transformation (verse).[39] Williams' own comments, however, stress fusion rather than difference. Thus he writes to Parker Tyler on 3 October 1948:

> All the prose [in *Paterson*] including the tail which would have liked to have wagged the dog, has primarily the purpose of giving a metrical meaning to or of emphasizing a metrical continuity between all word use. It is *not* an antipoetic device. . . . It *is* that prose and verse are both *writing*, both a

matter of words and an interrelation between words for the
purpose of exposition, or other better defined purpose of *the
art*. . . . I want to say that prose and verse are to me the same
thing, that verse (as in Chaucer's tales) belongs *with* prose. . . .
Poetry does not *have* to be kept away from prose as Mr. Eliot
might insist. . . .

And in the same year, to Horace Gregory:

The truth is that there's an identity between prose and verse,
not an antithesis. It all rests on the same base, the same measure . . . the long letter [at the end of *Paterson*, Book One] is
definitely germane to the rest of the text.[40]

In what sense can there be "an identity between prose and verse"; in
what sense does their juxtaposition emphasize "a metrical continuity
between all word use"? What Williams means, I think, is that once the
page rather than the foot or line or stanza becomes the unit of measure,
the typographic composition of that page can consist of prose as easily
as of verse, provided that there is some juxtaposition of the two so as to
create visual interest, provided that, in Hugh Kenner's words, "art lifts
the saying out of the zone of things said."[41] Poetry, in this larger sense
that would include both "verse" and "prose," is a form of writing, of
écriture, that calls attention to words as words rather than as referents to
a particular reality.

Take, for example, the passage in Book One, Part III in which the
poet meditates on the fragmentation of self:

Let it rot, at my center.
    Whose center?
I stand and surpass
    youth's leanness.

My surface is myself.
    Under which
to witness, youth is
    buried. Roots?

Everybody has roots.[42]

Abrupt quatrains full of word repetition give way to open tercets, in
which Williams lashes out at the university, a place ruled by "clerks /
got out of hand forgetting for the most part / to whom they are
beholden." The passage concludes with the single line:

Something else, something else the same.   (P, p. 32)

What is that "something else" which is the same as the *trahison des clercs?* We now read the following prose passage, printed in reduced type:

> He was more concerned, much more concerned, with detaching the label from a discarded mayonnaise jar, the glass jar in which some patient had brought a specimen for examination, than to examine and treat the twenty and more infants taking their turn from the outer office, their mothers tormented and jabbering. He'd stand in the alcove pretending to wash, the jar at the bottom of the sink well out of sight and, as the rod of water came down, work with his fingernail in the splash at the edge of the colored label striving to loose the tightly glued paper. It must have been varnished over, he argued, to have it stick that way. One corner of it he'd got loose in spite of all and would get the rest presently: talking pleasantly the while and with great skill to the anxious parent.

And this in turn gives way to four long free-verse lines, lines distinguished from normal prose only by the jagged right margin:

> Will you give me a baby? asked the young colored woman
> in a small voice standing naked by the bed. Refused
> she shrank within herself. She too refused. It makes me
> too nervous, she said, and pulled the covers round her.

The three visual units – lyric (quatrains and tercets), prose narrative, and free-verse block – are thematically related: they all center on the nature of "divorce," of alienation from others and from one's work, of the search for and loss of "roots." But the change in prosody signals a change in tone: if the lyric poet of the first part speaks to us directly, ruminating on the universal nature of pain – "Youth is / buried. Roots?" – the subject of the prose passage is that same poet carefully distanced by an urbane voice that uses the language of the lab report or case study, recording the poet-doctor's compulsive-neurotic behavior, his bizarre concentration on the label of the mayonnaise jar as an escape from all human contact. The intrusion of the free-verse passage:

> Will you give me a baby? asked the young colored woman

provides a third perspective: the personal account, evidently given by the doctor to whom the question is addressed, gives us a sense of what it is that the man obsessed with the mayonnaise jar (who is, of course, the same poet-doctor) is afraid of: the confrontation with another, "the young colored woman" whose demands he cannot satisfy.

Each of the three passages in question might have been in "verse" or "prose": it is not their metrical (or non-metrical) status or even their lineation (or non-lineation) that matters, but the very fact of transition from an A to a B and C, the shift in typographical format signalling a change in perspective, in tone, in mood. Thus the personal pathos of the lyric ("we go on living, we permit ourselves / to continue") gives way to the macabre humor of the mayonnaise-jar story, and in turn to the intimacy of the free-verse passage with its embedded speech.

Such consistent shifting of ground, such change in perspective propels the reader forward through the poem. Try to imagine *Paterson* without such prose-verse alternation, try to imagine all the prose anecdotes and letters and documentary catalogues absorbed into the larger free-verse fabric or vice-versa, and the point will become apparent. The difference between Williams' "verse" and his "prose" is thus *not,* as he rightly says, meter: it is the manipulation of tone implicit in the visual presentation of a small stanza versus a prose paragraph with justified left and right margins, and so on. The page is to be seen, its contrasting juxtaposed elements recalling the bits of newspaper or photographs pasted into Cubist or Dada collage.

4

James Laughlin has recently suggested that the influence of modern painting, regularly cited with respect to such earlier works as *Kora in Hell,* "extended to the composition of *Paterson*": "In the revolutionary works of those French painters he saw ways to revolutionize the very nature of writing in English."[43] Certainly, the collage-structure of *Paterson* would not have been possible without the Cubist or Dada model. Indeed, I would posit that when Williams exchanged this particular visual paradigm for the simple numerical grid of the geometer, as he was to do in the step-triads of his last decade, he denied himself the possibility of the *play* that makes poems of his middle years like "Between Walls" and "The Gay Wallpaper" so remarkable. The prosodic trick was to decenter, or, as Williams put it in "The Attic Which Is Desire":

Here

from the street
by

    ★ ★ ★
    ★ S ★
    ★O★
    ★D★
    ★ A ★
    ★ ★ ★

ringed with
running lights

the darkened
pane

exactly
down the center

is

transfixed   (CEP, p. 353)

NOTES

1   *I Wanted to Write a Poem: The Autobiography of the Works of a Poet,* reported
    and edited by Edith Heal (Boston: Beacon Press, 1958), pp. 66–67. Subse-
    quently cited as IWWP.

2   As early as 1913, Williams declared: "I do not believe in *vers libre,* this
    contradiction in terms. Either the motion continues or it does not continue,
    either there is rhythm or no rhythm. *Vers libre* is prose." See Mike Weaver,
    William Carlos Williams: The American Background (Cambridge, England:
    Cambridge University Press, 1971), p. 82. Weaver produces the whole
    unpublished essay, "Speech Rhythm" submitted to *Poetry* but returned by
    Harriet Monroe as being incomprehensible: see pp. 82–83. For other im-
    portant versions of this argument, see *The Selected Letters of William Carlos
    Williams,* ed. John C. Thirwall (New York: McDowell, Obolensky, 1957),
    p. 129; "Studiously Unprepared: Notes for Various Talks and Readings:
    May 1940 to April 1941," ed. Paul Mariani, in *Sulfur,* 4 (1982): 12–13;
    Walter Sutton, "A Visit with William Carlos Williams" (1961), in *Inter-
    views with William Carlos Williams,* ed. Linda Wagner (New York: New
    Dimensions, 1976), pp. 38–39; and William Carlos Williams, "Free
    Verse," in *Princeton Encyclopedia of Poetry and Poetics,* ed. Alex Preminger
    (Princeton: Princeton University Press, 1974), pp. 288–290. Ironically, it is
    customary to treat Williams as one of *the* inventors of free verse: see
    Charles O. Hartman, *Free Verse, An Essay on Prosody* (Princeton: Princeton
    University Press, 1980), pp. 93–106, and passim.

3   IWWP, p. 75. See also, "Note: The American Language and the New
    Poetry, so called," enclosed with a letter to H. L. Mencken, 17 December
    1934, cited by Weaver, p. 81; Williams, "Interview with Mike Wallace"
    (1957), in Wagner, *Interviews,* p. 74; Williams, "Some Hints Toward the
    Enjoyment of Modern Verse" (1952), in *Quarterly Review of Literature*
    (1953); rpt. in *Contemporary Poetry, A Retrospective from the Quarterly Review
    of Literature,* ed. Theodore Weiss and Renée Weiss (Princeton: Princeton
    University Press, 1974), p. 125.

As in the case with free verse, most commentators take Williams at his word. Thus David Perkins writes: "the lines are arranged to enact the movement of the voice speaking: they reinforce the natural rhythm by linear notion," *A History of Modern Poetry from the 1890s to Pound, Eliot and Yeats* (Cambridge, Mass.: Harvard University Press, 1976), p. 316.

4 A similar argument is advanced by Henry M. Sayre in *The Visual Text of William Carlos Williams* (Urbana and Chicago: The University of Illinois Press, 1983), p. 82. Sayre's book, published after I had completed my own essay, is a valuable adjunct.

5 See Cary Nelson, "Suffused-Encircling Shapes of Mind: Inhabited Space in Williams," *Journal of Modern Literature,* 1, no. 4 (May 1971): 549–564.

6 *A Homemade World, The American Modernist Writers* (New York: Alfred A. Knopf, 1975), p. 58.

7 John W. Gerber and Emily M. Wallace, "An Interview with William Carlos Williams" (1950), in Wagner, *Interviews,* p. 17. Subsequently cited as INTS.

8 My notation is a simplified version of the standard Trager-Smith scansion using 4 stresses: primary (´), secondary (ˆ), tertiary (ˋ), and weak ( ). A strong pause is indicated by the standard caesura (‖), a lesser pause (∣). The poem appears in *The Collected Earlier Poems of William Carlos Williams* (New York: New Directions, 1951), p. 354. Subsequently cited as CEP.

9 *The Autobiography of William Carlos Williams* (New York: Random House, 1951), p. 47. Cf. the slightly different versions Williams gives in IWWP, p. 4, and INTS, p. 8.

10 In *William Carlos Williams: A New World Naked* (New York: McGraw Hill, 1981), pp. 30–31, Paul Mariani, commenting on the cardiac episode, writes:

> Williams was shattered. He had fondly hoped that he would at least shine as a track star, and now he went into a black depression. It was, ironically, this touching bottom, this first descent into his private hell, that turned out to yield an unlooked-for gift: the gift of the poem. It was, as far as he could remember, the first poem he had ever written, a short, spontaneous thing, a single sentence containing a symbol of his own despondency. But writing it brought with it a sense of relief, of delight, as though he had done something truly extraordinary.

And Mariani quotes the four lines of the poem.

Similarly, Rod Townley, commenting on the awkwardness of Williams' early verse and exclamatory rhetoric, writes: "But these are all half-measures; none of the poems resulting from them has the clean quiet shock value of the enjambment that concludes the first poem Williams wrote: 'driven by fierce flying / rain.' " See *The Early Poetry of William Carlos Williams* (Ithaca: Cornell University Press, 1975), p. 63. Townley does not ask himself the question: how would the poet who used those "half-measures" as late as 1913, have devised the "clean quiet shock value of . . . enjambment" as early as 1900?

11   See on this point, Herbert Leibowitz, "You Can't Beat Innocence: *The Autobiography of William Carlos Williams,*" *American Poetry Review,* 10, no. 2 (March/April 1981): 35–47.

12   According to Emily M. Wallace, Williams' bibliographer and the editor of the Williams Correspondence now in progress, the original manuscript of this poem has not yet been found.

13   *Poems* (Rutherford, N.J.: Reid Howell, 1909), p. 14.

14   See *The Poetry Review,* I, x (October 1912): 479–81. Williams' poems in this volume are a selection from *The Tempers,* introduced by Ezra Pound, but the poems included in this selection are still very close to those in *Poems* (1909). For a list of these poems and for all subsequent bibliographical information on book and magazine publication, see Emily Mitchell Wallace's indispensable *A Bibliography of William Carlos Williams* (Middletown, Connecticut: Wesleyan University Press, 1968).

15   H. D.'s comment is made in a letter of 14 August 1916 which Williams reprints in the Preface to *Kora in Hell: Improvisations* (1920); rpt. in Williams' *Imaginations,* ed. Webster Schott (New York: New Directions, 1970), p. 13. Subsequently cited as IMAG. H. D.'s letter then goes on to object to the "flippancies" and "hey-ding-ding touch" of a slightly later poem, "March," and Williams responds with some asperity, IMAG, p. 13.

        For Pound's comment, see his review of *The Tempers* in *New Freewoman,* I, no. 11 (December 1913); rpt. in *William Carlos Williams: The Critical Heritage,* ed. Charles Doyle (London: Routledge & Kegan Paul, 1980), p. 53. Subsequently cited as Doyle. At Pound's request, "Postlude" was published in the June 1913 number of *Poetry* by Harriet Monroe; see Mariani, *A New World Naked,* p. 105.

16   The lines come respectively from "Und Drang," "The Return," "Sub Mare," and "N.Y.": see *Collected Early Poems of Ezra Pound* (New York: New Directions, 1976), pp. 173, 198, 194, and 185.

17   *The Cantos of Ezra Pound* (New York: New Directions, 1971), p. 24.

18   The phrase is Hugh Kenner's: see *A Homemade World,* p. 59.

19   *The Egoist,* 16, no. 1 (1914): 307–308.

20   *Others,* 3 (1916–1917): 31. Marianne Moore's poem appears on pages 4–5.

21   Hoyt's "Damask" appears in *Others,* p. 10; Aiken's "Illusions" on p. 16. The first version of Williams' "Love Song" adds three lines at the beginning ("What have I to say to you / When we shall meet? / Yet–") and fifteen more lines after "spoiling the colors / Of the whole world"); it does not have the final couplet. See *Poetry,* 9 (November 1916): 81–82; and CEP, pp. 173–174. The second version first appeared in *Al Que Quiere* (1917); see CEP, p. 174.

22   "Mr. Williams and His Caviar of Excessive Individualism," *Skepticisms: Notes on Contemporary Poetry* (New York, 1919); rpt. in Doyle, p. 58.

23   Review of *Paterson, Book Three,* in *Nation* (8 April 1950); rpt. in Doyle, p. 221.

24   *William Carlos Williams, An American Artist* (New York: Oxford University Press, 1970), p. 52.

25 "The Young Housewife" first appeared in the December 1916 issue of *Others*.

26 Bram Djikstra, *The Hieroglyphics of a New Speech: Cubism, Stieglitz, and the Early Poetry of William Carlos Williams* (Princeton: Princeton University Press, 1969); Dikran Tashjian, *Skyscraper Primitives: Dada and the American Avant-Garde, 1910–1925* (Middletown, Connecticut: Wesleyan University Press, 1975). See also, Bram Djikstra (ed.), *A Recognizable Image: William Carlos Williams on Art and Artists* (New York: New Directions, 1978); and, for an account of Williams' relationship with American artists in the twenties and thirties, Dikran Tashjian, *William Carlos Williams and the American Scene* (Berkeley and Los Angeles: University of California Press, 1978).

27 See my *The Poetics of Indeterminacy: Rimbaud to Cage,* Chapter Four; Ruth Grogan, "The Influence of Painting on Williams Carlos Williams" (1969), in *William Carlos Williams, A Critical Anthology,* ed. Charles Tomlinson (Baltimore: Penguin Books, 1972), pp. 265–298; Henry Sayre, "Ready-Mades and Other Measures: The Poetics of Marcel Duchamp and William Carlos Williams," *Journal of Modern Literature,* 8 (1980): 3–22. An excellent essay that does relate Williams' verse form to Cubist art is James E. Breslin's "William Carlos Williams and Charles Demuth: Cross-Fertilization in the Arts," *Journal of Modern Literature,* 6, no. 2 (April 1977): 248–263.

28 See William S. Rubin, *Dada, Surrealism, and their Heritage* (New York: The Museum of Modern Art, 1968), p. 27.

29 "Some Memories of Pre-Dada: Picabia and Duchamp" (1949), in *The Dada Painters and Poets: An Anthology,* ed. Robert Motherwell (New York: George Wittenborn, Inc., 1951), p. 261.

30 *Camera Work,* Special Number: June 1913, pp. 6–8. See *Poetics of Indeterminacy,* Chapter Three.

31 "The Work of Gertrude Stein" (1931), in *Selected Essays of William Carlos Williams* (New York: New Directions, 1954), p. 116. Subsequently cited as SE.

32 See *Poetics of Indeterminacy,* Chapter Three, passim.

33 Letter of 25 May 1948: see *Selected Letters of William Carlos Williams,* ed. John C. Thirwall (1957; New York: New Directions, 1984), p. 265. Subsequently cited as SL.

34 "To Daphne and Virginia," in *Pictures from Breughel and Other Poems* (New York: New Directions, 1962), p. 75. Subsequently cited as PB.

35 "Free Verse," *Princeton Encyclopedia of Poetry and Poetics,* p. 289. Cf. John C. Thirwall, "Ten Years of a New Rhythm," PB, pp. 183–184.

36 See Alan Stephens, "Dr. Williams and Tradition," *Poetry,* 101 (February 1963): 361; A. Kingsley Weatherhead, "William Carlos Williams: Prose, Form, and Measure," ELH, 33 (1966): 118–131.

37 Williams, letter to Richard Eberhart, 23 May 1954, in SL, pp. 326–327.

38 *Free Verse,* p. 35, and cf. p. 69.

39 See, for example, Walter Peterson, *An Approach to Paterson* (New Haven: Yale University Press, 1967), Chapter 1 *passim.*

40 Cited by James Laughlin in "William Carlos Williams and the Making of *Paterson:* A Memoir," *Yale Review,* 71 (Spring 1982): 193–194.

41 *A Homemade World,* p. 60.

42 *Paterson* (New York: New Directions, 1963), pp. 43–44. Subsequently cited in text as P.

43 Cf. Eleanor Berry, "Williams' Development Of A New Prosodic Form – *Not* The 'Variable Foot,' But The Sight-Stanza," *William Carlos Williams Review,* 7, no. 2 (Fall 1981): 28. Berry writes: "The sense of regularity, sometimes, inded, monotony, that is induced by Williams' triadic-line verse would seem to be due to the fact that the intervals between the prominent syllables of successive intonational units in spoken English tend to be perceived as equal." As I have argued above, I question the isochrony of the three parts of the Williams triad, but I do agree with Berry that this form is "essentially antithetical to the sight stanza [e.g., the quatrain or tercet used in the earlier poetry] in its operation."

5 "The shape of the lines": Oppen and the metric of difference

−I see the difference between the writing of Mr. Oppen and Dr. Williams, I do not expect any great horde of readers to notice it. They will perhaps concentrate, or no, they will concentrate, they will coagulate their rather gelatinous attention on the likeness.
         − Ezra Pound, Preface to *Discrete Series* (1934)[1]

Pound was quite right. From the beginning, the "likeness" between Williams and Oppen has been accepted as axiomatic; Williams himself, for that matter, introduced *Discrete Series* to the audience of *Poetry* magazine in a review that devoted more space to "our" Objectivist aims than to Oppen's poems, praising the latter rather off-handedly for their use of "plain words" and their "metric . . . taken from speech."[2]

Oppen himself has regularly protested to the contrary. In a 1968 interview, he tells L. S. Dembo,

> . . . some people think I resemble Williams and it seems to me that the opposite is true. Pound unfortunately defended me against the possible charge of resembling him in the original preface to *Discrete Series.* The fact has always haunted me. At any rate, my attitudes are opposite those of Williams. Certainly one would have needed a great deal more courage without his example, to begin to find a way to write. He was invaluable and many of his poems are beautiful, though I've always had reservations about *Paterson.*[3]

When Dembo remonstrates, "I was under the impression that one of the basic themes of *Paterson,* 'No ideas but in things,' would appeal to you," Oppen replies,

119

> I have always wondered whether that expression didn't apply
> to the construction of meaning in a poem – not necessarily that
> there are out there no ideas but in things, but rather that there
> would be in the poem no ideas but those which could be ex-
> pressed through the description of things. I took it that he
> meant the latter. . . .   (*CL,* p. 170)

Oppen's desire to separate himself from what he takes to be Williams'
Imagist aesthetic is not just a case of the Anxiety of Influence, the need
to dissociate oneself from the threatening Precursor. For although his
poems may look on the page like Williams' lyrics – minimalist, jagged,
free verse units, surrounded by much white space – Oppen's language,
his syntax, and especially his prosody are really quite different. For one
thing, the stress on "plain words" and a "metric taken from speech,"
attributed to Oppen by Williams, the faith that, as Williams puts it,
"The pronunciation as spoken must make [the poet's] line,"[4] is one that
Oppen emphatically rejects. "I don't subscribe," he tells Dembo, "to
any of the theories that poetry should simply reproduce common
speech and so on" (*CL,* p. 167). On the contrary, "I learned from Louis
[Zukofsky], as against the romanticism or even the quaintness of the
imagist position, the necessity for forming a poem properly, for achiev-
ing form" (*CL,* p. 160). Which is to say that the making of a poem
inevitably involves artifice. In a "Statement on Prosody" made in a
recent interview, Oppen says,

> I try one word and another word, reverse the sequence, alter
> the line-endings, a hundred, two hundred rewritings, revi-
> sions – This is called prosody: how to write a poem. Or rather
> how to write *that* poem.[5]

And again, "every *and* and *but* must be revelatory – a music. We must
think what is being asserted in the 'little' words." For "primarily and
above all, and note by note, the prosody carries the relation of things
and the sequence." Prosody is "the instant of meaning, the achievement
of meaning and *presence,* the sequence of disclosure which comes from
everywhere" (Schieffer interview, n.p.). And, in articulating that *sequence of disclosure,* nothing is more important than the decision where
to break the line:

> . . . I do believe in a form in which there is a sense of the
> whole line, not just its ending. Then there's the sense of the
> relation between lines, the relation in their length; there is a
> sense of the relation of the speed, of the alterations and mo-
> mentum of the poem, the feeling when it's done that this has

been rounded. I think that probably a lot of the worst of modern poetry . . . uses the line-ending simply as the ending of a line, a kind of syncopation or punctuation. It's a kind of formlessness that lacks any sense of line measure.

The meaning of a poem is in the cadences and the shape of the lines and the pulse of the thought which is given by those lines. The meaning of many lines will be changed . . . if one changes the line ending.   (*CL,* p. 167)

Or, to put it another way, "The line-break is just as much a part of the language as the period, comma, or parenthesis, and it shows that there are things that can only be said as poetry."[6] In this context, "syntax" refers to "those connections which can't be dealt with outside the poem but that should take on substantial meaning within it" (*Montemora,* p. 198).

To compare Oppen's line divisions and syntactic patterns to those of Williams is to learn a great deal about the fuzziness of the Objectivist label. Here is Williams' "Nantucket," which first appeared in *Poems 1921–1931,* published by George Oppen's Objectivist Press in 1934.

> Flowers through the window
> lavender and yellow
>
> changed by white curtains –
> Smell of cleanliness –
>
> Sunshine of late afternoon –
> On the glass tray
>
> a glass pitcher, the tumbler
> turned down, by which
>
> a key is lying – And the
> immaculate white bed[7]

Both rhythmically and visually, "Nantucket" is characterized by stability of pattern. Despite a somewhat variable syllable count (6-6; 5-5; 7-4; 7-6), each of the five couplets contains a three-stress followed by a two-stress line, the exception being line 10 which has three primary and one secondary stress – "immáculâte whíte béd" – and which therefore provides at least a degree of closure. In the first couplet, for that matter, both lines terminate with an amphibrach:

```
´ x   ´    x ´ x
´ x x    x ´ x
```

with the final words linked by rhyming feminine endings.

In the first half of the poem, the line breaks coincide with phrasal units, culminating in "Smell of cleanliness" and "Sunshine of late afternoon." But in the second half, the movement accelerates: cuts now come between noun and verb or between article and noun, as words in final position reach out for completion: "On the glass tray →," "by which →," "the tumbler →," "And the →." In Williams, says Hillis Miller, "the word reaches out with all its strength towards the other words which are for the moment absent. Conjunctions, prepositions, adjectives, when they come at the end of a line, assume an expressive energy as arrows of force reaching towards the other words."[8]

In reading "Nantucket," we are propelled forward by precisely such "arrows of force," as the camera eye of the poem pans from outside ("flowers through the window") to inside by means of the "white curtains" that connect the two, coming to rest on what we might call the still-life of the "glass tray," with its "glass pitcher, the tumbler / turned down, by which / a key is lying." This last clause contains the first indicative verb in the poem: indeed, the key is the poetic point of focus, and it leads, hesitantly but tantalizingly, to "the / immaculate white bed." Thus, although the poem can be read as no more than a charming verbal painting of an interior, of one of those simple and hence delightful rooms in which one spends a Nantucket holiday, it also has Williams' characteristic erotic overtones. In a neighboring poem, we are presented with "Gay Wallpaper" that bears "cerulean shapes / laid regularly round" and a "basket floating / standing in the horns of blue" (*CEP*, p. 345). "Nantucket" begins with the word "flowers" and ends with the word "bed." Perhaps the white bed won't, after all, remain "immaculate," especially with that key so near by. The erotic tension of the final couplet is, in any case, heightened by the line break after "And the" and the increasingly choppy rhythm:

$$x \, ' \quad x \, / \, x \quad \| \quad x \; x$$
$$x \, ' \, x \, x \quad | \quad ''$$

One would think that a poem like "Nantucket" would answer perfectly to Oppen's own demand for a "prosody that carries the relation of things and sequence." "The little words I love so much"[9] – surely we find them in "Nantucket" or in a related poem of the thirties like "Between Walls":

the back wings
of the

hospital where
nothing

will grow lie
cinders

in which shine
the broken

pieces of a green
bottle   (*CEP*, p. 343)

Yet the scrupulous bareness of these poems is oddly different from Oppen's own kind of minimalism. Here is a poem from *Discrete Series*, published the same year as "Nantucket":

She lies, hip high,
On a flat bed
While the after-
Sun passes.

Plant, I breathe –
            O Clearly,

Eyes legs arms hands fingers,
Simple legs in silk.[10]

Perhaps the first thing that strikes us as we read this unnamed poem is that Oppen's bedroom scene is much more disjointed than Williams'. For although Williams' lines are often fragmentary bits of incomplete grammar ("turned down, by which"; "of the"; "will grow lie"; "the broken"), the syntax itself, overriding line units, is perfectly straightforward. "Nantucket" is framed as a simple catalogue of noun phrases, into which a single clause is inserted in the ninth line: "by which / a key is lying." We can read the poem as a list:

Flowers through the window . . .
Smell of cleanliness . . .
Sunshine of late afternoon . . .
On the glass tray a glass pitcher . . .
And the immaculate white bed

Again, "Between Walls" is, despite the fragmentation of its line units, a complete sentence. We need only supply the word "of" at the beginning of the poem, and a comma after "grow," in order to read it as follows: "Between walls of the back wings of the hospital where nothing will grow, lie cinders in which shine the broken pieces of a green bottle." To destroy Williams' lineation in this way is, of course, to make a travesty of his poem;[11] I merely want to point out that "Between Walls" has a definite forward movement, a straight propulsion. Hillis Miller writes:

> When nothing remains but the bits of glass and the poet fixes these with his full attention, the presentness of things present becomes a revelation of that fugitive radiance which all things hide. The poem means, [Williams] says, "That in a waste of cinders loveliness, in the form of color, stands up alive" [*Selected Letters*]. In the same way words, cut off from past and future, and from all preformed literary tradition, are freed to reveal their innate linguistic energy as nodes of power in a verbal field.   (Miller, p. 346)

But what is the "revelation" that "all things hide" in Oppen's gnomic poem? Here lineation is not, as in Williams, a release of the "innate linguistic energy" of words, a removal of those words from their usual contexts so as to create new relationships between them. Rather, in *Discrete Series,* line division is, so to speak, the meaning of each poem. For try to transpose the eight lines of "She lies, hip high" as prose and see what happens:

> She lies, hip high, on a flat bed while the after-sun passes. Plant, I breathe–. O Clearly, eyes legs arms hands fingers, simple legs in silk.

It makes no sense: "Plant, I breathe–" and "O Clearly" follow neither from what comes before nor relate, in any reasonable way, to "Eyes legs arms. . . ." Indeed, when we try to define what is happening in Oppen's poem, we find no reliable guide-posts. "She lies, hip high / On a flat bed"–a woman in labor, perhaps, with "after-Sun" being some kind of play on "after-birth." But the poet's response to this woman (his wife, Mary Oppen) is so sexual ("Plant, I breathe–"), he is so interested in enumerating the parts of her body (hip, eyes, legs, arms, hands, fingers), that it seems more plausible to read the poem as describing a love scene: "She lies, hip high / On a flat bed"–a man is about to enter a woman. It is perhaps a late, lazy afternoon, the "after- / Sun" that "passes" referring to twilight. "O Clearly" the speaker is full of want, and yet the last line presents a puzzle. "Simple legs in silk"– the wearing of stockings–makes one wonder if the poet is, after all, describing an afternoon's love making or whether he is simply observing the object of his desire from a distance, taking pleasure in her movements. Perhaps he has just been with her; perhaps he is going to be. There is no way to be sure, and the exclamation "O Clearly," withheld as it is from the left margin and floating in space, functions as a false lead.

Now let us see what role sound structure plays. "She lies, hip high" is, strictly speaking, written in free verse, the syllable count being 4, 4, 4, 3 in the first stanza; 3, 3, 6, 5 in the second, and no two lines having precisely the same pattern of stresses. At the same time, the first stanza looks like a square and its qualitative sound features create a densely interwoven system of recurrences:

> She lies, hip high,

Four monosyllables with two punctuation breaks, the fourth word chiming with the second (assonance of long i's) as well as with the third (alliteration of h's). A phonemic transcription[12] of the line gives us:

> šiy layz ‖ hip hay ‖

What is startling is the way the poem now modulates these initial sounds. The following phonemes are foregrounded:

/iy/ glide:	breathe – clearly
/ay/ glide:	lies – high – while – I
high front vowel (/i/):	hip – fingers – simple – in – silk
lateral (/l/):	lies – flat – Plant – clearly – legs – simple – legs – silk
voiceless spirant (/s/):	sun – passes – simple – silk
voiced spirant in final position (/z/):	lies – passes – eyes – legs – arms – hands – fingers – legs

Sometimes more than one kind of sound repetition is involved: thus "eyes" rhymes with "lies"; there is consonance in "lies" / "legs," chiasmus in "lies" / "while," and so on.

When the recurrence of sound is so pervasive, one looks for places where the sounds don't chime. The final word of the poem, the word that gives an odd perspective to the whole "love scene," is "silk," which contains the only instance in the poem of the phoneme /k/. Again, Oppen's first word, "She," contains the only instance of /š/ and the "O Clearly" of line 6, the only instance of /ow/. When we look at these isolated instances against the larger structure of recurrence, we discover a kind of subtext that conveys the urgency of the poet's desire: "She – O – silk." The "little words" that Oppen loves so much – a vocabulary that looks like Basic English but that in fact deviates sharply from the inflections of common speech that Williams advocated – are welded into a tensile verbal structure, a carefully planned suspension system. We can see now what the poet means when he says, "I try one word and another word, reverse the sequence, alter the line-endings . . . This is called prosody: how to write a poem. Or rather how to write *that* poem." "She lies, hip high" is purposely set up as a structure of possible contradictions: its presentation of desire is arresting precisely because we don't know whether it has been or will be satisfied. Or even if it wants to be.

From the beginning, then, Oppen has displayed a penchant for what we might call a poetic of "discrete series." As he explains the term to L. S. Dembo,

> A pure mathematical series would be one in which each term is derived from the preceding term by a rule. A discrete series is a series of terms each of which is empirically derived, each one of which is empirically true. And this is the reason for the fragmentary character of those poems. I was attempting to construct a meaning by empirical statements, by imagist statements. (*CL*, p. 161)

Here the term "imagist" is misleading, for the point about a poem like "She lies, hip high" is precisely that the poem does not proceed, as do Williams' "Nantucket" or "Between Walls," from image to related image. Rather, Oppen lays out, side by side, a "discrete series" of empirical statements, of fragments that seem unrelated and that tend to be conceptual rather than sensuous:

> From this distance thinking toward you,
> Time is recession
>
> Movement of no import
> Not encountering you . . .   (*DS*, p. 26; *CP*, p. 10)

The very titles of Oppen's volumes – *The Materials, This in Which, Of Being Numerous, Primitive* – express a concern for cognition: the poem, Oppen implies, is the only way to reconcile one's disparate and contradictory perceptions of the external world, for here the recurrence of sound can mitigate against the undecidability of experience. Consider another love poem in *Discrete Series:*

Near your eyes –
Love at the pelvis
Reaches the generic, gratuitous
      (Your eyes like snail-tracks)
Parallel emotions,
We slide in separate hard grooves
Bowstrings to bent loins,
      Self moving
Moon, mid-air.   (*DS*, p. 28; *CP*, p. 11)

Here the fragmentary prepositional and noun phrases that make up most of the nine lines are suspended both phonically and visually, and yet forms of recurrence, unobtrusive as they seem, play a central role. Stress count, for example, brings items together that syllable count would distinguish. Thus "Near your eyes" (3 syllables) and "Love at the pelvis" (5 syllables) have corresponding stress patterns:

$$\acute{} \ \text{x} \ \acute{}$$
$$\acute{} \ \text{x} \ \text{x} \ \acute{} \ \text{x}$$

and even the long third line (10 syllables) has only three primary stresses:

$$\acute{} \ \text{x} \ \mid \ \text{x} \ \text{x} \ \acute{} \ \text{x} \ \mid \ \text{x} \ \acute{} \ \text{x} \ \text{x}$$

"the generic" repeating the rhythm of "at the pelvis." Again, the first line of the second stanza, "Parallel emotions," echoes the first line of the poem, repeating the amphimac (/ x /) and adding its mirror image in the form of an amphibrac (x / x). In the last three lines, the recurrence of what we might call "envelope" groups (/ x / /) and (/ / /) balanced by the falling rhythm of the enclosed line (/ / x) provides a sense of arrest and coalescence, a coalescence emphasized by the marked alliteration of b's and m's, the consonance of "strings" / "loins," and the assonance of "bent" / "Self," the two words forming a column. The final words, "moving" and "moon," nearly rhyme, "mid-air" breaking up this chiming ever so slightly.

Just as the relationship among the elements along the speech chain is thus repeated – but not quite – in the course of the poem, so the semantic elements involve both recurrence and suspension. "Near your eyes," to begin with, would seem to go with "Love," but "Love at the pelvis" is hardly a very pretty image, despite the near-rhyme of "Love" and "pelvis." What seems to be a suspended noun phrase, "Love at the pelvis," now turns out to lead to a complete sentence unit, but a sentence whose meaning is indeterminate. Love "Reaches the generic," the root, that which makes the woman what she really is. But why is the "generic" "gratuitous"? The two words, joined as they are by the alliteration of g's and r's – an alliteration that makes the line turn back upon itself to "Reaches" – are a puzzling pair. Is the generic gratuitous because freely given? Obtained without charge? For no apparent cause? Or given without receiving any return value? We cannot tell. We know only that the poet somehow hangs back, perceiving his beloved's eyes quite unromantically as "snail-tracks" – which is to say that her eyes follow his movements very slowly. But "snail-tracks" also looks ahead to the "separate hard grooves" of line 7, the "parallel" and hence never meeting "emotions" of the two lovers.

Is theirs then a failed love act? One might say yes and no. "Bow-strings to bent loins" suggests close and loving conjunction: the playing upon each other's instrument. In this context, "Self moving" may refer to the moment of orgasm, but the word "Self" also suggests separation, possibly isolation. The final line, "Moon, mid-air," does not dispel the mystery. The reference may be to the ejaculation of seed. But also, perhaps more humbly, to a mere shift in position of one or the other lover. Does the woman, like her counterpart in "She lies, hip high," thrust her legs into "mid-air"? Is she the moon? Or is the moon literally shining?

"The meaning of a poem," says Oppen, "is the cadences and the shape of the lines." Certainly in "Near your eyes" each line break acquires meaning, emphasizing a "discrete series" of emotions and perceptions that could not be stated in any other way. Making love, the poem implies, is at once an act of conjunction and separation. Love "Reaches the generic" – "Bowstrings to bent loins" – yet somehow the lovers' emotions remain parallel, a "sliding" in "separate hard grooves" like the "snail-tracks" of the woman's eyes. Just so, on the sound level, there is a rhythmic recurrence, a coming together that is consistently offset by the "separate hard grooves" of the unequal line lengths, the variation of syllable count, the move away from the left margin as the poet discovers the "Self moving." "Prosody," as Oppen says, "is the achievement of . . . *presence,* the sequence of disclosure that comes from everywhere."

Such "achievement of presence" often depends upon parody, the sly undermining of a traditional topos:

> Her ankles are watches
> (Her arm-pits are causeways for water)
>
> When she steps
> She walks on a sphere

Walks on the carpet, dressing.
Brushing her hair

Her movement accustomed, abstracted,
Declares this morning a woman's
"My hair, scalp –"   (*DS,* p. 11; *CP,* p. 5)

Here Oppen begins with a series of extravagant conceits: his wife, evidently emerging from the shower or bath in what is her morning ritual, is quite literally a kind of wet dream; the flow of her body (arm pits become "causeways for water" and ankles tick as she moves) meets the flow of his desire so that her mere footsteps across the room have the grace of a goddess "walk[ing] on a sphere." It is the sort of metaphoric indulgence Williams scorned, believing, as he did, that "the coining of similes is a pastime of very low order,"[13] that instead the poet's attention should attach itself to the forms of nature themselves – a young sycamore, a lily, a cat climbing over the top of a jamcloset – so as to extract their particularity, their unique erotic force. Indeed, reading the first half of Oppen's poem, one thinks of Yeats's tributes to Maud Gonne:

For she had fiery blood
When I was young
And trod so sweetly proud
As 'twere upon a cloud . . .[14]

But unlike Yeats, Oppen can't hold such a thought for more than a moment; he knows that women don't really walk on spheres, that in fact his wife "Walks on the carpet, dressing. / Brushing her hair." And now something happens. Once dressed, his wife has lost the capacity for metaphoric transformation; the fanciful conceits of the opening couplet give way to hard facts:

Her movement accustomed, abstracted,
Declares this morning a woman's
"My hair, scalp –"

Here the word "scalp" functions rather as does "silk" in "She lies, hip high." The first three couplets have stressed the recurrence of sounds (*watches – water – walks; ankles – arm-pits – steps – walks; dressing – brushing; sphere – hair*); what is ironically "accustomed" turns out to be the dissonance of the tercet: the nine syllables of line 7 yield only three stresses, arranged, so to speak, in clumps:

x ´ x | x ´ x | x ´ x

and the truncated last line comes down heavily on the hard voiceless stop /p/ of "scalp." It is not the first /p/ in the poem, but the others ("arm-pits," "steps") are not in final position, and "scalp" also contains a second voiceless stop /k/ following a spirant. The effect is harsh and it is meant to be. What was once flowing (arm-pits as causeways for water) gives way to a substance that is hard and possibly scaly: we prefer the scalp to be concealed by hair. Nor do we know what the woman, who speaks for the first time in the last abbreviated line of the poem, is about to say about her "scalp." We only know that the liquid flow of desire is, at least for the moment, suspended.

Oppen's best poems regularly display this curious tension between the image of desire and the hard fact, between metrical and phonemic recurrence and a curious disruptiveness. Here is a later poem called "A Theological Definition":

> A small room, the varnished floor
> Making an L around the bed,
>
> What is or is true as
> Happiness
>
> Windows opening on the sea,
> The green painted railings of the balcony
> Against the rock, the bushes and the sea running[15]

Thematically, this poem recalls Williams' "Nantucket"; indeed, Williams might have written the first couplet with its precise and loving description of the L-shaped varnished floor surrounding the bed. Again, the reference to the "green painted railings of the balcony" in the tercet bring to mind such Williams poems as "The Poor," with its reference to the "cast iron balcony / with panels showing oak branches / in full leaf" (*CEP,* p. 415).

But the middle couplet, which shifts abruptly from image to concept, reflects Oppen's own personal conviction that the "bare image," as Stevens called it, is not enough. The syntax of the passage is impossible to unravel because the "of" is equivocal: Oppen may be saying that "What is" (the phenomenology of perception) is the only truth since it can give us happiness. Or again, the other way around: "What is" (the delightful little room with its varnished floor and ocean view) is just an appearance but since it brings us happiness we accept it as "true." However we take these words, they clearly place the title of the poem in an ironic perspective: the only theological definition Oppen can give us is that there is none. The monosyllabic line "What is or is true as," with its function words and auxiliaries, suggests that knowledge comes only by fits and starts, and that, in any case, words like "true" and "happiness" are not sufficiently delimited. This suggestion is borne out by the last line of the poem, which is a pseudo-alexandrine, its twelve syllables containing no more than five primary stresses, and the dying fall of its feminine ending ("running"), gently mocking the preceding rhyme, "sea" / "balcony."

Oppen is not always able to sustain a syntax in which the "connections which can't be dealt with outside the poem . . . take on substantial meaning within it." "The Forms of Love," which appeared in *This In Which* (1965), is one of his better known poems, but I don't think it can match the formal achievement of the love lyrics in *Discrete Series:*[16]

> Parked in the fields
> All night
> So many years ago,
> We saw
> A lake beside us
> When the moon rose.
> I remember
>
> Leaving that ancient car
> Together. I remember
> Standing in the white grass
> Beside it. We groped
> Our way together
> Downhill in the bright
> Incredible light
>
> Beginning to wonder
> Whether it could be lake
> Or fog
> We saw, our heads
> Ringing under the stars we walked
> To where it would have wet our feet
> Had it been water   (*CP*, p. 86)

Questioned by L. S. Dembo as to the meaning of this poem, Oppen replies:

> The car is detached from emotion, from use, from necessity – from everything except the most unconscionable of the emotions. And that lake which appears in the night of love seemed to me to be quite real even though it was actually fog. (*CL*, p. 168)

And when Dembo suggests: "But only two lovers – because of their heightened state of mind or heightened sensitivity – would have thought that the fog was a lake," that "the vision was actually a form of love," Oppen agrees.

It is a lovely poem but after a decade of Deep Image and Confessional poetry, we are perhaps inured to such lyrics of "heightened sensitivity," lyrics in which "vision" becomes "a form of love" somewhat too easily. Of the first stanza of "The Forms of Love," one might say what Oppen said in criticism of much contemporary poetry: "the line ending [is used] simply as the ending of a line, a kind of syncopation or punctuation" (*CL,* p. 167). "Parked in the fields / All night / So many years ago" – these lines merely continue, phrases like "So many years ago" and the repetitive "I remember" acting as little more than padding. "We groped / Our way together / Downhill" – any number of poets might have written those lines. Only in the last stanza does Oppen's characteristic rhythm of suspension return. "We saw," for example, refers back to the fog, but the lineation also makes us read it as "We saw our heads . . . " By the time we reach the penultimate line:

> to where it would have wet our feet

with its eight hesitant monosyllables, at once disjointed and yet united by the repeated chiming of w's and t's, we know we are back in Oppen country.

In a five-part poem called "Images of the Engine," that appears in *The Materials* of 1962, we find these lines:

> *Also he has set the world*
> *In their hearts.* From lumps, chunks.   (*CP,* p. 21)

I can think of no better description of Oppen's characteristic prosody, his way of proceeding through a given poetic structure. If Williams' is a metric of action, the creation of a field of force in which the presence of the moment is made manifest, Oppen's "discrete series" of lines remains disjunctive, discriminatory, abrupt – a movement of fits and starts, "From lumps, chunks." Ellipsis, riddle, radical condensation, abstraction, equivocal syntax, and the fragmentation of semantic units – all these pull against the coalescence of sound, often extremely delicate, and the hammering of words into the firm structure of the line. Oppen wants us to pause on every word, to try to understand how and why just these words could possibly coexist in the same text, so far removed are his "connections" from those of ordinary discourse. The text itself is thus called into question even as the poet "*sets the world / In our hearts.*"

NOTES

1 (New York: Objectivist Press, 1934), p. v; rpt. *Paideuma*, 10 (Spring 1981): *Special Issue: George Oppen*, ed. Burton Hatlen, p. 13.
2 "The New Poetical Economy," *Poetry*, 44 (July 1934), 224.
3 L. S. Dembo, "George Oppen" (interview conducted on 25 April 1968), *Contemporary Literature*, 10 (Spring, 1969), 159–77. Subsequently cited as *CL*.
4 For a good summary of Williams' view of the relation of poetry to actual speech, see Mike Weaver, *William Carlos Williams: The American Background* (Cambridge: Cambridge University Press, 1971), pp. 78–84. As early as 1913, Williams sent an essay called "Speech Rhythms" to Harriet Monroe for publication in *Poetry*, but, according to Weaver, she found it incomprehensible. See also "The Poem as a Field of Action," *The Selected Essays of William Carlos Williams* (New York: Random House, 1954), p. 290.
5 Reinhold Schieffer, "Interview with George Oppen conducted on 1 May 1975," Unpub. MS, Archive of New Poetry, University of California at San Diego. Cited by permission of Michael Davidson, Director of the Archive for New Poetry.
6 Kevin Power, "An Interview with George and Mary Oppen," *Montemora*, 4 (1978), 195. Subsequently cited as *Montemora*.
7 *The Collected Earlier Poems of William Carlos Williams* (New York: New Directions, 1951), p. 348. Subsequently cited as *CEP*. For publication dates and information, see Emily Mitchell Wallace, *A Bibliography of William Carlos Williams* (Middletown, Conn.: Wesleyan University Press, 1968).
8 *Poets of Reality: Six Twentieth-Century Writers* (1965; rpt. New York: Atheneum, 1969), pp. 299–300.
9 See *Montemora*, 198, 203. The point is also made in the Dembo interview (*CL*, 1968) and the Schieffer interview (1975).
10 George Oppen, *Collected Poems* (New York: New Directions, 1975), p. 9. Subsequently cited as *CP*. Because the *CP* obscures the original divisions between poems, I cite the original text (New York: Objectivist Press, 1934), subsequently noted as *DS*, as well. "She lies, hip high" is found in *DS*, p. 21.
11 The distinctive statement on the function of lineation in Williams is made by Hugh Kenner in his discussion of "The Red Wheelbarrow" in *A Homemade World* (New York: Alfred A. Knopf, 1975), p. 60:
    Try to imagine an occasion for this sentence to be said:

    So much depends upon a red wheelbarrow glazed with rainwater beside the white chickens.

    Try it over in any voice you like: it is impossible. It could only be the gush of an arty female on a tour of Farmer Brown's barnyard. . . . Not only is what the sentence says banal, if you heard someone say it you'd wince. But hammered on the typewriter into a *thing made*, and this without displaying a single word typographically, the sixteen words exist in a different zone altogether.

Precisely, but this is not what Oppen's lineation does. In his case, the words are lifted, not out of "the zone of things said," but, so to speak, out of the poet's imagination, for his phrases and clauses are often non-grammatical.

12 For the terminology used here, see H. A. Gleason, *An Introduction to Descriptive Linguistics* (New York: Holt, Rinehart and Winston, 1961), pp. 14–50. *Glide* is the phonetic designation for a semi-vowel. In the interest of clarity, I use the term *caesura* rather than *plus juncture* for a mid-line pause and the traditional / x / for a weakly stressed syllable.

13 "Prologue," *Kora in Hell: Improvisations* (1920), in *Imaginations* (New York: New Directions, 1970), p. 18.

14 *The Collected Poems of W. B. Yeats* (New York: Macmillan, 1950), p. 88.

15 It appeared in *Of Being Numerous* (1968). See *CP*, p. 197.

16 It may be objected that Oppen's later lyric mode has its own particular strengths and that it is unfair to judge poems like "The Forms of Love" according to the norms of the Objectivist phase. See Eleanor Berry, "Language Made Fluid: The Grammmetrics of George Oppen's Recent Poetry," *Contemporary Poetry*, 25 (Fall 1984), 305–22.

6 Between verse and prose: Beckett and the New Poetry

The opening paragraph of Samuel Beckett's most recently published fiction, *Ill Seen Ill Said,* begins as follows:

> From where she lies she sees Venus rise. On. From where she lies when the skies are clear she sees Venus rise followed by the sun. Then she rails at the source of all life. On. At evening when the skies are clear she savors its star's revenge.[1]

How shall we characterize this strange discourse, a discourse that is surely no closer to *prose,* which I shall define here, following Northrop Frye, as "the arrangement of words . . . dominated by the syntactical relations of subject and predicate" – in other words, the sentence – than it is to *verse,* which is the arrangement of words dominated by "some form of regular recurrence, whether meter, accent, vowel quality, rhyme, alliteration, parallelism, or any combination of these."[2] Indeed, if we had to choose one term or the other to designate this passage we might as well want to call it verse:

From whére she líes
she sées Vénus ríse.

> Ón.

From whére she líes
    when the skíes are cléar
she sées Vénus ríse

> fóllowed by the sún.

Then she ráils at the sóurce of âll lífe.

> Ón.

At évening when the skíes are cléar
she sávors its stár's revénge.

135

Six dimeter lines, five of them rhyming, followed by three trimeters made up primarily of anapests, the whole bound together by the alliteration of voiced and voiceless spirants: "she lies," "she sees Venus rise" (twice), "skies" (twice), "sun," "she rails," "source," "she savors," "stars." The paragraph – or is it a strophe? – is punctuated twice by the refrain word "On" (which rhymes with "sun").

But of course the text is not, strictly speaking, verse either. For one thing, Beckett chose not to lineate it, and for many readers this very choice determines the status of the text as prose. For another, *Ill Seen Ill Said* is written in what are, despite the indeterminacy of reference, primarily normal grammatical sentences: "From where she lies she sees Venus rise" – adverbial modifier, subject-verb-object.[3] What makes us want to lineate this particular sentence are two things: its binary rhythm, reinforced by rhyme (x / x / x x / x /), and the appearance of the word "On" immediately following, where "On," pointing to nothing perceivable, breaks up the linear flow of successive sentences. Throughout *Ill Seen Ill Said,* we shall run into this odd prose-verse ambiguity; either a single unit can be construed both ways or a "poetic" unit is directly followed by a prose one, as in this example at the end of the second strophe:

> Rigid with face and hands against the pane she stands and marvels long.

A little imagist poem, one might say, followed by the matter-of-fact sentence, "The two zones form a roughly circular whole."

Whatever we choose to call Beckett's series of disjunctive and repetitive paragraphs (sixty-one in all), *Ill Seen Ill Said* surely has little in common with the short story or the novella. Yet this is how the editors of the *New Yorker,* where Beckett's piece first appeared in English in 1981, evidently thought of it, for like all *New Yorker* short stories, it is punctuated by cartoons and, what is even more ironic, by a "real" poem, Harold Brodkey's "Sea Noise" (see Figure 6.1). Notice that the reader immediately knows – or is supposed to know – that Brodkey is a poet and Beckett a fiction writer, not only because "Sea Noise" is designated a poem in the issue's table of contents, but also because its placement on the page, framed by white space, distinguishes it from *Ill Seen Ill Said,* which is printed in standard *New Yorker* columns. Yet if we examine the sound structure of Brodkey's poem, we find that the rhythm of recurrence is, if anything, less prominent here than in the Beckett "prose." The four stanzas are of irregular line length (9, 6, 9, 7); the stress count ranges from one ("and cúrsive") to five ("ínter-lócutóries [báritóne]"); rhyme occurs only once, at the end of the poem

50

curvature. To the point at certain moments of its seeming unfit for service.
Child's play with a pliers to restore it.
Was there once a time she did? Careful. Once once in a way. Till she
could no more. No more bring the
jaws together. Oh not for weakness.
Since when it hangs useless from the
nail. Trembling imperceptibly without
cease. Silver shimmers some evenings
when the skies are clear. Close-up
then. In which in defiance of reason
the nail prevails. Long this image till
suddenly it blurs.

   She is there. Again. Let the eye
from its vigil be distracted a moment.
At break or close of day. Distracted by
the sky. By something in the sky. So
that when it resumes the curtain may
be no longer closed. Opened by her to
let her see the sky. But even without
that she is there. Without the curtain's
being opened. Suddenly open. A flash.
The suddenness of all! She still without stopping. On her way without
starting. Gone without going. Back
without returning. Suddenly it is evening. Or dawn. The eye rivets the
bare window. Nothing in the sky will
distract it from it more. While she
from within looks her fill. Pfft oc-
culted. Nothing having stirred.

   Already all confusion. Things and
imaginings. As of always. Confusion
amounting to nothing. Despite precautions. If only she could be pure
figment. Unalloyed. This old so dying
woman. So dead. In the madhouse of
the skull and nowhere else. Where no
more precautions to be taken. No precautions possible. Cooped up there
with the rest. Hovel and stones. The
lot. And the eye. How simple all then.
If only all could be pure figment. Neither be nor been nor by any shift to be.
Gently gently. On. Careful.

   Here to the rescue two lights. Two
small skylights. Set in the high-
pitched roof on either side. Each shed-
ding dim light. No ceiling therefore.
Necessarily. Otherwise with the curtains closed she would be in the dark.
Day and night in the dark. And what
of it? She is done with raising her eyes.
Nearly done. But when she lies with
them open she can just make out the
rafters. In the dim light the skylights
shed. An ever dimmer light. As the
panes slowly dimmen. All in black she
comes and goes. The hem of her long
black skirt brushes the floor. But most

SEA NOISE

The professorial sea
scribbles mile after mile
of waves. Rustling
and cursive,
the script is crawling,
lullingly sunlit,
illegible,
a green thesis
              (of the sea).

Near the shore, it rises,
ranks of old men emeritus,
snuffling, green-gowned;
it propounds upon shoals
interlocutories (baritone):
"Tomb? Tomb?" Also, "Box? Box?"

Across the lower sand,
a bubbling push,
flat-disembodied beard,
vaporous spirit of tumbling
polar bears,
exploded brides,
gravel-scatteringly asks,
"Which human hunger
       is least respectable . . . tibble, tibble?"

To which the sand,
with a student hiss,
aglaze in a rushing film,
utters, in a withdrawn whisper,
the delicate lie,
the bubbling polysyllables
of its mostly uninteresting reply.
                           —HAROLD BRODKEY

                    •   •

often she is still. Standing or sitting.
Lying or on her knees. In the dim
light the skylights shed. Otherwise
with the curtains closed for preference
she would be in the dark. In the dark
day and night.

   Next to emerge from the shadows
an inner wall. Only slowly to dissolve
in favor of a single space. East the bed.
West the chair. A place divided by her
use of it alone. How more desirable in
every way an interior of a piece. The
eye breathes again but not for long.
For slowly it emerges again. Rises

from the floor and slowly up to lose
itself in the gloom. The semi-gloom.
It is evening. The buttonhook glim-
mers in the last rays. The pallet scarce
to be seen.

   Weary of the inanimate the eye in
her absence falls back on the twelve.
Out of her sight as she of theirs.
Alone turn where she may she keeps
her eyes fixed on the ground. On the
way at her feet where it has come to a
stop. Winter evening. Not to be precise. All so bygone. To the twelve
then for want of better the widowed
eye. No matter which. In the distance
stiff he stands facing front and the
setting sun. Dark greatcoat reaching
to the ground. Antiquated block hat.
Finally the face caught full in the last
rays. Quick enlarge and devour before
night falls.

   Having no need of light to see the
eye makes haste. Before night falls. So

Figure 6.1. Reprinted by permission; © 1981 by The New Yorker
Magazine, Inc.

("lie" / "reply"); and alliteration and assonance are not marked. Unless we assume that poetry is defined by the sheer decision of its maker to lineate the text, or unless we want to call "Sea Noise" a poem because it is built around a single extended metaphor (the witty analogy of sea:shore = professor:class), there is no rationale for the classification the *New Yorker* has implicitly adopted.[4]

The meaning of this classification is worth pondering, for it represents, in microcosm, the orthodoxy of every major literature textbook and literary history as well as of most classrooms in the United States and Britain, which is that Beckett is a writer who, like the young Joyce or the young Faulkner, wrote in his dim youth some negligible, clotted lyric poems but whose real work belongs to drama and fiction. As such, we don't teach Beckett in our poetry courses or include him in discussions of contemporary poetry and poetics. The index of any major book on the subject – say, Robert Pinsky's *The Situation of Poetry* – will bear this out. And yet the irony is that contemporary poets are increasingly using forms that cannot be properly understood without the example of Beckett's astonishing "lyrics of fiction" – to use Ruby Cohn's apt term[5] – or, as I shall call them, his "associative monologues." Perhaps, then, it is time to rethink our current procedures of canon making. In what follows, I shall use *Ill Seen Ill Said* as an example.

The landscape of *Ill Seen Ill Said* has familiar Beckett contours – a dying old woman, an empty room in an isolated cabin, a pasture with a "zone of stones" which may or may not be a cemetery, and a cluster of obsessive objects: a kitchen chair, a skylight, a buttonhook hanging from a nail on the cabin wall, an antique coffer, a trap door. The colors of Beckett's composition are stark black and white – black night, black figure of the woman, black room at night, black greatcoat of the unknown man silhouetted against the setting sun, "Black as jade the jasper" that flecks the white of the granite (tomb) stone (42); white moonlight, white stones "more plentiful every year" (22), white walls, long white hair that "stares in a fan" (25), white disc of the dial on the clock face, and, above all, the white face above the black dress. In the course of Beckett's narrative, the woman is seen as in a series of film shots, sitting in her chair and watching the moon rise outside her window, or eating a bowl of slop, or opening the antique coffer and finding a "scrap of paper" on whose "yellowed face" appear "in barely legible ink two letters followed by a number. Tu. 17. Or Th." (35). These indoor scenes are punctuated by outdoor shots of the woman, occasionally followed by a lamb but mostly alone, making her way through the pasture toward the zone of stones, where she is confronted by the enigmatic "twelve," alternately advancing and receding, as she is drawn again and again to one particular stone (apparently her husband's tombstone although Beckett never specifies): "Blindfold she could find her way" (5).[6] In this Stonehenge-like setting, she often sits in the moonlight, rigid against the stone. But in the course of the seasons, some things change: there is, for example, the moment when the third finger of the left hand is lost: "A swelling no doubt . . . preventing one panic day withdrawal of the ring" (29). At another later moment, she tears up the piece of paper found in the coffer:

> The sheet. Between tips of trembling fingers. In two. Four. Eight. Old frantic fingers. Not paper any more. Each eighth apart. In two. Four. Finish with the knife. Hack into shreds. Down the plughole. On to the next. White. Quick blacken.   [54]

After this moment, "only the face remains," and the time is envisioned when there will be no more trace even of it, when "the coats will have gone from their rods and the buttonhook from its nail" (56). "Farewell to farewell"(61).

Unlike such earlier monologues as *Enough* (1967), where the speaking voice is that of the old woman herself, *Ill Seen Ill Said* is the product of "the voice of us all" as Beckett calls it in *How It Is,*[7] the strange ventriloquist voice outside and detached from the woman's own consciousness, that obsessively recounts her every movement and guesses at her feelings as she moves from cabin to pasture and back again in the course of successive winters. We can surmise that the "relentless eye" (26) that "return[s] to the scene of its betrayals" (23) is Beckett's own, that the writer is trying to exorcise the painful image of what he imagines his mother's last days to have been, especially with respect to her response to his dead father. But, as always in Beckett, the autobiographical mode is turned inside out; the old woman's Book of Hours is recited by a debased or parody bard who can barely articulate the words to define her movements. Her "story," that is to say, comes to us only in broken fragments as it presents itself to the impersonal voice whose fate is to "ill see ill say" it.

Here the word "trace" is central, the bard's mission being to "erase" the "trace" of the "face" that forever haunts his sleep and his waking. *Ill Seen Ill Said* represents one of the rare cases in Beckett's oeuvre in which such erasure seems to be successful; here is the sixtieth strophe:

> Absence supreme good and yet. Illumination then go again and one return no more trace. On earth's face. Of what was never. And if by mishap some left then go again. For good again. . . . Till no more trace. On earth's face. Instead of always the same

> place. Slaving away forever in the same place. At this and that trace. And what if the eye could not? No more tear itself away from the remains of trace. Of what was never. Quick say it suddenly can and farewell say say farewell. If only to the face. Of her tenacious trace.

And so, in the final section "trace" gives way to "grace": "Not another crumb of carrion left. Lick chops and basta. No. One moment more. One last. Grace to breathe that void. Know happiness" (61).

Because the old woman is forever "ill seen" by the "relentless eye," just as her story is forever "ill said" by the speaking voice, the verbal units of which Beckett's narrative is made are like bits of flotsam: words, phrases, clauses – these do not cohere; indeed, the levels of discourse are entirely inconsistent. For what sort of English is this?

> The cabin. Its situation. Careful. On. At the inexistent center of a formless place. Rather more circular than otherwise finally. Flat to be sure. To cross it in a straight line takes her from five to ten minutes. Depending on her speed and radius taken. Here she who loves to – here she who now can only stray never strays. Stones increasingly abound. Ever scanter even the rankest weed. Meagre pastures hem it round on which it slowly gains. With none to gainsay. To have gainsaid. As if doomed to spread. How come a cabin in such a place? How came? Careful. [2]

One thinks immediately of Stephen Dedalus walking on the beach; Beckett's next strophe, for that matter, contains the phrase "Invisible nearby sea. Inaudible," confirming the allusion. The difference between *Ill Seen Ill Said* and the "Proteus" chapter of *Ulysses* is that the words of the latter monologue still have a center – Stephen's consciousness – from which they emanate, whereas the words and phrases in Beckett's passage emanate from no identifiable source. Is it, for instance, the woman who thinks "Careful. On," or is it the voice that "ill tells" her story? That voice is occasionally capable of straightforward articulation – "To cross it in a straight line takes her from five to ten minutes" – but then it lapses into riddle ("here she who now can only stray never strays"), into mock Elizabethan pentameter ("Éver scánter éven the ránkest wéed"), and into pun and archaism ("it slowly gains. With none to gainsay. To have gainsaid"). Sometimes we hear the voice of fairy tale ("Meagre pastures hem it round on which it slowly gains"), sometimes of nursery rhyme: "To have gainsaid / As if doomed to spread." But no tone lasts long: after this little jingle, we come back to modern colloquial speech – "How come a cabin in such a place?" – followed by the elliptical "How came?" and the repetition of "Careful."

Wherever we look in *Ill Seen Ill Said,* we find this curious mixture of voices and discourse patterns: straightforward reportage ("The two zones form a roughly circular whole" [3]); inversion, usually coupled with ellipsis ("To the twelve then for want of better the widowed eye" [18]); archaism ("In the way of animals ovines only" [3]; "Rigidly horrent it shivers at last" [26]); parodic literary allusion, usually in tetrameter or pentameter ("The lids occult the longed-for eyes," "On centennial leave from where tears freeze" [23]; "Sweet foretaste of the joy at journey's end" [57]; "Empty-handed she shall go to the tomb" [43]); mock balladry ("Time will tell them washen blue" [21]); tongue twister ("Winter in her winter haunts she wanders" [9]; "Panic past pass on," "Will they then never quiver" [29]; "To scrute together with the inscrutable face" [55]); and series of short staccato questions ("Who is to blame? Or what? They? The eye? The missing finger? The keeper? The cry? What cry?" [29]), where rhyme ("eye" / "cry") provides further formalization. The result is often a kind of babble:

> What is it defends her? Even from her own. Averts the intent gaze. Incriminates the dearly won. Forbids divining her. What but life ending. Hers. The other's. But so otherwise. She needs nothing. Nothing utterable. Whereas the other. How need in the end? But how? How need in the end? [10]

It is impossible to tell from whom or from what the woman is to be defended or even who "her own" are. "Avérts the intént gáze" (perhaps a garbled version of Herbert's "Bids the rash gazer wipe his eye" in "Virtue") is syntactically and rhythmically parallel to "Incríminates the déarly wón," but the second phrase doesn't follow from the first and indeed the referent of "the dearly won" is undecidable. Even if we conclude that death ("life's ending") will finally defend the woman against the vicissitudes of life, we still don't know to whom "The other's" refers. The abrupt phrase leads not to any semantically related but to wordplay: "The other's. But so otherwise. . . . Whereas the other." And so it goes on.

How should we interpret this querulous, compulsive, sometimes maddening babble? In the course of the sixty-one strophes, repetition, both of words and of phrases, becomes increasingly insistent, culminating, as I have shown, in the variations on the word "trace" contained in the final sections. The repetition of the title is particularly telling. The first allusion to it comes in the eighth strophe, and even then, only to its first part: "And only half seen so far as a pallet and a ghostly chair.

Ill half seen" (8). "Ill seen" does not recur until strophe 22 – "First zone rather more extensive than at first sight ill seen" – whereas "Ill said" does not appear until strophe 25: "Which say? Ill say." Both finally appear together at roughly the midpoint of the monologue: "Such bits and scraps. Seen no matter how and said as seen" (28). This is an important aphorism: what is "seen" is "said," no matter how badly. Or, as the voice says in strophe 23, "The eye will return to the scene of its betrayals." After this moment in the monologue, the words "ill seen ill said" become more prominent: the full title appears in strophe 41 – "Such the dwelling ill seen ill said" – and the phrase now becomes increasingly insistent: "Day no sooner risen fallen. Scrapped all the ill seen ill said. The eye has changed. And its drivelling scribe" (49). But although the "drivelling scribe" now seems inclined to scrap the whole story, to forget about that which is "ill seen, ill said," it takes another ten strophes to "efface" the "tenacious trace" of the "face," to cease seeing the "Full glare now on the face present throughout the recent future. As seen ill seen throughout the past neither more nor less" (58).

In charting this thematic development, the question of prosody is central. The peculiar babble of Beckett's monologue, its consistent and abrupt dislocations and deflations reflect the speaking voice's repeated attempt – and repeated failure – to articulate what it perceives or imagines, to achieve coherence out of what is ill seen and can only be, at best, ill said.[8] To express this peculiar inexpressibility, prose is inadequate, for prose, as Frye points out, "is the expression or imitation of directed thinking or controlled description in words. . . . It is not ordinary speech, but ordinary speech on its best behavior, in its Sunday clothes, aware of an audience and with its relation to that audience prepared beforehand" (*WTC*, p. 18). Rather what we hear in *Ill Seen Ill Said*, as in Beckett's related lyrics of fiction like *Imagination Dead Imagine* and *The Lost Ones*, is what Frye calls the *associative rhythm:*

> One can see in ordinary speech . . . a unit of rhythm peculiar to it, a short phrase that contains the central word or idea aimed at, but is largely innocent of syntax. It is much more repetitive than prose, as it is in the process of working out an idea, and the repetitions are largely rhythmical filler, like the nonsense words of popular poetry, which derive from them. In pursuit of its main theme it follows the paths of private association, which gives it a somewhat meandering course. Because of the prominence of private association in it, I shall call the rhythm of ordinary speech the associative rhythm. [*WTC*, pp. 21–22]

Because the "associative rhythm represents the process of bringing ideas into articulation, in contrast to prose or verse which normally represent a finished product" (*WTC,* p. 99), twentieth-century writers have been especially interested in formalizing its properties:

> The naive assumption that any poetry not in some recogniz-able recurrent pattern must really be prose clearly will not do, and we have to assume the existence of a third type of con-ventionalized utterance. This third type has a peculiar relation to ordinary speech, or at least to soliloquy and inner speech. We may call it an oracular or associational rhythm, the unit of which is neither the prose sentence nor the metrical line, but a kind of thought-breath or phrase. Associational rhythm pre-dominates in free verse and in certain types of literary prose. [*EPP,* p. 886]

In verse, Frye notes, the associative rhythm "very seldom predomi-nates over meter before Whitman's time; about the only clear examples are poems written in abnormal states of mind, such as Christopher Smart's *Jubilate Agno*" (*EPP,* p. 890). What Frye calls "free prose" ("the associative rhythm influenced, but not quite organized, by the sen-tence"), on the other hand, is found much earlier: in seventeenth- and eighteenth-century diaries and letters, in Swift's *Journal to Stella,* Sterne's *Tristram Shandy,* and before these in Burton's *Anatomy of Mel-ancholy,* that "tremendous masterpiece of free prose, where quotations, references, allusions, titles of books, Latin tags, short sharp phrases, long lists and catalogues, are all swept up in one vast exuberant associa-tive wave" (*WTC,* pp. 81, 83).

It should be clear by now that *Ill Seen Ill Said* similarly sweeps up references, allusions, short sharp phrases, neologisms, and contorted elliptical clauses into an associative monologue; indeed, Beckett's fiction *The Unnamable* (1958) is one of Frye's repeated examples of the associa-tive rhythm. Note that "associative" does not simply mean conversa-tional: the discourse of *Ill Seen Ill Said* is, on the contrary, highly formalized: "The eye will return to the scene of its betrayals. On cen-tennial leave from where tears freeze. Free again an instant to shed them scalding" (23). No one, surely, talks this way. But then if we want to be technical, we would have to say even more emphatically that no one writes this way either. Consider the following:

> It is now the left hand lacks its third finger . . . a swelling no doubt of the knuckle between first and second phalanges pre-venting one panic day withdrawal of the ring. The kind called

keeper. Still as stones they defy as stones do the eye. Do they as much as feel the clad flesh? Does the clad flesh feel them? Will they then never quiver? This night assuredly not. For before they have – before the eye has time they mist. Who is to blame? Or what? They? The eye? The missing finger? The keeper? The cry? What cry? All five. All six. And the rest. All. All to blame. All.   [29]

The abrupt phrases with their repetition – "a swelling no doubt," "as stones," "clad flesh," "eye," "finger," "keeper," "cry," and "all" (this last word five times) – follow the paths of private association in a radically nonlinear way. The panic experienced when the ring cannot be withdrawn has nothing to do with the kind of ring in question, yet the voice moves from "withdrawal of the ring" to "The kind called keeper" and from there to the stones in the ring: "Do they as much as feel the clad flesh?" In response to the questions, "Who is to blame? Or what?" further questions burst out like pellets – "They? The eye? The missing finger? The keeper? The cry? What cry?" – and the answers are framed around repetition of the word "all": "All five. All six. And the rest. All. All to blame. All." The pedantic talk of "phalanges" and "clad flesh" finally gives way to this stark reality.

"A kind of thought-breath or phrase," a rhythm neither that of regular recurrence as in verse nor of sentence-making as in prose – this is the mode of Beckett's associative monologue as it fumbles to articulate meaning only to lapse yet again into what is almost a dyslexic reading of the "still shadowy album" (8). Beckett has been extending the formal limits of this mode since the time of the trilogy (*Molloy, Malone Dies, The Unnamable* [1951–58]). In *How It Is* (1964), for example, the successive blocks of type are made up of abrupt phrasal groupings, each containing two or three stresses, whose truncated syntax, repetition, archaism, and foregrounding of rhyme and metrical units anticipate the poetic texture of *Ill Seen Ill Said:*

> to speak of happiness one hesitates those awful syllables first asparagus burst abscess but good moments yes I assure you before Pim with Pim after Pim vast tracts of time good moments say what I may less good to they must be expected I hear it I murmur it . . .   [*HII*, p. 25]

Note the pervasive rhyme ("happiness" / "abscess," "first" / "burst," "say" / "may"); the intricate patterns of alliteration and assonance ("asparagus burst abscess but," the repetition of "good," the parallelism of "before Pim with Pim after Pim" and "I hear it I murmur it"); and the interjection of "yes I assure you" cutting into the so-called narrative. The germ of *Ill Seen Ill Said* is literally found among these fragments:

> my life last state last version ill-said ill-heard ill-recaptured ill-murmured in the mud brief movements of the lower face losses everywhere   [*HII,* p. 7]

We can scan this as follows:

```
  ̋    ̋    ̋́X    ̋    ̋ ̋    ́X́X
  ̋ X   XX́   ̋́X   XX́X́
  ̋    ́X́
```

Here the spondees, some with an unaccented tail, and cretics create an almost liturgical rhythm.

Free prose as Beckett develops it is, in other words, very close to free verse. Once this point is understood, we can come to terms more readily with such anomalous texts of the seventies as John Ashbery's *Three Poems,* a book dismissed by certain critics as not being poetry at all because it is written in prose.[9] The book-cover blurb is not entirely helpful; it states that *Three Poems* "partakes of what amounts to a new literary form: not at all 'prose poetry' in the traditional sense, it is one in which the resources of prose are used toward an end which is nevertheless poetic."[10] The latter part of this assertion is certainly true: *Three Poems* is distinctly not a medley of prose poems in the tradition of, say, Baudelaire's *Spleen de Paris.* But neither has Ashbery quite invented a "new literary form"; readers of Beckett will recognize the mode of a typical paragraph unit:

> There are some old photographs which show the event. It makes sense to stand there, passing. The people who are there – few, against this side of the air. They made a sign, were making a sign. Turning on youself as a leaf, you miss the third and last chance. They don't suffer the way people do. True. But it is your last chance, this time, the last chance to escape the ball.   [P.4]

Like Beckett's free prose, Ashbery's contains sentences that are correct grammatically but have indeterminate referents: the "event" the photographs depict is not specified, nor does the text ever explain what it means to stand "there" or how one can "stand" and be "passing" at the same time. Repetition is used here as in Beckett's associative monologues to present the process of "working out an idea," of getting at a meaning: "They made a sign, were making a sign" and "But it is your last chance, this time, the last chance" bring to mind a tried and true fairy-tale motif—the story of the three caskets, for instance. Again, fairy tale yields to abrupt interjection—"True"—and little rhyming units are foregrounded:

> The people who are there
> few against this side of the air
>
> Turning on yourself
> as a leaf
>
> They don't suffer the way people do
> True

These jingles modulate, in turn, into elliptical abstractions. Ashbery's open-ended strophe continues in the next unit:

> of contradictions, that is heavier than gravity bringing all down to the level. And nothing be undone.   [P. 4]

"Down to the level" of what? one wonders. The faintly archaic phrase "And nothing be undone" provides no answer. Grammatically, it may be either an imperative ("And let nothing be undone!") or an indicative ("And nothing can be undone"); in either case, "And" acts as false conjunction.

From paragraph to paragraph, from present to past to future tense, and from "I" to "he" to "we" and back again to "I," often within the space of a single sentence or sentence fragment—Ashbery's prose repeatedly shifts, as does Beckett's, from the mundane ("an open can of axle grease" [p. 5]) to the recondite ("it sets the hydra in furious motion, pullulating beyond the limits of the imagination" [p. 36]), from colloquial speech ("That's the way it goes" [p. 90]) to formal locution ("There are dark vacancies the light of the hunter's moon does little to attenuate" [p. 8]). The appearance in discordant contexts of characters from fairy tales and classics—Childe Roland, the Red Queen, Don Quixote, Hop-o'-My-Thumb—recalls Beckett's parodic references to Shakespeare in *Ill Seen Ill Said* (Edmund's blinding of Gloucester in *Lear,* for example, appears in garbled version in strophe 51: "Closed again to that end the vile jelly or opened again"). *Three Poems,* however, is not as fully narrative as Beckett's associative monologue. Ashbery's interpolated stories and parodic film clips are subordinated to the larger meditation in which they are embedded. That meditation, despite its radical fragmentation and shifting reference, is never as detached as Beckett's "voice of us all." But the movement of the whole, its representation of the struggle to control thought and articulate meaning without ever quite finding a point of rest—this is strikingly reminiscent of the poetic mode Beckett had made his own by the early sixties.

In *The Poetics of Indeterminacy,* I have tried to show how this mode
has been assimilated and transformed by such performance poets as
John Cage and David Antin. Here let me just point briefly to some
recent examples of the associative paradigm:

> Thought you'd like to hear so having a minute, would just drop
> a line. To say, thought you'd like to hear, so having a minute. So
> have a minute, thought, to hear. You'd like to. All that sort of
> stuff you never put anywhere anyhow, it just comes in, goes
> out, up and down, in and out the system, as Buckminster Fuller
> says – one thinks one heard that – Or music: Go in and out the
> system, go in and out the system, go in and out the system –
> Words then misplaced, forgotten, i.e., how it ends there. Some-
> thing about roses, it seemed it was. Not a mulberry bush in any
> case.   – Robert Creeley, *A Day Book* (1972)

> Closure. Approaching the death it was the afterlife she insisted
> upon. Hell in the afterlife. But the afterlife held no promise.
> Brooked no quarter. How pale and lifeless the human body in
> its flowered dress, in its flowered dress. There is no effort
> being made. But then imagine in the imagining. The same
> faculty of those crossing the bridge imagining the workers
> falling. Specifically the Golden Gate bridge, specifically reddish
> rust-inhibiting paint. Specifically painting to inhibit decay of
> the bridge. Span.   – Barbara Einzig, *Disappearing Work* (1979)

> Nothing so old and so new, is no longer there. Full of all day.
> Awake awake. 5 a.m. she awoke, was awakened into a tight
> gut. A rip into that deep sleep. Something alarming, filling up
> the body. Filling inch by inch through the hours, designated as
> dark. Piling up. About to pour over the rim. Holding lids
> tight. One lie and then the next. They had their own lives and
> erased her.   – Kathleen Fraser, *Each Next* (1980)

> It is in the distance. It distances. She said that in the gorilla guilt
> is expressed in the passive voice. The typewriter was written.
> The mess was made. A composition occurred to him in which
> a man's acts preceded his reflections. It was being written at the
> moment it occurred to him. He made stairs and ramps in the
> time it took him to come to a point. Now he was being writ-
> ten. Now he was swimming.   – Michael Davidson, *The Prose
> of Fact* (1981)[11]

Each of these so-called prose blocks of print comes from longer
sequences composed of series of such paragraph units. In all four cases,

their authors present these sequences as poetry, perhaps because they all (with the exception of Einzig, the youngest poet in the group) began their poetic careers by writing free verse, as did Ashbery, and in their current work they continue to alternate free verse with the type of free prose quoted above.

None of these four poets seems to have been directly influenced by Beckett. Creeley comes, of course, out of Ezra Pound and William Carlos Williams via Charles Olson and the Black Mountain school; Davidson, some twenty years Creeley's junior, began his career as a student of Creeley, Olson, and especially Robert Duncan. Fraser, whose early free verse was strongly influenced by Frank O'Hara and Kenneth Koch, has been working closely with the L=A=N=G=U=A=G=E poets based in New York and San Francisco; and Einzig has been associated with the poets who write and edit the *New Wilderness Letter,* especially Jerome Rothenberg and David Antin. Yet despite individual differences and allegiances in the work of these contemporary poets (Creeley's *A Day Book,* for instance, surely owes something to Williams' *Kora in Hell,* a great early exemplar of the associative mode),[12] free prose, as found in Beckett's *How It Is* or *Ill Seen Ill Said,* has quite simply become an accepted norm. In all four cases, the basic unit is not the verse line or the sentence but the short phrase of irregular length and "primitive" syntax, often marked by inversion and ellipsis. In all four, repetition, whether of phoneme, word, or phrase, is the main binding device, sound often creating meaning as in the movement from "lids" to "lie" to "lives" in Fraser's strophe, and in the modulation of "thought," "hear," and "minute" in Creeley's. Davidson's "It is in the distance. It distances" and Einzig's "But then imagine in the imagining" are, whether consciously or not, distinct echoes of the later Beckett. To put it another way, our familiar modernist paradigms (especially Harold Bloom's account of contemporary poetry as a belated version of Romantic visionary lyric) may be less than adequate in accounting for a growing body of poetic discourse whose mainsprings seem to be elsewhere.

That world elsewhere is a domain in which "poems" refuse to follow the ground rules of modernist free verse even as "short stories" paradoxically become more "poetic" by foregrounding the rhythm of recurrence. Take the case of "Au Tombeau de Charles Fourier," placed at the center of *Da Vinci's Bicycle: Ten Stories by Guy Davenport.*[13] Davenport's story is more accurately construed as a collage composition that sets nineteenth-century belief in progress (exemplified by the utopian socialism of Fourier) in ironic collusion with two antithetical time frames: the revolutionary years of the early twentieth century (exemplified by Picasso, Gertrude Stein, and the Wright brothers) and the prehistoric culture of the Dogon (the primitive peoples of Upper Volta and Mali whose remarkable scientific understanding and mythology have been studied by the ethnologists Marcel Griaule and Germaine Dieterlen). As Davenport puts it in a related essay, "Prehistoric Eyes":

> Art . . . has not evolved. It has always been itself, and modern artists have notoriously learned more from the archaic discovered in our time than from the immediate centuries. . . . The Dogon, most primitive of men, can point to the star (western man found it only recently, with a telescope, and catalogued it with a number, and published the fact in the back pages of a newspaper, which was then used to wrap garbage) that contains the plan for the spiral inside the crabgrass seed, the source of life.[14]

In keeping with this faith that "History is not linear; it is the rings of growth in a tree," Davenport invents a structure for his "Tombeau" that is, at one level, rigidly mathematical and circular: the text has twenty-nine sections, each containing nine four-line paragraphs, with a two-paragraph (seven-line) coda in section 30. The only exception to this rule comes in section 10, which consists of a single sentence – "What works in the angle succeeds in the arc and holds in the chord" – an aphorism that acts as a kind of buried epigraph for the whole piece. The "Tombeau" moves full circle from an opening description of Stein, her hair rebelliously cut short, "chittering down the Boulevard Raspail in her automobile" on her way "home from reading the Katzenjammer Kids to Pablo" (p. 60), to the final image, taken from *The Autobiography of Alice B. Toklas,* of Stein's vision of French soldiers marching through the Arc de Triomphe on Armistice Day. The Parisian world fades in and out as the text relates items about the Dogon:

> They discover all and remember all that's useful to their lives. Yellow crumbles, soft meal, gum, grains on the grippers, bright. Green is crisp, gives water, ginger mint keen. Yellow is deep, green is long. Green snaps wet, a wax of mealy yellow clings.
>
> Yellow clings and our jaws crunch green. Crunch curls of dry wood. Cling around green, red shine is the line and red shine is wobble the happy and shimmy the sting. Dance the ripen red, hunch the yellow bounce. Red the speckle, green the ground. [P. 90]

Two sections later, "green" appears in a very different context:

> Wilbur Wright was Ohio and Ohio is flat and monotonous, green and quiet. And so was he, a splendidly tedious man. You cannot be a mechanic and not be tedious, nor the first man to fly and not be green as Ohio is green, nor a hero and not be quiet.[P. 92]

Twenty-nine times 9 such blocks of print arranged in no temporal or causal sequence; 261 strophes characterized by primitive syntax ("Wilbur Wright was Ohio and Ohio is flat and monotonous"), word repetition ("Green is crisp," "green is long," "Green snaps wet," "our jaws crunch green," "Cling around green," and so on), and the foregrounding of sound patterning:

> Gréen is crísp   gíves wáter   gínger mínt kéen
> réd shíne is the líne and réd shíne
> Dánce the rípen réd   húnch the yéllow bóunce

Here again is the associative paradigm as we have seen it in Beckett's work. Indeed, Beckett himself is introduced in section 24, chatting with the narrator about Joyce over Irish whisky. As Davenport explains in his autobiographical essay "Ernst Machs Max Ernst":

> I wanted to include a conversation of Samuel Beckett's about Joyce, and felt that this poignancy belonged to the pattern I was making and not to autobiography. The inscription on Fourier's tomb had been copied down in the cemetery at Montmartre the afternoon of the same day that I talked with Mr. Beckett at the Closerie des Lilas (in chairs once occupied by Apollinaire, Joyce, Picasso, Jarry, Braque); the story, or *assemblage,* was generated by this moment, with courage derived from the encounter.[15]

Because *"assemblage"* always involves what Davenport, follwing the filmmakers, calls *intercut,* Beckett dissolves, in the seventh strophe of section 24 into Ogotemmêli, the blind old Dogon metaphysician who explained his culture's astronomy to the modern ethnologists:

> You must understand, Beckett said, that Joyce came to see that the fall of a leaf is as grievous as the fall of man, *I am blind,* Ogotemmêli said, opening a blue paper of tobacco with his delicately long wrinkled fingers, his head aloof and listening. [P. 98]

Davenport's curious conjunction of time frames, narrative and lyric forms, and verse and prose elements (not to speak of the sixteen remarkable illustrations – drawings, photographs, pictograms, etchings – that in Davenport's words "turn the text into a *graph* ['to write' and 'to draw' being the same Greek verb]")[16] – creates a hybrid mode for which we do not yet have a generally accepted name. Pieces, texts, lyrics of fiction, associative monologues, collage, *bricolage, assemblage,* free prose – perhaps the name is after all less important than the recognition that we are living in a world of new literary organisms.

In a recent *Georgia Review* symposium prompted by Christopher Clausen's essay "Poetry in a Discouraging Time," a number of distinguished poets and critics try to come to terms with Clausen's contention that contemporary society no longer values poetry:

> The virtual extinction of poetry as a cultural force, though long predicted, is a recent event; it happened within living memory. Whether a second "rescue" is possible remains to be seen, for while the cultural changes attendant on the rise of science undoubtedly altered the position of poetry, they did not make its decline inevitable.[17]

Clausen speculates on what course of action might make poetry once again play a central role, but clearly both he and most of his respondents are gloomy about the prospect. There is much intelligent debate about the relationship of poetry to science as well as to the mass media, but what I find curious is that no one seriously questions Clausen's tacit assumption that when we talk about poetry we are referring to the lyric poem as that paradigm has come down from the Romantics. The names cited again and again in this symposium on "The Place of Poetry" today are those of Wordsworth, Shelley, Tennyson, and Eliot.

Perhaps it is time to question our continuing faith in Romantic and modernist paradigms for poetry. Can the "time" really be quite as "discouraging" as Clausen takes it to be in a year that witnessed the publication of a text as intricately poetic as *Ill Seen Ill Said* in a popular magazine like the *New Yorker?* Perhaps, in other words, the "death of poetry" Clausen and his fellow symposiasts talk about is more sensibly construed as the gradual and inevitable evolution of the free-verse lyric – a form that after a hundred years of use has become as conventionalized and trivialized as the Elizabethan love sonnet was by the end of the sixteenth century – into a literary mode that can accommodate verse and prose, narrative and lyric, fiction and nonfiction, the verbal and the visual. If, as Wayne Booth rightly points out in his response to

Clausen, sophisticated younger critics today may prefer to read *New Literary History* or *Critical Inquiry* rather than " 'the best novel, play, or collection of poems of the last year – one praised extravagantly by reviewers in whichever journals you respect most,' " perhaps it is because some of the so-called critical journals are currently publishing pieces that might well have more "literary" interest than, say, John Updike's *Rabbit Is Rich,* or Peter Shaffer's *Amadeus,* or Robert Bly's newest collection of poems, to mention just three "imaginative works" that have indeed been praised by a wide variety of reviewers.[18] Davenport's own "Ernst Machs Max Ernst" is a case in point: a lyrical collage essay, it first appeared in *New Literary History,* as did Cage's *assemblage,* "Diary: How to Improve the World (You Will Only Make Matters Worse) Continued, 1970–71."[19] Are these works we can dismiss as nonimaginative, as belonging to the discourse of the sciences?

Perhaps the familiar distinction Aristotle made between *poema* (the poem) and *poiesis* (the process of making a poetic construct) can point the way toward an understanding of what poetry is becoming in our time. Beckett, whose very earliest lines, in *Whoroscope* (1930), already displayed a curious resistance to lineation –

> Hey! pass over those coppers,
> sweet millèd sweat of my burning liver!
> Them were the days I sat in the hot-cupboard throwing
>   Jesuits out of the skylight –[20]

– has himself nicely defined the new associative paradigm in a strophe near the end of *How It Is:*

> but all this business of voices yes quaqua yes of other worlds yes of someone in another world yes whose kind of dream I am yes said to be yes that he dreams all the time yes tells all the time yes his only dream yes his only story yes   [*HII,* p. 145]

NOTES

1   *Ill Seen Ill Said* (New York: Grove Press, 1981), p. 7, par. 1; all further references to this work will be included in the text. *Ill Seen Ill Said* was translated by Beckett from his original French, *Mal vu mal dit* (Paris, 1981); the first English publication appeared in the *New Yorker,* 5 October 1981, pp. 48–58. Since the *New Yorker* edition is important to my argument, I refer to *Ill Seen Ill Said* by paragraph, or strophe, number rather than by page number.

2 *The Well-Tempered Critic* (Bloomington: Indiana University Press, 1963), p. 21; subsequently cited as *WTC*. See also Frye, "Verse and Prose," in *Princeton Encyclopedia of Poetry and Poetics*, ed. Alex Preminger (Princeton: Princeton University Press, 1974), p. 885; subsequently cited as *EPP*.

3 I discuss the question of reference in Beckett's poetry in *The Poetics of Indeterminacy: Rimbaud to Cage*, pp. 200–47.

4 Contemporary prosodists, perhaps because they must account for the difficult case of free verse, generally do equate verse – and hence implicitly the poem – with lineation. For example, Charles O. Hartman, in his recent *Free Verse: An Essay on Prosody* (Princeton: Princeton University Press, 1980), observes that, difficult as it is to define the word "poetry" "rigorously and permanently," verse can be distinguished from prose quite readily:

> *Verse is language in lines.* This distinguishes it from prose. . . . This is not really a satisfying distinction, as it stands, but it is the only one that works absolutely. The fact that we can tell verse from prose on sight, with very few errors . . . indicates that the basic perceptual difference must be very simple. Only lineation fits the requirements. [P. 11]

But, as I have just shown in the case of Beckett and Brodkey, what looks like verse may sound like prose and vice versa. The "basic perceptual difference" between the two is surely not as simple as Hartman suggests. I discuss the question from a somewhat different angle in "The Linear Fallacy," *Georgia Review* 35 (Winter 1981): 855–69.

5 See *Back to Beckett* (Princeton: Princeton University Press, 1973), chap. 5, "Lyrics of Fiction."

6 Twelve is, of course, a number with multiple symbolic connotations – especially in the New Testament and Book of Revelation. But I think Beckett has in mind especially the twelve signs of the zodiac, whose conjunction symbolizes cosmic wholeness; in this sense, "the twelve" relate to the astrological symbolism of the "zone of stones" (Stonehenge). Nevertheless, "the twelve" are purposely unspecified; their identity is finally as elusive as that of the man in the greatcoat or the stone itself.

7 *How It Is* (New York: Grove Press, 1964), p. 138; subsequently cited as *HHI*.

8 For a related discussion of voice in *How It Is,* see Hugh Kenner, "Shades of Syntax," in *Samuel Beckett: A Collection of Criticism,* ed. Ruby Cohn (New York: McGraw-Hill, 1975), pp. 30–31.

9 See, e.g., Charles Molesworth, " 'This Leaving-Out Business': The Poetry of John Ashbery," *Salmagundi,* 38–39 (Summer-Fall 1977): 30 and 39. In *Poet's Prose: The Crisis of American Verse* (Cambridge: Cambridge University Press, 1983), Stephen Fredman counters this charge; see his long chapter on Ashbery's *Three Poems,* pp. 99–133. Fredman's book, which appeared after I completed this essay, is an important treatment of "the new poet's prose" and I refer the reader especially to the introduction (pp.

1–11) and to the final chapter, "The Crisis at Present: Talk Poems and the New Poet's Prose," whose discussion of, among others, David Antin relates to my own in "Postmodernism and the Impasse of Lyric" (chap. 8).

10 *Three Poems* (New York: Viking Press, 1972); all further references to this work will be included in the text.

11 Robert Creeley, *A Day Book* (New York: Charles Scribner's Sons, 1972), unpaginated; Barbara Einzig, *Disappearing Work, a recounting* (Berkeley: The Figures, 1979), p. 105; Kathleen Fraser, "Piling up about to pour over," *Each Next, narratives* (Berkeley: The Figures, 1980), p. 42; Michael Davidson, "On a Distant Prospect of David Bromige," *The Prose of Fact* (Berkeley: The Figures, 1981), p. 23.

12 See Gerald L. Bruns, "De Improvisatione," *Iowa Review* 9 (Summer 1978): 66–78; rpt. in Bruns, *Inventions: Writing, Textuality and Understanding in Literary History* (New Haven: Yale University Press, 1982). Bruns' treatment of *Kora in Hell* as improvisation comes to conclusions that accord with Frye's definition of the associative rhythm; e.g., "an improvisation is a series of unforeseen discourse. . . . Its teleology is entirely in the present. . . . It is discourse that proceeds independently of reflection; it does not stop to check on itself. It is deliberate but undeliberated" (p. 66).

13 See *Da Vinci's Bicycle: Ten Stories by Guy Davenport* (Baltimore: Johns Hopkins University Press, 1979), pp. 59–107. All further refrences to "Au Tombeau de Charles Fourier" will be included in the text.

14 "Prehistoric Eyes," *The Geography of the Imagination: Forty Essays by Guy Davenport* (San Francisco: North Point Press, 1981), p. 67.

15 *Geography of the Imagination,* p. 380.

16 Ibid. Davenport appropriately compares the "Tombeau" to a Max Ernst collage (see p. 379).

17 "Poetry in a Discouraging Time," *Georgia Review* 35 (Winter 1981): 705. Clausen's essay summarizes the argument of his new book, *The Place of Poetry* (Lexington, Ky.: University of Kentucky Press, 1981).

18 "Becoming Dangerous Again," *Georgia Review* 35 (Winter 1981): 753.

19 "Ernst Machs Max Ernst," *New Literary History* 9 (Autumn 1977): 137–48; John Cage, "Diary: How to Improve the World (You Will Only Make Matters Worse) Continued, 1970–71," *New Literary History* 3 (Autumn 1971): 201–14.

20 *Collected Poems in English and French* (New York: Grove Press, 1977), p. 2.

7 From image to action: the return of story in postmodern poetry

I begin with a representative poem of the early sixties, James Wright's "Snowstorm in the Midwest":

Though haunches of whales
Slope into whitecap doves,
It is hard to drown here.

Between two walls,
A fold of echoes,
A girl's voice walks naked.

I step into the water
Of two flakes.
The crowns of white birds rise
To my ankles,
To my knees,
To my face.

Escaping in silence
From locomotive and smoke,
I hunt the huge feathers of gulls
And the fountains of hills,
I hunt the sea, to walk on the waters.

A splayed starling
Follows me down a long stairway
Of white sand.[1]

Let me summarize briefly the conventions I find operative here. (1) The voice of the poem is solitary and speaks out of a single moment in time. (2) The mode is emotive: the poem presents the response of the solitary speaker to the external world, in this case the landscape transformed by the snowstorm. (3) Because the emotion conveyed is not amenable to rational or discursive explanation, the poem conveys it in terms of animistic images: the governing metaphor is that of the white snow-fields as choppy ocean, its banks "the haunches of whales," its peaks "whitecap doves," its flakes "crowns of birds" flying, its drifts "the feathers of gulls." To make one's way through this silent white land-scape is to leave behind the real world of "locomotive and smoke," descending, as it were, "a long stairway / Of white sand." This, the poem implies, is what death is like. (4) The individual images coalesce to form a symbolic complex: the white snow world is the embodiment of the poet's naked ego, his keen sense of isolation, of mystery, a kind of ecstasy in loneliness that makes the voice of the unknown girl a living presence walking naked. (5) Because the "I" of the poem is concerned to utter rather than to address, his back turned to the audi-ence in a state of rapt self-communion, his speech takes the form of a series of short, gnomic, declarative sentences in the present tense: "I step into the water," "I hunt the huge feathers of gulls." (6) In keeping with this syntax, the short, irregular stanzas are made up of abrupt, end-stopped lines, ranging from three to ten syllables, from two to four primary stresses. Such free verse guarantees the authenticity of the emotion, as if to say "This is how it really *feels* while it's happening!" At the same time, phrasal parallelism ("To my ankles, to my knees, to my face"), and sound repetition (note the modulation from "spl*ay*ed *star*ling" to "*stair*way" and "*sand*" in the final stanza) emphasize the intensity of the moment.

At the time of their appearance, such poems as "Snowstorm in the Midwest" were labelled "Deep Image" or "American Surrealist" or perhaps "Regionalist"; they were thus distinguished from such rival modes of the period as the confessionalism of Robert Lowell or the plain-talk bardic poetry of social protest of Allen Ginsberg and the Beats. But from our vantage point in the eighties, we can now see that James Wright's poem is perhaps best understood as a late variant of the paradigmatic modernist lyric as that lyric has come down to poets like both Wright and Lowell from Emily Dickinson or Yeats or Stevens or Frost or Roethke. Pound and the early Eliot are, of course, the excep-tions to this rule: both *The Waste Land* and *The Cantos* are full of abortive stories, tales fragmented and never fully developed that weave in and out of the lyric fabric. Nevertheless, the dominant poetic mode of early modernism remains the lyric – what Goethe calls "die Ich-erzählung" – in which the isolated speaker (whether or not the poet himself), located in a specific landscape, meditates or ruminates on some aspect of his or her relationship to the external world, coming finally to some sort of epiphany, a moment of insight or vision with which the poem closes. For example:

> O body swayed to music, O brightening glance,
> How can we know the dancer from the dance?
> (Yeats, "Among School Children")

> I have it in me so much nearer home
> To scare myself with my own desert places.
> (Frost, "Desert Places"

> . . . until now I never knew
> that fluttering things have so distinct a shade.
> (Stevens, "Le Monocle de Mon Oncle")

What role, if any, does narrative play in such poetry? "Narrate," Victor Turner reminds us, "is from the Latin *narrare* ('to tell') which is akin to the Latin *gnārus* ('knowing,' 'acquainted with,' 'expert in') both derivative from the Indo-European root *gnâ* ('to know') whence the vast family of words deriving from the Latin *cognoscere*, including 'cognition' itself, and 'noun' and 'pronoun,' the Greek *gignōskein,* whence *gnōsis*. . . . Narrative is, it would seem, rather an appropriate term for a reflexive activity which seeks to 'know' (even in its ritual aspect, to have *gnōsis* about) antecedent events and the meaning of those events."[2] In this sense, the poetry of high modernism does incorporate autobiographical narrative: from the Yeats of "The Tower" to the Robert Lowell of *Life Studies* and the Adrienne Rich of "Snapshots of a Daughter-in-Law," we find retrospective accounts in which the solitary "I" remembers or even relives a particular situation or set of events in the past so as to come to terms with, understand, have *gnosis* about the present.

Modernist poets, then, do narrate, but they rarely use the third person and they rarely tell stories. For a story is the imitation of an action (the Aristotelian *mimesis praxeos*); the resultant plot is a particular arrangement or structuring of the incidents (*ton pragmaton systasis*). "By plot," writes Paul Ricoeur, echoing Aristotle, "I mean the intelligible whole that governs a succession of events in any story. . . . A story is *made out of* events to the extent that plot *makes* events *into* a story."[3] And in a similar vein Robert Scholes observes: "A story is a narrative with a very specific syntactic shape (beginning–middle–end or situation–transformation–situation). . . . When we speak of narrative, we are usually speaking of story, though story is clearly a higher (because more rule-governed) category."[4]

As such, *story* held little interest for early twentieth-century poets, at least in Anglo-America. It was not spurned because poets like Yeats or Stevens or Crane questioned, as postmodern writers have increasingly done, the very nature of the *order* that a systematic plot structure implies. Rather, the poetry of modernism was wedded to a sharp distinction between *poetry,* the lyric expression of personal emotions, and *prose,* the language of fiction, of the novel. Behind this separation of the literary modes stands the Poe of "The Philosophy of Composition" (1846), who argued that a long poem is a contradiction in terms, for "a poem is such, only inasmuch as it intensely excites, by elevating, the soul; and all intense excitements are, through a psychal necessity, brief."[5] For "long" and "brief" we can easily substitute the words "narrative" and "lyric," Poe's point being that only the condensed lyric utterance – the cry of the heart – can produce the elevation of soul and "psychic intensity" that is the aim of all art. Mere story, it would seem, could never produce the Longinian transport.

Poe's first and greatest disciple, Baudelaire, expressed the same view when, in his dedication to his collected prose poems, *Le Spleen de Paris* (1863), he assured Arsène Houssaye:

> Nous pouvons couper où nous voulons, moi ma rêverie, vous le manuscrit, le lecteur sa lecture; car je ne suspends pas la volonté rétive de celui-ci au fil interminable d'une intrigue superflue.[6]
>
> (We can cut wherever we please, I my dreaming, you your manuscript, the reader his reading; for I do not keep the reader's restive mind hanging in suspense on the threads of an *interminable and superfluous plot.)*

Ironically, Baudelaire's prose poems often take the form of parody versions of the fable or the fairy-tale so that plot does play a central part. But the story element is played down, even as Yeats, half a century later, divided his *Collected Poems* into two unequal halves: *Lyric* (the first four hundred pages, containing all the major poems), and *Narrative and Dramatic* (the last hundred, in which we find such early works as "The Wanderings of Oisin" and "The Old Age of Queen Maeve." Narrative, Yeats suggests, belongs at the back of the book. For, as Albert Lord observes, "when poetry is thought of as form and ecstasy, then narrative poetry is an anomaly."[7] The reader of fiction is put off by its verse form, the reader of poetry by its dissipation of intensity. And so poetry (lyric) and the novel (narrative) have increasingly played to separate audiences.

The equation of poetry with the lyric is almost axiomatic in contemporary criticism. In her recent *Lyric Time: Dickinson and the Limits of Genre,* Sharon Cameron writes:

> . . . both novels and drama distinguish themselves from the lyric (whose speaker plots out his concerns in the absence of both action and others). . . . Unlike the drama, whose province is conflict, and unlike the novel or narrative, which connects isolated moments of time to create a story multiply peopled and framed by a social context, the lyric voice is solitary and generally speaks out of a single moment in time. . . . The lyric's propensity [is] to interiorize as ambiguity or outright contradiction those conflicts that other mimetic forms conspicuously exteriorize and then allocate to discrete characters who enact them in the manifest pull of opposite points of view.[8]

What interests me here is the tacit assumption that lyric is to be opposed to "drama" or to "the novel or narrative"; the possibility of writing poems that tell stories is not considered. Not surprisingly, then, when Cameron turns, in her final chapter, to the larger problem of time in romantic and modern poetry, she uses the words "lyric" and "poem" interchangeably. And indeed, when we see the title *Collected Poems* in a bookshop or library or newspaper article, most of us assume that the book will contain short lyrics or lyric sequences of an emotive or descriptive kind.

Theory, however, usually lags behind practice and, curiously, in the same year that James Wright was composing such epiphany poems as "From a Bus Window in Central Ohio before a Thunder Shower" or "Snowstorm in the Midwest," Frank O'Hara wrote a snow poem that goes like this:

Poem

Lana Turner has collapsed!
I was trotting along and suddenly
it started raining and snowing
and you said it was hailing
but hailing hits you on the head
hard so it was really snowing and
raining and I was in such a hurry
to meet you but the traffic
was acting exactly like the sky
and suddenly I see a headline

> LANA TURNER HAS COLLAPSED!
> there is no snow in Hollywood
> there is no rain in California
> I have been to lots of parties
> and acted perfectly disgraceful
> but I never actually collapsed
> oh Lana Turner we love you get up[9]

The wonderfully absurd event that is announced in the opening line of this poem (what a world in which such "news" makes the headlines!) is absorbed into the lyric fabric of O'Hara's discourse in an ingenious way. For O'Hara, narration, the reflexive activity which seeks to "know" antecedent events and the meaning of those events, replaces the momentary *einfühlung* into the cosmos that we find in the poems of a James Wright. For here the event (or rather pseudo-event, the act being known only through a newspaper headline) allows the poet to assess, however comically, his own place in the universe. Life, we know, is chaotic; even the poem's piling up of paratactic clauses (and . . . but . . . so . . . and), spilling over line-ends and rushing on to the comic finale in a single breath, suggests jumble. The poet's "trotting" is met, both semantically and syntactically, by raining, snowing, and possibly even (so his friend mistakenly posits) hailing; the chaos, moreover, is almost by design: "the traffic was acting exactly like the sky." But the event itself – the collapse of Hollywood's leading sweater girl – is wonderfully reassuring and puts the chaos of the poet's life into perspective:

> there is no rain in Hollywood
> there is no snow in California
> I have been to lots of parties
> and acted perfectly disgraceful
> but I never actually collapsed

To hear the story of Lana Turner is thus to triumph over contingency: grandly, the poet does a turn-about, declaring "oh Lana Turner we love you get up."

Notice how this declaration suggests possible story lines. Perhaps Lana Turner was merely drunk when she "collapsed"; not to collapse when drunk, as is O'Hara's case, is thus a kind of victory. Or perhaps some man has spurned the star (but no man has spurned our speaker, who has made his way through the traffic snarl to meet his friend over lunch and tell him about Lana), and so the poet must assure her that "we love you." But O'Hara doesn't follow up these leads. It is his poetic strategy, here and elsewhere, to *allude* to story ("The main thing," he says in "Fantasy," "is to tell a story. / It is almost / very important") and then to turn story fragments inward, applying their possible meanings to himself.

What I am suggesting is that when story reappears in postmodern poetry, it is no longer the full-fledged *mythos* of Aristotle, the "specific syntactic shape" Robert Scholes speaks of, but a point of reference, a way of alluding, a source – as we shall see in the case of Edward Dorn's *Slinger* – of parody. To tell a story is to find a way – sometimes the only way – of *knowing* one's world. But since, in the view of many of our poets, as in the view of comparable fiction writers, the world just doesn't – indeed shouldn't – make sense, the *gnosis* which is narration remains fragmentary. By frustrating our desire for closure ("Well, what *did* happen to Lana Turner?"), such "stories" foreground the narrative codes themselves and call them into question. Consider what happens in another narrative poem of the sixties, John Ashbery's " 'They Dream Only of America' ":

> They dream only of America
> To be lost among the thirteen million pillars of grass:
> "This honey is delicious
> *Though it burns the throat.*"
>
> And hiding from darkness in barns
> They can be grownups now
> And the murder's ash tray is more easily –
> The lake a lilac cube.
>
> He holds a key in his right hand.
> "Please," he asked willingly.
> He is thirty years old.
> That was before
>
> We could drive hundreds of miles
> At night through dandelions.
> When his headache grew worse we
> Stopped at a wire filling station.
>
> Now he cared only about signs.
> Was the cigar a sign?
> And what about the key?
> He went slowly into the bedroom.

> "I would not have broken my leg if I had not fallen
> Against the living room table. What is it to be back
> Beside the bed? There is nothing to do
> For our liberation, except wait in the horror of it.
>
> And I am lost without you."[10]

There is no question that the narrator of this poem is telling some kind of story, but what is it about? " 'They Dream Only of America' " is itself a dream narrative, our expectations being defied at every turn. In the first place, the orderly four-line stanzas and straightforward syntax call to mind a "normal" lyric poem; indeed, on the page Ashbery's 25-line poem does not look all that different from Wright's 20-line "Snowstorm in the Midwest." Like the latter, " 'They Dream Only of America' " also foregrounds complex patterns of sound repetition as in "The *lake* a *lilac* *cube*." Secondly, Ashbery's first stanza provides what purports to be the beginning of a coherent plot. "They dream only of America" is not really a very odd thing to say: all sorts of people all over the world have dreamt and continue to dream of the great American continent, the promised land, the Hollywood image of affluence, materialism, and success. Even the next line seems to bear this out: "the thirteen" brings to mind the thirteen colonies of our founding fathers, and "pillars of grass" immediately recalls Whitman's *Leaves of Grass,* that great celebratory American poem. However, a note of doubt already creeps in: "thirteen million pillars of grass" is a contradictory image, suggesting the constriction of the city rather than the natural landscape. By the time we read the third line, " 'This honey is delicious / *Though it burns the throat,*' " we are left in a sort of limbo, knowing neither who is speaking nor who "They" are.

Ashbery keeps us guessing by setting up at least two possible story lines: a tale of murder (a parody detective story) and a tale of love that plays upon Hollywood movies. The detective story has to do with "hiding from darkness in barns," with a "murderer's ash tray" that relates mysteriously to the lake as "lilac cube," with the puzzling reference, in the third stanza, to a "He" who "holds a key in his right hand" – a key which, like the cigar of the fourth stanza, may or may not be a "sign." At the end, someone has broken a leg by falling against the living room table and announces that "There is nothing to do / For our liberation, except wait in the horror of it." At the same time, what we may call the poem's "murder mystery code" can just as easily be read as an erotic one. "Hiding from darkness in barns / They can be grownups now" – these lines may refer to the sexual encounter of two adolescents, just as the later dialogue about the key may have to do with a rendezvous. The "We" who "could drive hundreds of miles / At night through dandelions" may be passionate lovers. Whatever it is that happens, at any rate, terminates in the bedroom, and the last line of the poem is like the refrain of a popular song: " 'And I am lost without you.' "

" 'They Dream Only of America' " can be glossed by an interesting comment Ashbery made about Gertrude Stein's *Stanzas in Meditation:*

> *Stanzas in Meditation* gives one the feeling of time passing, of things happening, of a "plot," though it would be difficult to say precisely what is going on. Sometimes the story has the logic of a dream . . . at other times it becomes startlingly clear for a moment, as though a change in wind had suddenly enabled us to hear a conversation that was taking place some distance away. . . . But it is usually not events which interest Miss Stein, rather it is their "way of happening," and the story of *Stanzas in Meditation* is a general, all-purpose model which each reader can adapt to fit his own set of particulars. The poem is a hymn to possibility.[11]

Just so, in Ashbery's poem, we have the feeling of time passing ("now," "he is thirty years old," "That was before"), of things happening ("When his headache grew worse we / Stopped at a wire filling station," "He went slowly into the bedroom"), of a "plot," but it is impossible to say precisely what is going on. For, like Stein, Ashbery is less interested in "events" than in a "way of happening," and his story is intentionally set up as an "all-purpose model which each reader can adapt to fit his own set of particulars."

This is not to say that the narrative has no meaning. Ashbery's dreamscape is like a cut-up version of a Hollywood film epic, the sort where wistful immigrants come to America only to find themselves embroiled, before they know it, in events more sordid than those they left behind. Whatever is happening, it clearly has to do with pleasure (" 'This honey is delicious' "), fear ("hiding from darkness in barns"; "There is nothing to do . . . except wait in the horror of it"), and loss. "To be lost among the thirteen million pillars of grass" of our great continent is ultimately to be "lost without you" – to end up in a world where the lake has become a "lilac cube." A parable, one might say, for the times.

A poem like " 'They Dream Only of America' " is thus indirectly a commentary on the sort of poem James Wright was writing in "Snowstorm in the Midwest." The two poems are exactly contemporary. Wright's speaker communes with nature: the "haunches of whales" and "whitecap doves" create a magic water world in which "it is hard to drown"; indeed, the poet comes to feel that he can "walk on the waters." Difficult as it may be to express his particular emotions except in terms of images and metaphors, the poet never doubts their validity, their ability to signify. It is such doubt that we meet in the longer narrative poems of the past decade.

Here the great example is perhaps *Slinger* (1975), Edward Dorn's four-book epic of the Wild West, a narrative poem in which "action" is consistently put in question. In the little border town of Mesilla, New Mexico, the "I" of the poem meets "The Cautious Gunslinger / of impeccable personal smoothness / and slender leather encased hands / folded casually / to make his knock."[12] The "Slinger" (Dorn evidently prefers this epithet to "Gunslinger" because he can play on its meanings: a "slinger" is a heavy drinker – one who imbibes "sling" – as well as, in British parlance, one who plays the stock market) is a curious blend of cowboy hero, robber baron, philosophy professor, and sometime bard; he can, at will, "unroll the map of locations" and, like the Pied Piper, entice others to join him in his "gothic search" (p. 2). So "I" – designated as both "an initial" and a "single" – sets out on a journey with the Slinger and his "constella-tion," ostensibly in search of "Hughes / Howard," who is, they say, in Las Vegas. Other members of the party include a Stoned Horse, sometimes called Heidegger ("Hi digger!") and sometimes Claude Lévi-Strauss, a "character" who has conveniently forgotten his tradi-tional role as beast of burden and rides inside the coach he should be pulling, and who rolls giant Tampico bombers even as he engages in debates on hermeneutics; a traveling minstrel known only as "The Poet," who strums his "abso-lute" and sings sentimental love songs that refer curiously to ampersands and cybernetics; and Lil, the "gaudy Madam of the cabaret" and the Slinger's sometime mistress, a lady given to speeches like the following:

> Shit, Slinger! you still got that
> marvelous creature, and who is that
> funny talker, you pick him up
> in some sludgy seat of higher
> learnin, Creeps! you always did
> hang out with some curious refugees.   (p. 6)

In Book II, the company meets two other characters, the sixties acid freak Kool Everything, who is hitchhiking to Universe City, and Dr. Flamboyant, who conducts scientific researches into "post-ephemeral subjects" and "fan[s] his neck / with . . . Scientific American" (p. 37).

These pilgrims travel from town to town, but despite the accompanying STRUM of the guitar and the references to the Rio Grande and to Wurlitzers, Dorn's West is no longer the West of heroic exploits but the West created by the movies, television, and comic books – a West in which the real sharpshooters are the businessmen and storekeepers who direct the flow of money. Accordingly, although Slinger and his friends make a fairly consistent journey that we could trace on a map (from Mesilla, to Truth or Consequences, then on toward Four Corners, site of a big industrial power plant, and finally to Cortez, Colorado, in the southwestern part of the state), the purpose of the pilgrimage gradually disappears as we come to see that travel makes little difference, all places being essentially the same. At the end, Las Vegas has become an eternal mirage. Howard Hughes is forgotten (perhaps because he and the Slinger are really one and the same person), and the friends disperse to various places: Lil to Wyoming, the Poet, "Moving to Montana soon / going to be a nose spray tycoon" (p. 187), and so on. But then, none of these places have any real identity anyway, as witness the rechristening of Hot Springs with the name of a TV quiz show, *Truth or Consequences*.

The role of the "I" in this context is particularly puzzling and interesting, especially when we compare this "I" to that of the lyric voice that speaks in James Wright's poem. At the beginning of *Slinger,* "I" is the person who tries to interpret the meaning behind events, who needs to know what is happening and to whom. "I" is forever asking questions. For example:

> And where will you now I asked.
> Five days northeast of here
> depending of course on whether one's horse
> is of iron or flesh
> there is a city called Boston
> and in that city there is ahotel
> whose second floor has been let
> to an inscrutable Texan named Hughes
> Howard? I asked
> The very same.
> And what do you mean by inscrutable.
>   oh Gunslinger?
> I mean to say that He
> has not been seen since 1833.
>
> But when you have found him my Gunslinger
> what will you do, oh what will you do?   (p. 4)

At first, the Slinger is more or less tolerant of "I's" questions, but, as they become more and more insistent, he becomes "hos-tile":

> What does the foregoing mean?
> I asked. Mean?
> my Gunslinger laughed
> *Mean?*
> Questioner, you got some strange
> obsessions, you want to know
> what something *means* after you've
> seen it, after you've *been* there
> or were you *out* during
> That time? No.
> And you want some *reason*.   (pp. 27–26)

To the Slinger, the word "mean" is a "mortal sin / And Difference I have no sense of" (p. 29). But because "I" does have a sense of this "Difference," he is an anachronism in the poem. Accordingly, he dies in Book II and is preserved in LSD until he emerges, at the end of Book III, as the secretary of Parmenides, which is to say as a representative of the pre-Socratic philosophy that Dorn finds closest to our own postmodern deconstructions. Michael Davidson, in a superb essay on *Slinger,* calls "I" the "last vestige of the self-conscious, rationalizing ego":

> As Dorn kills off the ego he destroys the primacy of the first-person narrative. In creating a character who is also a pronoun, Dorn illustrates the predicament of a post-Cartesian ontology in which man's being is defined both by his thought and his ability to call that thought into doubt. The reader becomes caught in a double-bind by following a first and third person narration at the same time. Dorn's strategy thus collapses subjective upon objective poles without, at the same time, having to posit a transcendental principle.[13]

This is, I think, a very important point. In an interview with Barry Alpert, asked whether he wanted *Slinger* to rival a novel, Dorn replied:

> Well, that's one of its great pleasures. Originally, before I understood any of the ontology of the situation, I was interested in getting rid of I. To get rid of I, in the most literal sense, and, in fact, my intentions toward I in the beginning were rather ruthless, to give *me* that kind of freedom. . . . I didn't want to have any truck with that first person singular excuse which I find one of the most effective brakes on current verse practice.[14]

And he adds, somewhat portentously, "I believe in the shared mind."

Some readers will undoubtedly find such talk of the shared mind and the getting rid of what Olson called "the lyrical interference of the individual as ego," pretentious, but it makes sense in terms of Dorn's central distrust of the metaphysical tradition based on the primacy of Being as presence, the Cartesian separation of man from the objects of his knowledge. As Lévi-Strauss (alias Horse) tells "I":

> I study the savage mind.
> And what is that I asked.
> *That,* intoned Claude leaning on my shoulder
> is what you *have*
> in other words, you provide
> an instance
> you are purely animal
> sometimes purely plant
> but mostly you're just a
> classification, I mean it's conceivable
> but so many documents
> would have to be gone through
> and dimensions of such *variety*
> taken into account to realize what
> you are, that
> even if we confined ourselves
> to the societies for which
> the data are sufficiently full,
> accurate, and comparable
> among themselves
> it could not be "done"
> *without the aid of machines.*   (p. 33)

Thus the realm of inherent human values, of a logocentric universe is called into question, and with it the centrality of persons. Accordingly, Dorn's "characters" – Lil, Kool Everything, Dr. Flamboyant – are "flat," and they appear, as it were, on a shallow screen. Although they seem to represent classic Western or comic book types, they finally have no identity or, to put it another way, their identities can merge even as Gunslinger himself is both sharpshooter and Howard Hughes. For the real hero of Dorn's narrative poem is not, of course, the title character but language itself, the language of our time – an ingenious mix of scientific jargon, structuralist terminology, junkie slang, Elizabethan sonneteering, Western dialect, and tough talk about kicking a gorilla "in the balls" – the language that we actually hear around us and see in print, refracted, distorted, heightened, but always recognizable in its "presyntactic metalinguistic urgency" (p. 69).

Near the end of *Slinger,* the Gunslinger tells Lil his heart now "beats to another radio signal":

> *Whats it like* Lil asked
>
> Our Source is self refracting
> and when it rises it actually plays a tune
> on one's eyeballs, Maximum Deum
> and our birds have two heads and sing duets
>
> Holy xit, Everything wept
>
> and the cows have the ability
> to convert their teets
> in the summertime
> they give a substance
> not unlike tasty-freeze
> Rather convenient said the Horse
> who was speaking on the phone
> to Frank Chrystler Canlid, the great producer
>
> Yes, since the trees
> bear a double cone
> Where, then, Lily are you off to?
> as this company scatters on the marvellous winde   (p. 187)

Homonyms, puns, nonsense words, coinages, archaisms, learned allusions, advertising jargon, a play on proper names like "Chrystler" – *Slinger* is a collage of all these things. In keeping with the emphasis on what Ashbery calls "an open field of narrative possibilities," Dorn's poem also accommodates every possible verse form from blank verse and rhymed ballad stanzas to free verse paragraphs and prose interludes. When, at the end of the story, the Slinger tells the company that "this has been such fine play / and I'll miss this marvellous accidentalism," the reader can only agree.

Now let us come back to our beginning, James Wright's epiphany poem, "Snowstorm in the Midwest." It is never easy to predict what course the poetry of the future will take, but I would guess that the conventions I discussed as being operative in that poem – the solitary "I" in the timeless moment, the emotive response to the landscape, the reliance on the consort of images to create meaning, the ecstatic

present-tense mode, the structured free verse stanzas – all these hall-
marks of the late modernist lyric will become less prevalent as our
conceptions of the relation of self to world become more closely ad-
justed to the phenomenology of the present. In understanding that
present, a narrative that is not primarily autobiographical will once
again be with us, but it will be a narrative fragmented, dislocated, and
often quite literally non-sensical.

There are signs that this is already happening. To cite just one example: in *The Wishing Bone Cycle* (1976), the young ethnopoet Howard
Norman, who has done field work with the Swampy Cree Indians in
Northern Manitoba, gathers together a series of name-origin poems,
riddling fables translating and re-enacting tales told him by the Cree
elder Samuel Makidemewa'be. Each poem purports to explain how a
given person in the community got his or her name, for example:

> *Larger Ears*
> She had large ears, and this seemed
> to please her. Even the time a man joked at her ears
> and said they were BATS,
> she chose to believe it! She said to him, "Yes,
> you are right. They are bats!
> I'm glad you came to tell me.
> And I will send them into your house
> THIS VERY NIGHT to hover
> and listen over your face!"
>
> This quickly stopped
> his joking.
>
> Also, she liked to listen to *large* sounds
> with those large ears.
> Maybe the two things
> went together.
> Before storms, she would sit along the edge
> of a lake, EVEN AFTER IT BEGAN RAINING,
> and listen to thunder!
> Sometimes she shouted back
> to it, "Louder, I can hardly hear you!"
> Even though the rest of us
> had our hands over our ears, as we sat
> inside our houses.
>
> Listening with our smaller ears.[15]

The strangeness of this and related Cree name-origin poems, as Norman recreates them, is that although the narrator can record *how* the girl known as "Large Ears" got her name, he cannot really explain why her ears were different in the first place or whether her "larger ears" turned out to be an asset or a liability. As Gary Snyder says of Norman's naming poems, "The mystery is, how do events and names cross paths and marry?"[16] Clearly, we cannot today read *The Wishing Bone Cycle* in the spirit intended by the Cree elder who is Norman's informant, for we bring to the poetic tale the modern assumption that events should make sense, that we should work together to puzzle out their latent meanings. Or, as Ursula Le Guin puts it in her superbly witty essay-fiction, "It was a Dark and Stormy Night; or, Why Are We Huddled about the Campfire?":

> The *histoire* is the what
> and the *discours* is the how
> but what I want to know, Brigham,
> is *le pourquoi*
> *Why* are we sitting here around the campfire?[17]

Le Guin herself concludes that "there is no reliability in the telling" of any tale, but that "by remembering it," we make the story ours: "Take the tale in your teeth . . . and bite till the blood runs, hoping it's not poison; and we will all come to the end together, and even to the beginning: living, as we do, in the middle" (p. 199). To put it another way: the lyric of the solitary self, engaged in the ceaseless longing for disclosure, may well be giving way to a more communal poetry, a poetry in which narrative once again becomes the locus for *gnosis*. In the words of John Cage, himself a narrative poet:

> . . . more and more this concern with personal feelings of individuals, even the enlightenment of individuals, will be seen in the larger context of society. . . . The path to self knowledge has been mapped out by psychiatry, by oriental philosophy, mythology, occult thought, anthroposophy, and astrology. We know all we need to know about Oedipus, Prometheus, and Hamlet. What we are learning is how to be convivial. "Here comes Everybody."[18]

NOTES

1 *Collected Poems* (Middletown, Conn.: Wesleyan University Press, 1971), pp. 130–31.

2 "Social Dramas and Stories about Them," *Critical Inquiry*, 7 (Autumn 1980), 167.

3 "Narrative Time," *Critical Inquiry*, 7 (Autumn 1980): 171.

4 "Language, Narrative, and Anti-Narrative," *Critical Inquiry*, 7 (Autumn 1980): 210.

5 *The Portable Poe*, ed. Philip Van Doren Stern (New York: Penguin Books, 1973), p. 552.

6 *Le Spleen de Paris* (Texte de 1869), in Baudelaire, *Oeuvres complètes*, ed. Y. G. Le Dantec et Claude Pichois (Paris: Gallimard, Bibliothèque de la Pléiade, 1961), p. 229. The translation is that of Louise Varèse, *Paris Spleen* (New York: New Directions, 1970), p. lx.

7 "Narrative Poetry," in *Princeton Encyclopedia of Poetry and Poetics,* ed. Alex Preminger, Frank J. Warnke, and O. B. Hardison, Jr., Enlarged edition (Princeton: Princeton University Press, 1974), p. 550. Interestingly, this view is regularly expressed by poets of the sixties: Robert Bly, for example, remarks: ". . . for reasons no one understands the narrative line which was useful in the old poem is no longer useful." And again, "since the narrative has failed there may be another way to write which we literally haven't found." See "A Craft Interview with Robert Bly," *New York Quarterly* (1972); rpt. in *Talking All Morning* (Ann Arbor: University of Michigan Press, 1980), pp. 191, 193.

8 (Baltimore: The Johns Hopkins University Press, 1979), pp. 22–23.

9 *The Collected Poems of Frank O'Hara,* ed. Donald Allen (New York: Alfred A. Knopf, 1971), p. 449.

10 *The Tennis Court Oath* (Middletown, Conn.: Wesleyan University Press, 1962), p. 13.

11 "The Impossible," *Poetry,* 90, no. 4 (July 1957): 251.

12 (Berkeley, Wingbow Press, 1975), p. 1. The pages of this volume are unpaginated, but I have paginated them here for the sake of convenience.

13 " 'To Eliminate the Draw': A Reading of *Slinger* by Edward Dorn," *American Literature,* 53 (November 1981): 447–98. I am indebted to this illuminating essay throughout my discussion.

14 "An Interview with Barry Alpert," 31 July 1972, *Vort,* 1 (Fall 1972); rpt. in Edward Dorn, *Interviews,* ed. Donald Allen (Bolinas: Four Seasons Foundation, 1980), pp. 29–30.

15 *The Wishing Bone Cycle* (New York: Stonehill Publishing Co., 1976), p. 78.

16. Dust Jacket, Howard Norman, *Born Tying Knots, Swampy Cree Naming Stories told by Samuel Makidemewa'be* (Ann Arbor: Bear Claw Press, 1976).

17 *Critical Inquiry,* 7 (Autumn 1980): 192. Le Guin is writing as respondent in the symposium "On Narrative," to which I refer in notes 2–4 above, specifically to the essays of Derrida ("The Law of Genre") and Hayden White ("The Value of Narrativity in the Representation of Reality").

18 "The Future of Music," in *Esthetics Contemporary,* ed. Richard Kostelanetz (Buffalo: Prometheus Books, 1978), p. 291.

8 Postmodernism and the impasse of lyric

I

In a recent symposium on "The Place of Poetry" in our time, Christopher Clausen declares:

> Nearly everyone agrees that poetry in the twentieth century – at least in English–speaking countries – is not so highly honored or widely read as it once was. Few doubt that the rise of science has had something to do with displacing it as a publicly impor-tant vehicle for those truths that people accept as being cen-trally important. The attempt to persuade the reading public that figurative, ironic, or connotative modes of thought and discourse retain their value in an age of computer language has not been notably successful. Few educated Americans today have any confidence in their ability to understand metaphor or detect irony; most undoubtedly believe that anything of real importance can be better said in prose.[1]

What are the assumptions behind this statement, a statement not untypi-cal of discussions of poetry in our leading journals? First, that "poetry" and "science" have mutually exclusive modes of discourse. Second, that "poetry" is the opposite of "prose." Third, that poetry once served and should serve as a vehicle for "truth" – that is to say, "truths that people accept as being centrally important." And, fourth, that poetry is inher-ently "figurative, ironic, or connotative" and, as such, stands opposed to "computer language," which is presumably non-figurative, straight-forward, and denotative. Further, if we relate (3) and (4), the implication is that the "truth" of poetry is one of subjectivity, of personal feeling and experience. As Clausen puts it later in his essay:

172

> Poetry remains an essential form of knowledge because of its
> unique ability to embody the particular in subtle and powerful
> form; its comparative lack of generalization is in fact its main
> advantage. If we are after the truths of moments, situations,
> relationships, the case of art (and particularly poetry) to eluci-
> date is a strong one, for such insights are unique. . . .   (GR,
> p. 711)

Clausen's fellow symposiasts, a group of distinguished poets and
critics, do not quarrel with these basic assumptions. Some, like Maxine
Kumin and Linda Pastan, suggest that Clausen is not sufficiently critical
of television, which they regard as the villain behind poetry's demise;
others, like Joel Conarroe, observe that ours is "an age of remarkable
prose and that the presence of masterly novelists may have something
to do with the invisibility of even our leading poets" (GR, p. 746); still
others, like Donald Hall, point out that Clausen is possibly too gloomy
about the state of poetry since its audience has, after all, never been
exactly large. Wayne Booth, finally, remarks ruefully that it is not just
"poetry" but all "imaginative writing" that is in trouble at a time when
the best young critics would rather read the latest copy of *New Literary
History* or *Critical Inquiry* than "the best novel, play, or collection of
poems of the last year" (GR, p. 753).

The causes of the malaise Clausen describes, as well as its extent, are
thus regarded as subjects open to debate, even as his characterization of
poetry is accepted as a given. No one, for example, seems to find it
unusual that Clausen uses the words *poetry* and *lyric* interchangeably;
lyric, furthermore, refers less to any form of *melopoeia* (the word originally refers, of course, to a poem composed to be sung) than to a
particular decorum of subject matter and tone. Thus, in assessing Modernist poetry, Clausen remarks:

> . . . we can look back on an entire century in which the longer,
> more public genres of poetry have been moribund. Gone from
> the mainstream of literature are the poetic autobiography, the
> extended elegy, the philosophical meditation in verse, the long
> satirical poem. Prose fiction has largely replaced narrative
> verse; the lyric has largely replaced all other kinds. With rare
> exceptions, the question of whether a contemporary poem is a
> lyric or not is meaningless.[2]

Poetry, then, means lyric, and by *lyric,* Clausen evidently refers to a
short verse utterance (or sequence of such utterances) in which a single
speaker expresses, in figurative language, his subjective vision of "the

truths of moments, situations, relationships," a vision culminating in a "unique insight" or epiphany that unites poet and reader.

A much more sophisticated version of what I take to be an essentially Romantic theory of lyric may be found in the writings of Harold Bloom. In *The Anxiety of Influence* (1973), we read:

> The greatest poet in our language is excluded from the argument of this book for several reasons. One is necessarily historical; Shakespeare belongs to the giant age before the flood, before the anxiety of influence became central to poetic consciousness. Another has to do with the contrast between dramatic and lyric form. As poetry has become more subjective, the shadow cast by the precursors has become more dominant.[3]

Indeed, "the whole tradition of the post-Enlightenment, which is Romanticism, shows a further decline in its Modernist and post-Modernist heirs. The death of poetry will not be hastened by any reader's broodings, yet it seems just to assume that poetry in our tradition, when it does, will be self-slain, murdered by its own past strength" (AI, p. 10).

Notice that, as in Clausen's argument, the poetry whose death we are about to witness is equated with lyric, with Romantic subjectivity. The possibility that poetry might deal with anything outside the enclosed self is immediately brushed aside. In *Agon* (1982), Bloom puts it this way:

> Poetry from Homer through Alexander Pope (who died in 1744) had a subject matter in the characters and actions of men and women clearly distinct from the poet who observed them, and who described and sometimes judged them. But from 1744 or so to the present day the best poetry internalized its subject matter, particularly in the mode of Wordsworth after 1798. *Wordsworth had no true subject except his own subjective nature,* and very nearly all significant poetry since Wordsworth, even by American poets, has repeated Wordsworth's inward turning.[4] (my italics)

What form does this poetry of "inward turning" take? Bloom formulated an answer to this question as early as 1968 in an essay called "The Internalization of Quest Romance":

> Wordsworth's Copernican revolution in poetry is marked by the evanescence of any subject but subjectivity, the loss of what a poem is "about." . . . the central problem of Romantic (and post-Romantic) poetry [is] what, for men without belief and

even without credulity, is the spiritual form of romance? How can a poet's (or any man's) life be one of continuous allegory . . . in a reductive universe of death, a separated realm of atomized meanings, each discrete from the next? Though all men are questers, even the least, what is the relevance of quest in a gray world of continuities and homogenized enterprises?

The answer is that the Romantic (and hence, by Bloom's logic, the Modern as well) quest takes the form of "internalized quest romance," whose hero is the poet himself, and whose "antagonists" are "everything in the self that blocks imaginative work." The fulfillment of such quest is "never the poem itself but the poem beyond that is made possible by the apocalypse of imagination."[5]

In subsequent studies, Bloom submits "internalized quest romance" or, as he often calls it, "the Romantic crisis poem," to his famed revisionary ratios and his theory of the three crossings.[6] These refinements have often been questioned even as Deconstructionists have questioned Bloom's humanistic stance toward poetry, his arguments for origin and presence, indeed for the ability to make statements about poetic meaning. But the historical issue – the validity, for example, of the mid-eighteenth-century watershed Bloom sets up – has rarely been confronted.[7] It has not been suggested, for instance, that if there was a poetry "before the flood," "before the anxiety of influence became central to poetic consciousness," there might well be a poetry *after* the flood has receded, after, that is to say, the Romantic (and Modernist) lyric has been, in Bloom's words, "murdered by its own strength."

"Post-flood" poetry, it seems only reasonable to assume, may well take its impetus from texts quite unlike those of internalized quest romance; it may well prefer narrative and satire, parody and play, to the lyric epiphany. My sense is that, as we approach our own *fin de siècle,* the subjectivity that haunted the latter Romantics, and, to a large extent, the Moderns, is not at all, as Bloom insists, the only subject for poetry. "Minor authors," the semiotician Maria Corti observes, "tend to guarantee the constant validity and stability of a [given] genre, which is why the process of transformation is so slow that it can be noticed only across the distance of many links in the chain."[8] Thus we take note of the "belatedness' of this or that poetic text (say, a set of lyrics by A. R. Ammons or Mark Strand) without stopping to consider that it may be the genre itself, not the particular poet, that is "belated." The "virtual extinction of poetry as a cultural force," says Clausen, is an "event" that has "happened within living memory" (GR, p. 705). Substitute "Romantic lyric" for "poetry" in that sentence and Clausen may well be right. But it may also not matter very much, for what has become "extinct" is not, I shall suggest, *poetry*, but only a particular species of it. Postmodern poetics, it may yet turn out, has more in common with the performative, playful mode of eighteenth-century ironists than with Shelleyan apocalypse. It wants, that is to say, to re-inscribe its initial letter into the story of its arrival – to turn a Poe into a Pope.

II

Before I turn to Postmodern paradigms, however, it may be well to clear the air by probing, a little more closely, the lingering hold Romantic norms for poetry continue to have among us. The equation of *poem* with what Bloom calls "the Wordsworthian crisis lyric" is not fortuitous; it is the logical end product of a century in which this ideology was dominant. I want briefly to consider two versions of that ideology, one "low-brow" and one "high-brow," so that we can see how strong the actual consensus was.

The first or "low-brow" version is to be found in a pocket-sized book published by Macmillan in 1861 under the name *The Golden Treasury of the Best Songs and Lyric Poems in the English Language.*[9] The *Golden Treasury*, which was to become the most popular poetry anthology in the English-speaking world (it has gone through countless editions and is still a staple of public libraries and surburban bookstores), was assembled by a young Oxford graduate named Francis Turner Palgrave, who was to be elected to the Oxford Chair of Poetry in 1885. The first edition is appropriately dedicated to Tennyson, who was a close friend.

In his Preface, Palgrave defines *lyric* largely by exclusionary principles:

> Lyrical has been here held essentially to imply that each Poem shall turn on some single thought, feeling, or situation. In accordance with this, narrative, descriptive, and didactic poems – unless accompanied by rapidity of movement, brevity, and the colouring of human passion – have been excluded. Humorous poetry except in the very unfrequent instances where a truly poetical tone pervades the whole, with what is strictly personal, occasional, and religious, has been considered foreign to the idea of the book. (p. a)

The Idea of the Book – here, more than twenty years before Mallarmé's *Quant au livre,* to which I shall return, is the notion of the Poetic Book as Sacred Text, as special language removed from the chaos and triviality, the strictly "personal" and the "occasional," of everyday life. Note that the "religious" is dismissed along with these, presumably because the Religion of Art can have no truck with the credulity and superstitiousness of ordinary people.[10] For the same reason, narrative, didacticism, and humor are excluded from the canon: presumably, such incursions into the world of ordinary discourse (the world of satires, lessons, and jokes) would undermine what Palgrave refers to as "a truly poetical tone." The word "poetical" in this last phrase is, evidently, synonymous with the earlier "lyrical," the question of verse form or structure being much less important than the equation of lyric with expressivity – "the expression of some single thought, feeling, or situation" – special stress being laid on "the colouring of human passions." The commonsense view of a Samuel Johnson ("Poetry is a species of metrical composition") thus gives way to a definition by subject matter and tone; Palgrave's one concern, as regards metrics, is that the anthology should contain as little blank verse or heroic couplets as possible since these forms "rarely conform to Lyrical conditions in treatment" (p. a).

Brevity, rapidity of movement, passion – all these were to be subsumed under the principle that was to become a cornerstone of the New Criticism: organic unity. "Excellence," says Palgrave, "should be looked for rather in the whole than in the parts" (p. b); indeed, not only must each poem be an intense, unified whole, but "It is hoped that the contents of this Anthology will . . . be found to present a certain 'unity,' 'as episodes,' in the noble language of Shelley, 'to that great Poem which all poets, like the cooperating thoughts of one great mind, have built up since the beginning of the world' " (p. c).

The "great Poem," like Mallarmé's "Grand Oeuvre," is thus construed as an organic sequence of highly charged, emotive lyrics, whose brevity is in direct proportion to their intensity. "Poetry gives treasures more golden than gold, leading us in higher and healthier ways than those of the world . . ." (p. c). In keeping with this view, the *Golden Treasury* includes Herbert but not Donne (evidently too intellectual), Shelley but not Blake (evidently too religious).[11] The eighteenth century is represented chiefly by Gray, Thompson, Collins, and Cowper: Pope has only one selection (the little lyric "The Quiet Life"), Swift none. Again, the Romantic section gives more attention to Campbell and Scott, Hood and Moore, than to Byron: Palgrave's Byron is, predictably, the poet of "She Walks in Beauty" or "When We Two Parted."

The *Golden Treasury* can thus be seen as emblematic of the codification of Romantic theory, with its gradual privileging of the lyric above the other literary modes, a process whose history is well documented by such critics as Meyer Abrams and Tzvetan Todorov.[12] The anthology provided the Victorians and early Moderns with a poetic canon: Hardy, for example, first received a copy in 1862 and annotated it throughout the years, remarking to his wife, shortly before his death, that it was his ambition to have "some poem or poems in a good anthology like the *Golden Treasury*."[13] Again, Wallace Stevens, who received the 1896 revised edition while a student at Harvard, marked key passages by Wordsworth and Shelley or noted cross-references between, say, Wordsworth and Arnold's *Essays in Criticism*.[14] Indeed, by the turn of the century, for most would-be practitioners of the craft in England and America, poetry meant Palgrave.

The additions and omissions made by C. Day Lewis, himself a leading poet of the time, for the 1954 revised edition are especially interesting. Bemused by Palgrave's omission of Blake, Lewis hastens to reinstate this great lyric poet; he also adds a large twentieth-century section which includes Lawrence and Frost, Moore and Sitwell, Owen and Blunden, Auden. But although he obviously admires Eliot – "The Hollow Men," "Marina," and "Journey of the Magi" are in the anthology – he omits "Gerontion" along with Yeats's "The Second Coming" as being "outside the lyrical class" (p. 17). As for Pound and Williams, Lewis makes no mention of either: presumably, theirs are not poems of sufficient intensity of feeling; besides, they surely suffer from the introduction of all sorts of narrative and descriptive matter, not to mention their frequent humor. A decade after World War II, then, poetry still means lyric, and lyric means the expression of personal feeling in language divorced from "ordinary prose."[15] Pound, for one, never forgave Macmillan for continuing to publish revised editions of *The Golden Treasury*. His 1918 essay on Joyce begins with the sentence, "Despite the War, despite the paper shortage, and despite those old-established publishers whose god is their belly and whose godfather was the late F. T. Palgrave, there is a new edition of James Joyce's *A Portrait of the Artist as a Young Man*." He regularly referred to Palgrave as "that doddard" or "that stinking sugar teat."[16] In Pound's eyes, *The Golden Treasury* was nothing less than a Chinese wall against modern poetry.

Christopher Clausen posits that the clash between Modernists like Pound and "most ordinary readers [who are] the heirs of Palgrave" has been largely responsible for the crisis of poetry today.[17] The fact is, however, that despite its alleged advocacy of indirection, impersonality, and fragmentation, Modernist poetry is not nearly so different from "the Palgrave version" as one might think. Mallarmé, for example, whose Symbolist poetic is at the very heart of Modernism, shares the Romantic belief that poetry is lyric, and that lyric is the expression of what Stevens was to call the "Supreme Fiction" or the "First Idea":

It is not *description* which can unveil the efficacy and beauty of monuments, seas, or the human face in all their maturity and native state, but rather evocation, *allusion, suggestion.* These somewhat arbitrary terms reveal what may well be a very decisive tendency in modern literature, a tendency which limits literature and yet sets it free. For what is the magic charm of art, if not this: that beyond the confines of a fistful of dust or of all other reality, beyond the book itself, beyond the very text, it delivers up that volatile scattering which we call the Spirit, Who cares for nothing save universal musicality.

Speech is no more than a commercial approach to reality. In literature, allusion is sufficient: essences are distilled and then embodied in *idea*.[18]

Accordingly, there are two entirely separate modes of discourse: the *poetic*, which is to say, the *lyric*, and the journalistic or *vulgar*, which includes everything else:

One of the undeniable ideals of our time is to divide words into two different categories: first, for vulgar or immediate, second, for essential purposes.

The first is for narrative, instruction, or description. . . . The elementary use of language involves that universal *journalistic style* which characterizes all kinds of contemporary writing, with the exception of literature.[19]

The language of poetry thus becomes entirely self-reflexive: "When I say: 'A flower!' then from the forgetfulness to which my voice consigns all floral form, something different from the usual calyces arises, something all music, essence, and softness: the flower which is absent from all bouquets."[20] Or, as Stevens was to put it, "The Poem that Took the Place of a Mountain."

But doesn't Mallarmean self-reflexivity stand opposed to Romantic subjectivity, to "the colouring of human passion" which Palgrave held to be so important? I think not. From our vantage in the late twentieth century, we can see that Modernist "objectivity" or "impersonality" was no more than an extreme version of the interiority it claimed to reject. For from where does the image of the "flower which is absent from all bouquets" come if not from the innermost recesses of the self? As Eliot put it, "Poetry is not a turning loose of emotion, but an escape from emotion; it is not the expression of personality, but an escape from personality. But, of course only those who have personality and emotions know what it means to want to escape these things."[21] Implicit in this statement is that whether we are confronted by Self ("personality") or Mask ("escape from personality"), the stress is on subjectivity, there being nothing outside it. For, as Harold Bloom puts it, and Mallarmé would surely have agreed, the poem can no longer be "about" any subject external to the poet's self; it can no longer present "the characters and actions of men and women clearly distinct from the poet who observed them."

In *Quant au livre* (1895), Mallarmé carries his "separatist" doctrine further by setting up a dichotomy between "The Newspaper" and "The Book." The newspaper is the sea; literature flows into it at will; the newspaper is "large-sized" and "open," whereas the "foldings" of the book have "an almost religious significance"; the newspaper inflicts on us "the monotonousness of its eternally unbearable columns"; the "fragile and inviolable book," on the other hand, "is perfect Music, and cannot be anything else." The Book, as Mallarmé defines it, is both sacred rite and, metaphorically, the moment of passionate discharge, of ecstasy. The Newspaper knows no such moments: "with its endless line of posters and proof sheets it makes for improvisation."[22]

Improvisation thus becomes the enemy of art, a curious state of affairs when one remembers that in the *Poetics,* Aristotle devotes a separate paragraph to that branch of *mimesis* that does not use *rhythmos* and *harmonia* (as do epic and tragedy) but "employs words alone either in bare prose or in meters–for example the mimes of Sophron and Xenarchus and the Socratic dialogues" (1447B). Improvisation, central to mime, was dearly loved by such early Romantic poets as Heine (see *Germany: A Winter's Tale*), and in *Don Juan,* Byron refers to himself as an *improvissatore.* But by the end of the nineteenth century, the "impurities" that "improvisation" would of necessity produce were ruled out of court. Such purification of the text created its own problems. As Michel Beaujour suggests:

> . . . an absolute distinction between journalistic cacography and artful writing is purely ideological and does not stand up to linguistic or rhetorical scrutiny: it is all a question of taste, and should ideology so decree, *bad* taste might become axiological king of the castle. We know this upset did indeed take place with futurism, Dadaism, surrealism, and their sequels: posters and newspapers became paradigms of artfulness.[23]

Precisely. Postmodernism in poetry, I would argue, begins in the urge to return the material so rigidly excluded–political, ethical, historical, philosophical–to the domain of poetry, which is to say that the

Romantic lyric, the poem as expression of a moment of absolute insight, of emotion crystallized into a timeless patterns, gives way to a poetry that can, once again, accommodate narrative and didacticism, the serious and the comic, verse *and* prose. It does not need to be the enemy of "science" as Clausen believes, for it seeks to incorporate the "computer language" of which Clausen is so contemptuous into the lyric fabric. Indeed, we are now witnessing, at least in America, an interesting phenomenon. Minor poets continue to write neo-Romantic lyric; in this context, the attack on television and the media as the enemy can be seen to be a kind of defensive nostalgia. At the same time, a new poetry is emerging that wants to open the field so as to make contact with the *world* as well as the *word*. In the space that remains, let me now turn to some concrete examples.

III

In the English-speaking world, the pivotal figure in the transformation of the Romantic (and Modernistic) lyric into what we now think of as postmodern poetry is surely Ezra Pound. When Pound came on the scene in the early 1900s, Mallarmean norms were largely dominant: the domain of "poetry" had become so restricted that any writer who still cared to relate literature to what Georg Lukacs called "the extensive totality of life,"[24] inevitably turned to the novel. For how could *poetry* deal with the social and political world? "By the end of the First World War," says Michael A. Bernstein in his important study of *The Cantos*, "a verse epic was not so much a form as an oxymoron, an anachronism that seemed to violate what many poets as well as critics had come to regard as the characteristic structure and horizon of poetic discourse."[25] Indeed, Pound himself began his career as a maker of small chiselled lyrics, not so different from those of the Yellow Nineties. He programmatically called these "Imagist" and declared that "It is better to present one *image* in a lifetime than to produce voluminous works."[26] Yet, as Pound's poetic evolved, he came to recognize, if reluctantly, that "The main expression of nineteenth-century consciousness is in prose," that the novels of Stendhal and Flaubert, at any rate, contain "language charged with meaning" that any poet might envy (see LE, p. 32). By 1938, in the *Guide to Kulchur*, he was defending his *Cantos*, then numbering fifty-one, as follows: "There is no mystery about the *Cantos*, they are the tale of the tribe – give Rudyard [Kipling] credit for his use of the phrase."[27] Bernstein, who takes the title of his book from this comment writes:

Traditionally the words ["the tale of the tribe"] have been regarded as only another version of the Mallarmean exhortation
to "donner un sens plus pur aux mots de la tribu," and yet
between the two statements lies the entire gap separating the
"poésie pure" of *Un coup de dès* from the modern verse epic,
The Cantos. (TT, p. 8)

This is an important point. By definition, the "tale of the tribe"
means *narrative,* and the narrative presents, in Bernstein's words, "its
audience's own cultural, historical, or mythic heritage, providing models of exemplary conduct (both good and bad) by which its readers can
regulate their lives and adjust their shared customs" (TT, p. 14). Again
sagetrieb, as Pound, borrowing the term from Leo Frobenius, called it
(*trieb* = drive; *sage* = tale or fable, hence the drive or urge to tell the
tale, to speak the fable) inevitably involves a departure from the lyric
voice, from the subjectivity Bloom takes to be the *only* subject of
poetry "after the flood." Pound's "tale of the tribe" is, of course,
hardly a classical linear epic; its baffling "circle of fragments" (Yeats's
phrase) demands quite new ways of construing the "story." Nevertheless, its repeated shifting of ground between what Bernstein calls the
"mythological" and "historical" codes – between lyric epiphany (the
Mallarmean crystallization) and the "prose tradition" of the novel –
challenges the hegemony of late Romantic and Modernist lyric. Of the
Malatesta Cantos (8–11), Bernstein writes:

> . . . Pound builds his presentation not just of Sigismundo him-
> self, but of the entire era, out of a series of brief memorable
> incidents. He transposes quotations from Sigismund's corre-
> spondence, papal missives, ambassadors' reports, and the re-
> corded conversations of contemporary witnesses directly into
> *The Cantos,* thereby showing for the first time in over a cen-
> tury, that poetry can actually *incorporate* prose, that the modern
> verse epic is a form sufficiently strong to absorb large chunks
> of factual data into its own texture (something the nineteenth-
> century verse epic has always avoided), without ceasing to be
> poetry. . . . The seemingly unobtrusive moment in Canto
> VIII, when the first series of historical letters is introduced into
> *The Cantos* and the personality of Sigismundo is shown by
> juxtaposing his prose instruction concerning a painter he wishes
> to engage with a lyric poem he writes for Isotta degli Atti,
> *without privileging either medium,* represents one of the decisive
> turning-points in modern poetics, opening for verse the capac-

ity to include domains of experience long since considered alien
territory.   (TT, p. 40)

This is a very suggestive statement, not just about *The Cantos* but
about a whole body of poetry that was to be written in its wake, from
Williams' *Paterson* down to Guy Davenport's *Eclogues* of 1981. *Without
privileging either medium*, lyric poem or "prose instruction" – this has,
more and more come to be our own poetic domain. A corollary,
equally important for postmodernism, is that the lyric voice gives way
to multiple voices or voice fragments: "the poem's judgments can now
appear, not as anxious intrusions into the text, but through the silent
arrangement, juxtaposition, and the selection of the historical *exempla*"
(TT, p. 170).

The mode, in other words, is that of *collage,* the setting side by side
or juxtaposition of disparate materials without commitment to explicit
syntactical relations between elements. In a collage-text like Pound's
Canto IX, such normal syntactical relations as subordination or implication are suppressed in favor of relations of similarity, equivalence, or
identity; thus the last thirteen lines of the Canto juxtapose a passage
from the *Commentaries* of Pius II ("*et amava perdutamente Ixotta degli
Atti . . .*") with bits from Horace, Walter Savage Landor, modern short-
hand ("i.e., Sigismund"), and travel-book narrative ("And the old sar-
cophagi, / such as lie, smothered in grass, by San Vitale"), without
subordinating one element to another, so that the reader must puzzle
out their various values and connections. But it is a puzzle that can
never be resolved, for collage, in David Antin's words, "operates in a
middle space between representation on the one hand and the kind of
constructional game of Mondrian on the other; and its operation
oscillate[s] between the two possibilities of representational reference
and compositional game."[28] For is the newspaper fragment in, say, a
Picasso collage to be read as a compositional unit, a luminous plane
juxtaposed to the neighboring planes (or, from another angle, the outline of a table leg), or are we to read it as a block of newsprint and focus
on its content? "The situation," as John Cage, himself a great *collagiste,*
puts it, "must be Yes-and-No not either-or."[29]

Since I have discussed the collage poetics of *The Cantos* elsewhere,[30] I
shall not rehearse the subject again here. Rather, let me say something
about a more recent collage poem that is now exerting a considerable
influence on younger poets, namely, Louis Zukofsky's 800-page poem
called "*A*," written over the half century between 1928 and 1974 but
not published as a whole until 1978.[31] I take as my sample of this
encyclopedic poem the 1950–51 segment "*A*"-12.

Following hard upon the two-page "*A*"-11, which is a formal love song, a *ballata* based on Cavalcanti's "Perch'io non spero,"[32] the long (138-page) "*A*"-12 begins on a musical note that takes us back to the opening line of "*A*"-1 – "A round of fiddles playing Bach" – with the lines:

> *Out of deep need*
> Four trombones and the organ in the nave
> A torch surged –
> Timed the theme Bach's name
> Dark larch and ridge, night. . . .   ("*A*," p. 126)

Not only is the subject here music, but the lines have an intricate sound pattern: *tromb* – *time* – theme – name; *Four* – *organ* – *torch*; *dark* – larch; *surge* – *larch* – *ridge*. The musical motif comes back again and again in references to his son Paul's violin playing, to "H- playing / The Turkish Concerto / By Mozart" (p. 161), and so on. Here, then, is what we might call the lyric derivation of the poem, the reminder that poetry, even when, as here, there is no fixed meter or syllable count, begins in *melopoeia*.

But "lyric," in Zukofsky's scheme of things, no longer means the individual framed poem; rather, lyric passages everywhere "cut" into narrative fragments. Bach the composer, for example, is also treated as Bach the father, and so, throughout "*A*"-12, we find interwoven stories of fathers and sons: Odysseus and Telemachus, the physician Nichomaeus and Aristotle (p. 236), the groaning old father of Gertrude Stein's *The Making of Americans*, who protests to his son, when the latter drags him through his own orchard, "Stop! I did not drag my father beyond this tree" (p. 168), and, centrally, Zukofsky's own father and grandfather in their relationships to him and his own relationship to Paul as well as to the "Poor Pay Pfc. Jackie," neighborhood kid and surrogate son, who is sent off to the Korean War and writes in slangy, non-orthographic prose, a series of letters to the poet, like the following:

> Friday, April 13. we derk at the port of
> Yokohama 5,263 miles from San Francisco.
> We derk about 1 o'clock in the afternoon
> and stay on the ship until midnight. (What
> for I don't now).   (p. 219)

These letters function as found objects – as "real" writings addressed to the poet even as a Schwitters collage will juxtapose "real" bits of newspaper or metal rings to painted canvas.

Reading fragment after fragment about the poet's childhood on the

Lower East Side and then about Paul's young life, one realizes that the materials of a whole novel are contained in the pages of "*A*"-12. But the narrative cannot be linear, for Zukofsky, like Pound, regards experience as always unfinished, indeed as always only potential – moving toward something that never quite happens. There is no unifying principle in "*A*"-12, no Supreme Fiction that will bring all the fragments together because, in Don Byrd's words about "*A*," "the structure of history is not to be found in logic or mythologic . . . but in language and the complex web by which language is involved with perception."[33] Accordingly, the literary pastiches and borrowings (for example, the dialogue between Titania and Bottom, the speech of Stephen Dedalus on Aristotle, or the condensed version of a Reznikoff narrative)[34] are arranged in a verbal-visual structure that accords with Zukofsky's declaration:

> I'll tell you.
> About my *poetics* –
>
>   music
> $\int$
>   speech
>
> An integral
> Lower limit speech
> Upper limit music
>
>   (p. 138)

Between these "limits," we find pictograms like the valentine on page 129:

Or the playful graph on pages 163–64, that begins:

MAN ⟶ EARTH ⟶ WORLDS

Thus the discourses of commerce (the greeting card) or of science (the graph), dismissed by Mallarmé as "journalistic," as discourses having nothing to do with poetry, are absorbed into the fabric of the poem. Again, "*A*"-12 follows the example of *The Cantos* in juxtaposing the found object to the moment of metamorphosis: Zukofsky's father, for example, becomes for young Paul the image of Aristotle:

> P. Z. remembers the day "Aristotle" died,
> Still owns his snowshoes
> Indispensable in Macedonia
> I bought him two balloons:
> "Plato" and "Aristotle"
> Filled with air they had faces
> Mounted on snowshoes
> As expected. . . .   ("*A*," p. 164)

Such moments occur against the backdrop of historical events – "the first John Jacob Astor / Landing in Baltimore / With \$25 and seven flutes to sell" – within ever shifting political and geographic frames. The "Upper limit / Music" appears in odal hymns, chants, and sonnets; the "Lower limit / Speech" in the conversations of the poet with his relatives and friends.

Where in this collage of documentary prose, song, Imagist lyric, pictogram, and free-verse autobiography, do we find the speaking subject? He functions, in Bernstein's words about the Pound of *The Cantos*, as a kind of "unspoken marginal presence which silently articulates (makes sense out of) the gaps in the printed text, a voice we only really discover in the process of a 'speaking it' ourselves" (TT, p. 170). This is not to say that Zukofsky doesn't have very strong views on, say, Roosevelt or Marx or the meaning of history. But the truths are ones we have to *find*, caught up as they are in the network of everyday living. A poem like "*A*" does, then, concern itself with what Christopher Clausen calls "Truths that people accept as being centrally important," but these "truths" must be discovered phenomenologically; they remain poised as possibilities revealing the difficulties of human choice.

IV

In the *Paideuma* issue honoring Zukofsky (Winter 1978), Gilbert Sorrentino takes one of the poet's short stanzas:

> Red alder berry
> Will singly break
> But you – how slight – do:
> So that even
> A lover exists.

and comments:

> "But"? What does "but" mean? And is "even" an adjective or
> an adverb? This "metaphysical" nicety of expression, the lyric
> turning on the most delicate changes in the meanings of words,
> is as subtle and exact as Donne's great gold/circle imagery in
> "A Valediction Forbidding Mourning" and gives Zukofsky's
> poetry its persistent hold on the mind.[35]

What interests me here, and in the commentaries of other poets in the
issue (Duncan, Tomlinson, Silliman, Taggart) is that attention is directed, not to questions of Zukofsky's "subjectivity," much less a possible "apocalypse of imagination" (Bloom's term), but to the niceties of
language – the poet's puns and word play, his complex allusions and
borrowings – what oft was thought, one might say, but ne'er so well
expressed.

Such concern for the pleasures of language brings to mind W. H.
Auden's witty definition of the critic who really understands poetry:

> Do you like, and by like, I really mean like, not approve on
> principle:
> 1. Long lists of proper names such as Old Testament genealo-
> gies or the catalogue of ships in the *Iliad?*
> 2. Riddles and all other ways of not calling a spade a spade?
> 3. Complicated verse forms of great technical difficulty, such
> as Englyns, Drott-Kvaetts, Sestinas, even if their content is
> trivial?
> 4. Conscious theatrical exaggeration, pieces of Baroque flattery
> like Dryden's welcome to the Duchess of Ormond?
> If a critic could truthfully answer "yes" to all four, then I
> should trust his judgment implicitly on all literary matters.[36]

Auden's own work – say, *The Sea and the Mirror,* everywhere gives
evidence of precisely such ability to master arcane catalogues, riddles,
complicated verse forms, and conscious theatrical exaggeration. The
performative aspect of the poem – its conflation of pop ballad ("Sing
first that green remote Cockaigne / Where whiskey-rivers run, / And

every gorgeous number may / Be laid by anyone"), terza rima (Antonio's speech), sestina (Sebastian's), villanelle (Miranda's), and rotund after-dinner speech in prose (Caliban's), creates a work of profound wit and intellectual complexity. Space precludes analysis of Auden's poetry here; I mention it only because it represents a variant on the Pound model that has had great influence on such poets as James Merrill and John Ashbery. Unlike that of Pound and Zukofsky, Auden's poetry is not collage; it does not, for example, destroy or fragment the prose syntax, nor does it incorporate found objects such as pages from history books or newspaper fragments. But Auden resembles Zukofsky in his conviction that "verse" and "prose," "lyric" and "didacticism," are not wholly separate entities. Thus he remarks shrewdly:

> Valéry bases his definitions of poetry and prose on the difference between the gratuitous and the useful, play and work, and uses as an analogy the difference between dancing and walking. But this will not do either. A commuter may walk to his suburban station every morning, but at the same time he may enjoy the walk for its own sake; the fact that his walk is necessary does not exclude the possibility of its also being a form of play. Vice versa, a dance does not cease to be play if it is also believed to have a useful purpose like promoting a good harvest. (DH, p. 24)

Here Auden oddly anticipates the recent manifesto of a very different poet, Jerome Rothenberg. In his "New Models, New Visions" (1977), Rothenberg insists that "there is a continuum, rather than a barrier, between music and noise, between poetry and prose (the language of inspiration and the language of common and special discourse); between dance and normal locomotion (walking, running, jumping), etc."[37] *Collage*, we might argue, is one way this erosion of the boundaries between modes and genres manifests itself. A second way, to which I now turn, is the use of what looks like "prose" by poets. In a new book called *Poet's Prose, The Crisis in American Verse*, Stephen Fredman writes:

> I was initially led to undertake this study through my engagement – both as writer and reader – with contemporary prose by poets. I have felt for a number of years that the most talented poets of my own postwar generation and an increasing number from previous generations have turned to prose as a form somehow most consonant with a creative figuration of our time. It would be difficult to mistake these works for fic-

tion or for purely discursive prose; they evidence a fascination with language (through puns, rhyme, repetition, elision, disjunction, excessive troping, and subtle foregrounding of diction) that interferes with the progression of story or idea, while at the same time inviting and examining the "prose" realms of fact and anecdote and reclaiming for poetry the domain of truth.[38]

Here certain qualifications are in order. Fredman's initial observation, that many of our most talented poets are turning to prose, is entirely correct, but I am not sure one can say that this has happened because "prose is a form . . . most consonant with a creative figuration of our time" any more than one can make a case for, say, Williams' free verse of the thirties as being a "radical" embodiment of his then "radical" political perspective. Poetic forms are, after all, "radical" or innovative only intertextually: "prose" may well become the preferred mode (as might a return to, say, folk ballad) at a time when free verse, once revolutionary, has become the orthodoxy of our time and hence the vessel to be shattered. Thus Henry Sayre writes, "Throughout the modernist period free verse was not so much an anti-structural gesture, though it was often confused for one, as it was a highly formalized device for conveniently depicting the disorder one feels before both world and mind,"[39] and a young Polish poet named Jerzy Kutnik, who is writing a dissertation on the performative aspect of poetic discourse, recently wrote me: "My favorite work of poetry is John Ashbery's *Three Poems,* since it's not poetry at all, so it powerfully demonstrates the tendency toward a merger of prose and poetry."

Prose or, as I prefer to call it, following Northrop Frye, the *associative rhythm* – the rhythm equidistant from both verse and prose, whose unit is the abrupt, discontinuous, repetitive, heavily accented phrase of ordinary speech[40] – currently exercises an important metapoetic function: it calls attention to itself as *discourse,* refusing to fulfill what John Cage would call our "either-or" expectations. What Fredman calls "poet's prose" is, like collage, a kind of *mise en question* of the romantic lyric: as he puts it, "the most encompassing freedom that these poets seek is the freedom to construct a poetic entity capable of including what poetry has been told to exclude" (PP, p. 7). As such, "poet's prose" is by no means the same thing as the "prose poem," which, in its classic nineteenth-century form is, as Fredman says, "a highly aestheticized, subjective, idiolectal artifact, a paean to the isolated genius" (PP, p. 8). The same point is made by Michel Beaujour, who points out that, once the Mallarmean distinction between "ordinary" and "poetic" language is accepted, the question of verse becomes a kind of irrelevancy. The prose poem, that is to say, becomes another version of the autonomous lyric, the lyric now freed from the slavery of rhyme and meter and hence all the more suited to become "the sacred homeland of verbal alchemy," "the place of revelation and epiphanies."[41]

Contemporary "poet's prose" – Ashbery's *Three Poems*, Creeley's *Presences: A Text for Marisol*, Cage's performance pieces, David Antin's talk pieces, the language works of Lydia Davis or Michael Davidson – thus derives, not from the Mallarmean prose poem, but from very different sources, for example the "flat" language constructions of Gertrude Stein. Consider the following composition from *Tender Buttons* (1914):

MILK

A white egg and a colored pan and a cab-bage showing settlement, a constant increase.

A cold in a nose, a single cold nose makes an excuse. Two are more necessary.

All goods are stolen, all the blisters are in the cup.

Cooking, cooking is the recognition be-tween sudden and nearly sudden very little and all large holes.

A real pint, one that is open and closed in the middle is so bad.

Tender colds, seen eye holders, all work, the best of change, the meaning, the dark red, all this and bitten, really bitten.

Guessing again and golfing again and the best men, the very best men.[42]

We might note to begin with that here every assumption about "poetry" made by such critics as Christopher Clausen is challenged. Stein's discourse is not at all opposed to "science"; on the contrary, her observation of what happens when milk comes to a boil has something of the lab report about it. Second, the text is not written in language detached from ordinary speech; indeed, there is barely a word in "Milk" that an eight-year-old wouldn't know. And third, the poem does not manifest organic unity; there is no conceptual order transcending perceptual fact, no centering principle.

But consider the figure of sound, not fully metrical (not even linear) and yet hardly that of "normal" prose.

A whíte égg   and a cólored pán   and   a cábbage
a cónstant íncrease
A cóld in a nóse
A réal pínt . . .

Or again, the phrasal repetition of

> A cóld in a nóse   ‖   a síngle cóld nóse
> Áll the góods are stólen   ‖   all the blísters
> are ín the cúp
> Cóoking   ‖   cóoking is the récogní-
> tion   ‖   between súdden and néarly súdden
> Gúessing agáin ‖ and gólfing agáin ‖
> and the bést mén   ‖   the véry bést mén.

This syntactic pattern is crossed by a number of phonemic ones: for example, an alliterative pattern of hard *c*'s is immediately established – *c*olored, *c*abbage, *c*onstant, *c*old – but, more important, look at the following progression:

*c*ol*d* – *n*ose – *st*olen – *h*oles – *o*pen – *c*lose*d* – *h*olders

where sexual innuendo is created by what the Russian formalists called "orientation toward the neighboring word."

Stein's phonemic play is repeated on the semantic level. "Milk" contains no coherent image (say, of a glass of milk on a table), nor does Stein's analysis follow normal patterns of induction or deduction. Rather, the title undergoes systematic transformation. To watch milk boiling is to see it as a white egg (oval) in the pan; as it rises and settles (shows settlement, a constant increase), it resembles a cabbage. But there are other associations: "A cold in the nose" suggests the milky substance called mucus; "a single cold nose" is itself as white as milk; it also serves as an excuse to drink a glass of warm milk. Maybe even two glasses. "Two are more necessary."

Yet with all these oddities, a kind of Jamesian pragmatism operates throughout. "Cooking, cooking is the recognition between sudden and nearly sudden, very little and all large holes." Of course. It takes an experienced cook to know when milk is sufficiently scalded. And when the container is emptied into the cup, "All the goods are stolen, all the blisters are in the cup." Stein is at once matter-of-fact and playful; her text oscillates between reference and compositional game. "Holes" – "stolen" – "blisters": are we hearing about "milk" or about female parts and liquids? The latter seems possible, especially when the text suddenly introduces "the meaning, the dark red, all this and bitten, really bitten." Is this a reference to the red nose of the cold victim, frostbitten? The red tongue? The "wound" made emptying the container? The "pint" is described as "open and closed and in the middle bad." Does this suggest that when we come to the last phrasal unit – "Guessing again and golfing again and the best men, the very best

men" – that a good man, like an open pint, is "in the middle so bad"?
Or again, the golf balls the best men hit have the same shape as the
blisters in the cup, and this milk, it seems is not what is desired.

Stein's images, as I have suggested in *The Poetics of Indeterminacy,* are
characterized by their undecidability: the more we probe the word play
in a text like "Milk," the more possible references manifest themselves
and we can never say with any assurance that the poem is "about" milk
boiling or "about" sexual aggression, and so on. What "Milk" is assuredly not, in any case, is a crisis-poem or lyric epiphany. Stein's discourse is closer to the language of philosophy than to psychological
self-projection; as such, it has paved the way for the moment when, in
Stephen Fredman's words, "poetry, philosophy, and criticism begin to
coalesce" (p. 10).

Take, for example, David Antin's so-called *talk poem* called "the death
of the hired man," performed at the Baxter Art Gallery at Cal Tech in
1982 on the occasion of Siah Armajani's construction of a poetry lounge
(a version of a New England schoolroom, with handcrafted wooden
benches and desks, whose tops have lines from Robert Frost's "Mending
Wall" stencilled across them; see Figure 8.1). Antin's poetic monologue
proceeds from the premise that, as he puts it in his essay "Modernism
and Postmodernism," "phenomenological reality is 'discovered' and
'constructed' by poets," that "reality is inexhaustible or, more particularly, cannot be exhausted by its representations because its representations modify its nature."[43] As such, "the death of the hired man" begins
flatly with the words, "when i was invited to come here i realized that
siah armajani had gotten here first" – a remark Antin now proceeds to
turn inside out. For one thing, the *present* of the performance is immediately undercut by Antin's references to "talking" versus "reading," and
by our knowledge that what we now hear in a particular place will be
transcribed on tape and later printed as text, often with extensive
changes. Conversely, those who have not attended the performance and
come to the text in print must mentally recreate the performance situation within which it was articulated. Which, then, is *real,* the oral performance or the written text?[44] Again, the present of the talk situation
quickly gives way to incidents that happened in the past, both to Frost
and to Antin himself. And thirdly, "armajani had gotten here first" must
be construed ironically because, as Antin discovers in the course of talking, it is questionable what "getting here" means, given that the book-
shelves have fake hinges, that indeed the whole schoolroom is a parodic
gesture to be exposed. Then too, the whole installation is temporary so
that we are forced to consider the relationship of the poetry lounge to the
space in which it has been placed.

Figure 8.1. Siah Armajani, "A Poetry Lounge," Installation, South Gallery, Baxter Art Gallery, California Institute of Technology, Pasadena, California (March–April 1982). Reprinted by permission of the Baxter Art Gallery.

Just as Gertrude Stein begins "Milk" with an observation on the phenomenon of milk boiling in a pan, so Antin begins with the observation that the poem "Mending Wall" is printed across the schoolroom desks. What follows may look at first like "just talk" (or just prose with white spaces and ragged left and right margins), but it follows a very particular process of discovery.

First, the "Mending Wall" of Frost's title metaphorically acts as a barrier between poet and audience – in Frost's case, "something mechanical and wooden about the way the lines are nearly all end stopped and tacked on one to the other like siding" (SA, p. 23); in Antin's, the foolish barrier between his "pulpit" and the desks behind which the audience sits in Armajani's comically bogus schoolroom situation. How to get rid of this "mending wall" – this is Antin's subject, although it is never stated as such. The discursive disquisition on the false bookcase hinges, hinges that are "not hinges at all but images of images or synecdoches that as individual hinges expend all their energy calling up the class of hinges of which they are merely representatives" (p. 27), brings forward the whole question of metaphor, which is Antin's central question about Frost's poetry. Why, given its real strength, is Frost's poetry committed to metaphoricity, to Poetic Diction and artificial ornament rather than to the New England landscape as such which Frost ostensibly wants to celebrate?

To answer this question, Antin turns to a consideration of metaphor:

> aristotle says
> there are the right names and the wrong names   the
>   wrong names are metaphors   now as he says this he
> also says other things about names   that there are
>   foreign names and common names and specially strange
> and deformed ones   but metaphor is the wrong name
>   you get something that is not the right name for
> something and you call it by that name   for example
>   you call this woman "george"   she won't answer to
> that name but it doesn't matter   what does matter is
>   that you refer to her as george in such a way that she
> or others hear her referred to as george   well she
> isn't really a george . . .   (p. 32)

Once we accept this *faux-naif* definition of metaphor, everything in the talk piece follows. The "wrong name" is likened to putting on a hat, a comparison that leads to a series of "hat" and "beard" narratives: Antin, being mistaken for a blond Scandinavian when his bald head is hidden by a hat; Antin linked to other Vietnam protesters, identified as having shaved off a beard he never had, and so on. Again, the poet's son Blaise (for Blaise Cendrars) insists on being called by the "wrong name" Blaze – Blaze Antin – in keeping with his California jock image; he is embarrassed to be named for some early twentieth-century French poet.

Ironically, however – and this marks the turn in the discourse – Blaise really *is* like Blaise Cendrars, who was a very "cheerful" poet and knew his America so well. And now we read:

> blaise cendrars was not a metaphorical writer in the
> way that robert frost is a metaphorical writer
>   blaise cendrars could once in a while be accused
> of lying honestly   telling a story the way it
>   should be told to make it luminously clear   blaise

```
cendrars was a writer of luminous and questionable truth
      in this sense he was far superior to robert frost
      who apparently had the problem of trying to make
the truth poetical     not in a wild but in a
      professional way     as if he considered it a poets
job     and when you hear a poem of robert frosts you
      know hes not simply telling you how it is or how he
might desperately want it to be     hes simply raising
      it to put it on the shelf with literature     at
the same time hes not the sort of poet who fails to
      respond to the things in life that just come up
            that simply happen     and you can see this in
a poem like the death of the hired man . . .          (p. 38)
```

The seemingly random discourse has thus circled back to the discussion of Frost's poem near the beginning of the monologue. But the circle now makes a final loop. Again Antin discusses the problem of Frost's diction, again he suddenly shifts into narrative, this time about his mother-in-law's Catskill hotel and her paranoia about burglers, culminating in the moment when, upon her request that he find the source of a scary noise from a neighboring building, Antin opens a linen closet and finds the real hired man, Joe Brizo, not dead but asleep, smelling "of whiskey and dirty clothes and vomit":

```
                  i closed the door and went back to
      tell jeanette     theres no one there     the door
was banging in the wind     the next morning he was
      gone
            now i could have killed him off in the story
            slowly or quickly it wouldnt have been too hard
            i could have given him a heart attack or pneumonia
            something terrible could have happened     but i
was thinking of him in terms of what had happened to
      the hired man     and that level of escalation i
            dislike so intensely in robert frost     and thats
where joe brizo comes in                          (p. 48)
```

With these words, the text breaks off. By this time, the audience has been brought round to consider, not only the connection between Frost's "hired man" and Antin's, but also between the status of Armajani, who was hired to design the poetry lounge, and Antin who was hired to speak in it. One of the ironies, of course, is that it takes more than a single hearing (or reading) to understand that Antin's casual talk has been, all along, a discovery process moving inexorably from relational thread to relational thread, that "the death of the hired man" is really a critique of Frost's way of writing poetry with reference to Antin's own poetic, his faith that poetry must be based on actual observation and natural language, that it should not hide behind a series of "hats" called Poetic Diction, Gentility, and Ornament. But the text puts forward that poetic not by any kind of general statement, but through a series of narratives, images, and discursive patterns so that we are finally not quite sure what we have witnessed: prose discourse or poetry? Lecture or story? Philosophical argument or sleight-of-hand? As Antin himself puts it, the pleasure of the text depends upon the "play and interchange of possibilities."[45]

Such an "interchange of possibilities" (compare Cage's "Avoid a polar situation") is obviously hard to reconcile to Clausen's definition of poetry with which I began. Antin does not regard "computer language" or the "rise of Science" as the enemy; he substitutes typographical patterning for verse form, metonymy for metaphor; and although he regards "truths" as indeed of central importance, he is more interested in questions of appropriateness (what does it mean to do x in this context?) and inconsistencies than in what Clausen calls "the truths of moments, situations, relationships."

Poetry, said Pound, is news that *stays* news. In this sense, the increasingly didactic, intellectual, and playful poetry of the present is finding a much wider audience than Clausen and like-minded critics might think. When Cage gave a reading of *Theme and Variations* at the MLA convention in New York in 1981, the standing-room-only crowd seemed to hang on every syllable of what was a highly formalized and often obscure set of permutations. Afterwards, when I asked friends and colleagues what it was they liked so much, they spoke of Cage's suggestive ideas, his play of language, the complex musical rhythms that underlie his intonation, contours, and pauses. Certainly, they did not doubt that what they were listening to was *poetry*. In this connection, Cage makes an interesting comment in an interview with Daniel Charles (1970):

> The real [is not] the world as it is . . . it is not, it becomes! It moves, it changes! It doesn't wait for us to change. . . . It is more mobile than you can imagine. . . . The world, the real is not an object. It is a process. . . . The function of art at the present time is to preserve us from all the logical minimizations

that we are at each instant tempted to apply to the flux of events. To draw us nearer to the process which is the world we live in.[46]

Surely romantic lyric – the internalized quest romance – is one such "logical minimization." In the poetry of the late twentieth century, the cry of the heart, as Yeats called it, is increasingly subjected to the play of the mind – a play that wants to take account of the "process which is the world we live in."

NOTES

1 *Georgia Review* 35 (Winter 1981): 703. Subsequently cited as GR.
2 *The Place of Poetry: Two Centuries of an Art in Crisis* (Lexington: University Press of Kentucky, 1982), p. 66. The *Georgia Review* essay is a précis of Clausen's book.
3 *The Anxiety of Influence: A Theory of Poetry* (New York: Oxford University Press, 1973), p. 11. Subsequently cited as AI.
4 *Agon: Toward a Theory of Revisionism* (New York and London: Oxford University Press, 1982), p. 287.
5 *The Ringers in the Tower: Studies in Romantic Tradition* (Chicago: University of Chicago Press, 1971), pp. 18–19.
6 See especially *Wallace Stevens: The Poems of our Climate* (Ithaca, N.Y.: Cornell University Press, 1977), pp. 1–26, 375–406.
7 Bloom's fellow Yale critic, Paul de Man, for example, takes the position that "all remnants of a genetic historicism have to be abandoned" in that the "loss of representational reality" and "loss of self," so often taken to be the hallmark of modernity, are merely reflections of "the absolute ambivalence of a language." Literature, in this case, "has always been essentially modern." See *Blindness and Insight: Essays in the Rhetoric of Contemporary Criticism* (New York: Oxford University Press, 1971), pp. 167–68.
8 *An Introduction to Literary Semiotics,* trans. Margherita Bogat and Allen Mandelbaum (Bloomington: Indiana University Press, 1978), p. 132.
9 (London and Cambridge: Macmillan & Co., 1861). All further references are to this edition unless otherwise specified. The preface has pages numbered a, b, c, etc.
10 Cf. Matthew Arnold's famous statement in "The Study of Poetry" (1880), in Matthew Arnold, *Poetry and Prose,* ed. John Bryson (Cambridge: Harvard University Press, 1967), pp. 663–64:

>More and more mankind will discover that we have to turn to poetry to interpret life for us, to console us, to sustain us. Without poetry, our science will appear incomplete; and most of what now passes with us for religion and philosophy will be replaced by poetry. . . . our religion, parading evidences such as those on which the popular mind

relies now; our philosophy, pluming itself on its reasonings about causation and finite and infinite being; what are they but the shadows and dreams and false shows of knowledge?

11 See *The Golden Treasury, with an Introduction and Additional Poems,* selected and arranged by C. Day Lewis (London and Glasgow: Collins, 1954), p. 16.

12 See M. H. Abrams, *The Mirror and the Lamp: Romantic Theory and the Critical Tradition* (New York: W. W. Norton, 1953), pp. 84–88 and *passim;* Tzvetan Todorov, "La Crise romantique," in *Théories du symbole* (Paris: Seuil, 1977), pp. 179–260.

13 See Evelyn Hardy, *Thomas Hardy: A Critical Biography* (London: Hogarth, 1954), p. 52. This story is told by Clausen, *The Place of Poetry,* p. 68, as part of a discussion on the impact of the *Golden Treasury.* Clausen argues (pp. 65–82) that "the Palgrave version" reflected valid norms for poetry that Modernism could not meet. I take issue with this view below.

14 *The Golden Treasury,* rev. and enl. (London: Macmillan & Co., 1896); Stevens's copy is in the Wallace Stevens Collection, Huntington Library, San Marino.

15 The equation continues to be made by most critics today. Helen Vendler, for example, in an essay on Wallace Stevens, writes: "Since feeling – to use Wordsworthian terms – is the organizing principle of poetry (both narratively, insofar as poetry is a history of feeling, and structurally, insofar as poetry is a science or analysis of feeling), without feeling the world of the poet is a chaos." See *Part of Nature, Part of Us: Modern American Poets* (Cambridge: Harvard University Press, 1980), p. 42.

16 See "Joyce," *The Future,* vol. 2, 6 (London, May 18); rpt. in *Literary Essays of Ezra Pound,* ed. T. S. Eliot (London: Faber & Faber, 1954), p. 410; "How to Read," *Literary Essays,* pp. 17–18; *Letters to Ibbotson, 1935–62,* ed. Vittoria I. Mondolfo and Margaret Hurley (Orono, Maine: National Poetry Foundation), p. 24.

17 See *The Place of Poetry,* pp. 83–96.

18 "Crisis in Poetry" (1886–95), trans. Bradford Cook, in Richard Ellmann and Charles Feidelson, eds., *The Modern Tradition: Backgrounds of Modern Literature* (New York: Oxford University Press, 1965), pp. 110–11. For the original, see *"Crise de vers," Oeuvres complètes,* ed. Henri Mondor and G. Jean-Aubry (Paris: Gallimard, Bibliothèque de la Pléiade, 1945), p. 366. subsequently cited as OC.

> Les monuments, la mer, la face humaine, dans leur plénitude, natifs, conservant une vertue autrement attrayante que ne les voilera une description, évocation dites, *allusion* je sais, *suggestion* cette terminologie quelque peu de hasard atteste la tendance, une très décisive, peut-être, qu'ait subie l'art littéraire, elle le borne et l'exempte. Son sortilège, à lui, si ce n'est libérer, hors d'une poignée de poussière ou réalité sans l'enclore, au livre, même comme texte, la dispersion volatile soit l'esprit, qui n'a que faire de rien outre la musicalité de tout.

Cf. Walter Pater, *Appreciations,* in *Selected Writings of Walter Pater,* ed. Harold Bloom (New York: Columbia University Press, 1974), p. 104: "the essential dichotomy [between poetry and prose] is between imaginative and unimaginative writing"; and again, "Music and prose literature are, in one sense, the opposite terms of art" (p. 122).

19 See Ellmann and Feidelson, p. 112; OC, p. 368:

Un désir indéniable à mon temps est de séparer comme en vue d'attributions différentes le double état de la parole, brut ou immédiat ici, là essentiel.

Narrer, enseigner, même décrire, cela va. . . . l'emploi élémentaire du discours [est le] dessert l'universel *reportage* dont, la littérature exceptée, participe tout entre les genres d'écrits contemporains.

20 See Ellmann and Feidelson, p. 112; OC, p. 368:

Je dis une fleur! et, hors de l'oubli où ma voix relègue aucun contour, en tant que quelque chose d'autre que les calices sus, musicalement se lève, idée même et suave, l'absente de tous bouquets.

21 "Tradition and the Individual Talent" (1919), *Selected Essays* (London: Faber & Faber, 1952), p. 21.

22 "The Book: A Spiritual Instrument," trans. Bradford Cook, in Stéphane Mallarmé, *Selected Poetry and Prose* (New York: New Directions, 1982), pp. 80–84; cf. OC, pp. 378–82.

23 "Short Epiphanies: Two Contextual Approaches to the French Prose Poem," in *The Prose Poem in France, Theory and Practice,* ed. Mary Ann Caws and Hermine Riffaterre (New York: Columbia University Press, 1983), pp. 55–56.

24 *The Theory of the Novel* (1920; rpt. Cambridge: Harvard University Press, 1971), p. 56.

25 *The Tale of the Tribe, Ezra Pound and the Modern Verse Epic* (Princeton: Princeton University Press, 1980), p. 4. Subsequently cited as TT.

26 "A Retrospect". (1918) in *Literary Essays of Ezra Pound,* p. 4. Subsequently cited as LE.

27 *Guide to Kulchur* (New York: New Directions, 1938), p. 194. Cf. letter to John Lackay Brown (April 1937), in *Selected Letters of Ezra Pound 1907–1941,* ed. D. D. Paige (New Directions, 1971), p. 294:

. . . the Cantos are in a way fugal. There *is* at start, descent to the shades, metamorphoses, parallel (Vidal-Actaeon). All of which is mere matter for little. . . . rs and Harvud instructors *unless* I pull it off as reading matter, singing matter, shouting matter, the tale of the tribe.

28 "Some Questions about Modernism," *Occident* 8 (Spring 1974): 21–22.

29 "Jasper Johns: Stories and Ideas," *A Year from Monday: New Lectures and Writings* (Middletown, Conn.: Wesleyan University Press, 1967), p. 79.

30 See *The Poetics of Indeterminacy: Rimbaud to Cage,* pp. 155–99.

31 "*A*" (Berkeley and Los Angeles: University of California Press, 1978). All further references are to this edition.

32 For a good account of Zukofsky's adaptation of Calvalcanti, see Barry

Ahearn, *Zukofsky's "A"* (Berkeley and Los Angeles: University of California Press, 1982), pp. 118–24.

33   "The Shape of Zukofsky's Canon," *Paideuma,* Louis Zukofsky Issue, 7, no 3 (Winter 1978): 464.

34   In "The Transfigured Prose," *Paideuma:* Louis Zukofsky Issue, Cid Corman gives an interesting account of this reworking, which transforms a passage from Reznikoff's *The Manner Music* into free verse.

35   "Louis Zukofsky," *Paideuma* 7 (Winter 1978): 401.

36   *The Dyer's Hand and Other Essays* (New York: Vintage Books, 1968), pp. 47–48. Subsequently cited as DH.

37   "New Models, New Visions: Some Notes toward a Poetics of Performance" (1977), in *Pre-Faces & Other Writings* (New York: New Directions, 1981), p. 168.

38   *Poet's Prose, The Crisis in American Verse* (Cambridge: Cambridge University Press, 1983), p. 1. Subsequently cited as PP.

39   "David Antin and the Oral Poetics Movement," *Contemporary Literature* 23 (Fall 1982): 430. Subsequently cited as DAOP.

40   See "Verse and Prose," in *Princeton Encyclopedia of Poetry and Poetics,* ed. Alex Preminger (Princeton: Princeton University Press, 1974), pp. 885–90; Marjorie Perloff, *Poetics of Indeterminacy,* pp. 39–42, 316–18.

41   "Short Epiphanies," *The Prose Poem in France,* pp. 40, 55.

42   *Selected Writings of Gertrude Stein,* ed. Carl Van Vechten (New York: Vintage, 1962), p. 487.

43   "Modernism and Postmodernism: Approaching the Present in American Poetry," *boundary 2,* 1, no. 1 (Fall 1972): 132–33. For "the death of the hired man," see *Siah Armajani, a Poetry Lounge,* catalogue of the exhibition, March 3–April 25, 1982 (Pasadena: Baxter Art Gallery of California Institute of Technology, 1982). Subsequently cited as SA.

44   For an interesting discussion of the relation of oral to written in Antin's work, see Henry Sayre, DAOP, pp. 443–44.

45   "Talking in Roy Harvey Pearce's Seminar on 'The Long Poem' " (August 1, 1978), audiotape in the Archive for New Poetry, University of California, San Diego. Cited by Henry Sayre, DAOP, p. 448.

46   *For the Birds, John Cage in Conversation with Daniel Charles* (Boston and London: Marion Boyars, 1981), pp. 80–81.

9 "Unimpededness and interpenetration": the poetic of John Cage

> —One does not then make just any experiment but does what must be done.[1]

John Hollander, reviewing *Silence* for *Perspectives of New Music* in 1963, complained that, however amusing and inventive Cage's verbal and musical compositions may be, "something seems to be missing":

> Perhaps what Mr. Cage's career as a composer lacks is a certain kind of hard work. Not the unbelievably elaborate effort merely, of planning, arranging, constructing, rationalizing (however playfully or dubiously); not the great pains of carrying off a production, but something else. The difference between the most inspired amateur theatricals and the opera, between the conversation that one would like to record and the poem, between the practical joke and the great film, is not one of degree of effort or of conviction. It is that peculiar labor of art itself, the incredible agony of the real artist in his struggles with lethargy and with misplaced zeal, with despair and with the temptations of his recent successes, *to get better*. The dying writer in Henry James' "The Death of the Lion" puts it almost perfectly: "Our doubt is our passion and our passion is our task. The rest is the madness of art." The rest, to be sure; but Mr. Cage's sense of indeterminacy is not this profound doubt, and his métier is not task.[2]

The Romantic myth of the artist as suffering hero, as dying Lion undergoing the Agony (Hollander's own word) and the Ecstasy – it is ironic that the Cagean enterprise should be judged to be deficient by the very standard it has consistently and resolutely called into question.

201

"The difference between the most inspired amateur theatricals and the opera" – a difference Hollander accepts as a given – is one that Cage has never recognized, committed as he is to the erasure of boundaries between genres, modes, and media – indeed, between what we call "art" and "life." Again, what Hollander calls the artist's "struggle with lethargy and misplaced zeal" seems curiously beside the point in the case of an artist like Cage, who, by his own account, refused to be psychoanalyzed when, at a preliminary meeting, the analyst told him: "I'll be able to fix you so that you'll write much more music than you do now." "I said, 'Good heavens!' " Cage recalls, " 'I already write too much it seems to me' " (*S*, 127). As for "the temptations of . . . recent successes," Cage has always gone by the precept that if something works once, you must not repeat it, that "Whenever I've found what I'm doing has become pleasing, even to one person, I have redoubled my efforts to find the next step."[3] "Doubt as our passion," "passion as our task," "the madness of art" – these are phrases not only alien to Cage's aesthetic; they represent, in terms of that aesthetic, a neo-Romantic self-centeredness to be resisted by all the discipline at one's command.

I mention discipline because readers of *Silence, A Year from Monday,* and the later writings are often misled by Cage's repeated insistence that "art is not an attempt to bring order out of chaos . . . but simply a way of waking up to the very life we're living, which is so excellent once one gets one's mind and one's desire out of its way and lets it act of its own accord" (*S*, 12). Isn't this to imply that anyone can be an artist, that all we have to do is to be *open* to the world around us and the rest will take care of itself?

In order to answer such questions, we must distinguish between what Hollander calls "the peculiar labor of art itself" and what Cage means by "true discipline" (*RK*, 13). A good place to begin is with a Cage interview of 1965, conducted by Richard Schechner and Michael Kirby and published in the *Tulane Drama Review.* The subject of discussion is the nature of theatre and the theatrical. At one point, Cage becomes quite angry, recalling a symposium on the performing arts held at Wesleyan University, led by George Grizzard, then playing Hamlet at the Tyrone Guthrie, and the director Alan Schneider:

> I certainly wouldn't have gone had I known what was going to take place. It was a warm evening and they began by taking their coats off, and trying to give the feeling of informality, and they went so far as not to use the chairs but to sit on the table which had been placed in front of them. They proceeded to say that they had nothing to tell the audience, in other words they

wanted to have a discussion. Of course there were no questions. So they had to chat and supplement one another's loss of knowledge of what to do next. The whole thing was absolutely disgusting: the kind of ideas and the kinds of objectives, the vulgarity of it, was almost incomprehensible.[4]

The irritation expressed here is at first quite puzzling to anyone familiar with Cage's usual equanimity, his belief that "rather than using your time to denounce what someone else has done, you should . . . if your feelings are critical, reply with a work of your own" (*RK*, 30). Why is Cage so annoyed by the behavior of Grizzard and Schneider? Hasn't he said, earlier in the same interview, that art is "setting a process going which has no necessary beginning, no middle, no end, and no sections"? Why then can't the director and actor sit silently on the platform, waiting to see what process will unfold? After all, if, as Cage says in *Silence*, "There is no such thing as an empty space or an empty time" (*S*, 8), isn't something interesting likely to happen?

The problem has to do with the authenticity – or lack thereof – of the situation. As Cage explains:

> I was quite heated. I normally don't like to talk against things, but I had been asked to [by the chairman of the meeting]. When we couldn't discuss Happenings because they had no knowledge nor interest and didn't think it was as serious as *Hamlet* and thought they were being virtuous, then I said, "Well, what do you think about TV?" They weren't interested in TV. And yet they're living in an electronic world where TV is of far more relevance than the legitimate theatre.   (*TDR*, 71)

What Cage finds so irritating about this "performance" is that the speakers claim to have no ideas about theatre, when the fact is that they conceive theatre quite narrowly as what Cage calls "the *Hamlet* situation," with its accompanying rejection of "low" art forms like Happenings and "low" media like television. The audience, understanding that its response is not really being solicited, predictably says nothing; the two speakers just as predictably move to break the silence, a silence that has nothing to do with the natural "silence" – really full of sound-events – that is central to Cage's aesthetic, by engaging in chitchat. By this time, the symposium has become pure power play, defying Cage's aphorism, "We are involved not in ownership but in use" (*RK*, 10). Here the discussion leaders *are* involved in "ownership" and so nothing of artistic interest can possibly happen.

"True discipline," Cage tells Richard Kostelanetz in an interview of

1966, "is not learned in order to give it [self-expression] up, but rather in order to give oneself up. . . . It is precisely what the Lord meant when he said, give up your father and mother and follow me" (*RK*, 13). Such self-surrender has nothing in common with what John Hollander calls "the incredible agony of the real artist," an agony that Cage would surely associate with excessive ego. "When I say that anything can happen I don't mean anything that I *want* to have happen" (*TDR*, 70). Rather, as Cage puts it in "Happy New Ears!" (1965), "I have for many years accepted, and I still do, the doctrine about Art, occidental and oriental, set forth by Ananda K. Coomaraswamy in his book *The Transformation of Nature in Art*, that the function of Art is to imitate Nature in her manner of operation" (*YFM*, 31). Here the phrase "manner of operation" is tricky. Cage writes:

> Our understanding of "her manner of operation" changes according to advances in the sciences. These advances in this century have brought the term "space-time" into our vocabulary. Thus, the distinctions made . . . between the space and the time arts are at present an oversimplification.   (*YFM*, 31)

To put it another way, the scientific and technological advances of our own time inevitably demand a reinterpretation of the very nature and role of art; the "Death of the Lion" is, so to speak, no longer our "death." In this context, an art that is to be genuinely avant-garde must, first of all, acknowledge the present.[5]

This has been, from the start, one of Cage's central themes. Consider the following exchange between Cage and Richard Kostelanetz, prompted by Cage's complaint that his work is too frequently interrupted by phone calls, often from total strangers:

> Kostelanetz: Why do you keep your name in the phone book?
>
> Cage: I consider it a part of twentieth-century ethics, you might say. I think that this thing I speak of about fluency is implied by the telephone, and that is partly why I have these ideas I have. If I were to have a totally determined situation in my own conception, then of course I would be unlisted.
>
> Kostelanetz: Well, if you want to close yourself off, it is the easiest way.
>
> Cage: Yes but it would fail. Morris Graves, an old friend of mine, is searching for a place to live that is removed from the twentieth century; but he can't find it, even in Ireland. The airplane flies overhead. If he finds a beautiful property, he has to bring a bulldozer in.

Kostelanetz: You want very much yourself to live in the twentieth century?

Cage: I don't see that it would be reasonable in the twentieth century not to. (*RK*, 6)

We are now in a better position to understand the famous Cage aphorism, "PERMISSION GRANTED, BUT NOT TO DO WHATEVER YOU WANT" (*YFM*, 28). To be false to one's art is to impose inappropriate restraints that impede the process of creation – nostalgia for the past, for example, or needless repetition of oneself or of others, or the refusal to recognize what is actually going on around us, as in the case of George Grizzard's ignorance of television. But this is not to say that one can make any experiment one pleases:

> Paraphrasing the question put to Sri Ramakrishna and the answer he gave, I would ask this: "Why, if everything is possible, do we concern ourselves with history (in other words with a sense of what is necessary to be done at a particular time)?" And I would answer, "In order to thicken the plot." (*S*, 68)

What does this mean in practice? In the Foreword to *Silence*, Cage writes: "As I see it, poetry is not prose simply because poetry is in one way or another formalized. It is not poetry by reason of its content or ambiguity but by reason of its allowing musical elements (time, sound) to be introduced into the world of words" (*S*, x). This distinction may strike us at first as decidedly unCagean, for doesn't the composer-poet always argue that "structure" must give way to "process," and that, as he declares in the prefaces to such sound poems as *Mureau* and *Writing through Finnegans Wake*, it is essential to "demilitarize the language" by getting rid of conventional syntax? Why, then, the concern for formalizing the language by means of sound repetition or, in other cases, by means of visual patterning?

Here a Zen proverb is applicable: "To point at the moon a finger is needed, but woe to those who take the finger for the moon." To write a poem – say, a series of mesostics or a sound text like *Empty Words* or a prose meditation on Jasper Johns – one submits oneself to a particular rule, generated, in Cage's case, by an *I Ching* "change" or chance operation, so as to free oneself from one's habitual way of doing things, one's stock responses to word and sentence formation. Once the rule (for example, telling one story per minute as in "Indeterminacy" [*S*, 260]) or using twelve typefaces and forty-three characters per line without ever hyphenating a word as in "Diary: How to Improve the World" (*YFM*, 3) has been established, it generates the process of composition. What the rule is, in other words, matters much less than the fact that one *uses* it.

Consider how this works in Cage's "36 Mesostics Re and not Re Duchamp" (*M,* 26–34). The words "Marcel" or "Duchamp" form a vertical column of capital letters down the middle of each stanza, which has, accordingly, either six or seven lines. The stated rule is that "a given letter capitalized does not occur between it and the preceding capitalized letter" (*M,* 1). Here is the first stanza:

> a utility aMong
> swAllows
> is theiR
> musiC
> thEy produce it mid-air
> to avoid coLliding.

Our first reaction to this little mesostic is likely to be one of skepticism: isn't this merely game-playing? And if Cage wants to restrict his movements by imposing rule, why not use such traditional prosodic devices as a fixed stress or syllable count, the repetition of vowel and consonant sounds, rhyme?

The fact is that these devices *are* used. "Their" rhymes with "-air," and the first and last lines chime with the near-rhyme "Am*ong*" / "collid*ing*." The fifth line has another such near rhyme internally – "avoid" / "coLlid-," and there is marked assonance throughout of short, lightly stressed *a*'s ("a," "avoid," "*a*Mong," "*air*") and *i*'s ("ut*i*lity," "*is*," "mus*i*C," "*it*," "mid-air," "coLlid*i*ng"), as well as alliteration of laterals and nasals ("uti*l*ity," "sw*All*ows," "coL*l*iding," "a*M*ong," "*m*usiC," "*m*id-air"). Further, the syllable count is 7-2-2-2-6-6 – hardly an arbitrary pattern, the number of stresses remaining within the limit of one ("músiC") and three (thÉy prodúce it mîd-áir"). But because our usual way of processing poems today is to read them silently, Cage provides us with the column "MARCEL," a column designed for the eye only since it is obviously impossible to hear the embedded letters as forming the word "Marcel." One might thus say that Cage's lyric pays tribute to what he calls "twentieth-century ethics," to the world of typographic layout and print format in which we all live, at the same time as it slyly sneaks poetic conventions in by the back door. In this sense, the mesostics for Marcel Duchamp nicely exemplify Cage's "concern . . . with history in order to thicken the plot."

Cagean *plot* is generally characterized by what Jung, in his Foreword to the Bollingen edition of the *I Ching,* designates as "sychronicity":

. . . the configuration formed by chance events in the moment of observation, and not at all the hypothetical reasons that seemingly account for the coincidence. While the Western mind carefully sifts, weighs, selects, classifies, isolates, the Chinese picture of the moment encompasses everything down to the minutest nonsensical detail, because all of the ingredients make up the observed moment.[6]

How such a "configuration" is created out of what seems to be "the minutest nonsensical detail" may be observed in Cage's longer lecture-poems or collage-essays, for example, the recent *Where Are We Eating? and What Are We Eating? (38 Variations on a Theme by Alison Knowles)*, originally written for a collection of essays and photographs on Merce Cunningham (1975) and reprinted in *Empty Words* (1979).

The preface to the "38 Variations" begins with a neat distinction:

No one need be alarmed by the exercises dancers give their stomachs. Dancers are furnaces. They burn up everything they eat. Musicians as furnaces are not efficient; they sit still too much. (*EW*, 79)

As such, Cage himself began in his late forties to suffer various aches and pains, for example, arthritis, for which the doctors prescribed huge doses of aspirin – a remedy that, so Cage tells us matter-of-factly, did no good at all. Finally, in 1977, on the advice of Shizuko Yamamoto, he adopted a macrobiotic diet and "For two days I lived in shock. I ate almost nothing. I couldn't imagine a kitchen without butter and cream, nor a dinner without wine." But as soon as the diet has gotten under-way, "The pain behind the left eye went away. After a month the toes began to move. Now my wrists, though somewhat misshapen, are no longer swollen and inflamed. I've lost more than twenty-five pounds."

It all sounds very virtuous, rather like one of those ads for Granola or Raisin Bran. But Cage's account of his new cooking habits – his use of sesame oil and tamari to flavor mushrooms, of dill and parsley to flavor brown rice – is only the framework for his text, a framework that is wholly exploded by the outrageously funny food catalog contained in the "Variations" themselves. Eating miso soup and nuka pickles, the piece implies, is all very well – indeed essential if you are a musician rather than a dancer – but don't think it will make you forget the joys of *real food*. Or, in Cage's own words, "One does not seek by his actions to arrive at the establishment of a school (truth) but does what must be done. One does something else. What else?" (*S*, 68).

Where Are We Eating? and What Are We Eating? is thus the elaborate food fantasy (paradoxically straight fact) of the artist as macrobiotic dieter. The "38 Variations" range from 15 to 24 lines with irregular left and right margins, the lines themselves averaging around 10 syllables. This stanzaic structure is visual only, for the discourse is that of a diary, written in short sentences and sentence fragments that regularly override line endings. But not quite a diary either, for Cage's prose has no continuity: each variation catalogs items and incidents unconnected in time and space, the only point of reference being that everything mentioned refers to *where* and to *what* members of the Merce Cunningham troupe ("America's Best Fed Dance Company," as Cage calls it in "Variation 31"),[7] eat as they travel around the world. For example:

> We were invited to the Riboud's in
> Paris. They had just received a large
> box full of fresh mangoes from India. We
> kept on eating until they were finished.
> In a Buffalo hotel Sandra and Jim stayed on
> the eighth floor. They had a large can of
> sardines for breakfast. Five they didn't
> eat they flushed down the toilet.
> After paying the bill at the desk, Sandra
> went to the ladies' room. There in the
> bowl of the toilet were two of her five
> sardines. We stopped at a small
> crowded restaurant on the road between
> Delaware and Baltimore. After our orders
> were taken, we waited a long time.
> The waitress finally came with some of
> our food. Hastily, she said to Carolyn,
> "You're the fried chicken," to
> Viola, "And you're the stuffed shrimp."   (*EW,* 87)

The fresh mangoes from India eaten at the Riboud's in Paris have no connection to the sardines eaten for breakfast in a Buffalo hotel room (two of which turn up the the toilet downstairs) or with the crowded restaurant, somewhere between Delaware and Baltimore, where the waitress pronounces Carolyn a fried chicken and Viola a stuffed shrimp. But Cage's curious lamination has the effect of making the world quite literally the poet's oyster, for it is a world defined by only two or three things: the quality of the performance space ("Zellerbach, in Berkeley, / is one of the most comfortable theatres / we've ever performed in. Stage is / wide and deep, has big wings" [*EW,* 81]), the setting for food intake, and, most important, the 1001 attributes and species of the food itself.

Cage's settings are carefully chosen so as to take us around the world in 38 Variations, but we come back, again and again, to Joe's in Albany ("Variations" 1, 9, 21, 30), where one eats a "number 20 (Old English): Beef, / ham, tongue, lettuce, tomato, with / Russian dressing"; to the Moosewood Inn in Ithaca, New York (15, 21, 25, 26, 36), whose luncheon menu features "Spinach and mushroom soup," "asparagus soufflé," and "yoghurt cream cheese pie (nuts in the crust)" (*EW*, 91); and to the Sri Lanka in London (6, 32, 34), where dinners generally begin with egg hoppers: "An egg hopper is an / *iddiapam* made with rice flour and coconut / milk in the bottom of which fried egg / sunny-side up is placed. On top of / the egg your choice of condiments from a / tray of many" (*EW*, 95).

In between these points, the journey takes the Cunningham troupe to every conceivable variety of eating place: the Cafe de Tacuba in Mexico City (4), the Big Tree Inn in Geneseo, New York (7), a motel in Malibu, whose "miserable" Chinese restaurant is perceived as serving "delicious" food once the company is sufficiently "plastered" (7), a truck stop outside Chicago (12), a restaurant inside a gas station in Eau Claire, Wisconsin (16), a California bungalow Japanese restaurant on the Sunset Strip (19), the lawn in front of Howard Johnson's (19), an Amish farm (22), a Durango whorehouse (26), a super-market in Ljubljana (29), a Ceylonese restaurant in Boulder, Colorado (32), and the Whole Earth in Santa Cruz (36) – not to mention private homes, hotels, open-air restaurants, and clubs in Paris, Warsaw, Grenoble, Amsterdam, St. Paul de Vence, Tennessee, Bremen, the Hague, Oklahoma City, and Delhi. There is even one dinner in "a lodge in a meadow surrounded by / a forest near the north rim of the Grand Canyon" (*EW*, 80).

The descriptions of food become more and more elaborate in the course of the "Variations." The poem begins on a low key: dancers need, Cage explains, a good steak restaurant with a liquor license so they can have some beer. But by the end of the first variation, we are already taken to Sofu Teshigahara's house: "room where we ate had two parts: one / Japanese; the other Western. Also, two / different dinners; we ate them both" (*EW*, 80). From here on out, we move into a world of "tequila sangrita" (4,5) and Pernod (10), of "risotto with truffles" (6) and "*mousse au chocolat*" served with "a large pot of *crème fraîche*" (6), and then on to moments when food seems to come alive and take over the human scene:

> Picnic preparation in hotel room.
> Chicken, marinated in lemon and *sake,*
>   wrapped'n foil, left overnight, next day
> dipped in sesame oil and charcoal-broiled.
> Broccoli, sliced, was put in ginger in
>   twenty-five packages; corn, still in
>   husks, silk removed,
>   butter 'n' wrapped. Noticing bathtub was
> full of salad, David said, "I don't want any
>   hairs in my food." In addition to the
>   roast beef and cheese on rye, Robert had
> triscuits, a sour orange from Jaffa, a
> banana, and some apple pie. David's sticky
>   fermented Passion-fruit juice geysered on
>   the way to Grenoble. Bus floor and
>   handbags were cleaned and the windows
>   were opened. Then it geysered again.
>   (*EW*, 87–88)

Here David (Tudor's) "Passion-fruit juice geyser[ing]" in the bus becomes a kind of fountain of love, the jet stream that keeps this wild group of people going.

But don't dancers do anything but eat? Cage's narrative playfully takes the great art of Merce Cunningham (to whom he has paid frequent tribute)[8] as a given, as if to say, "Well, of course the dancing is marvelous, so why say anything more about it?" Deflecting our expectations, his text presents, under the guise of simple record – a logbook in fact – a Gargantuan eating dream that outdoes Leopold Bloom's Lestrygonian fantasies. Cage's technique is to collage individual – and often quite unrelated – events (conscientiously providing every name and date – what Jung calls "the minutest nonsensical detail"), in keeping with the Zen belief that it is only the coincidence of events in space and time that reveal to us the "UNIMPEDEDNESS AND INTERPENETRATION" (*S*, 46) at the heart of the universe. The narrative is, moreover, entirely autobiographical ("this happened to me and then this and then that") without being in the least "confessional": we learn nothing whatever about Cage's personal life. The Zen precept followed is "Never explain, indicate," for there is no such thing as final understanding. Accordingly, everyone is called by name – Carolyn, Rick and Remy, Carroll Russell, Meg Harper, Kamalini – but the names are entirely opaque; they point to no hidden truth, no conceptual reality. Again, Cage's Orient is not the Exotic East, any more than his Paris is the City of

Light; indeed, the Japanese restaurant on the Sunset Strip (where the
waitress who brings Cage a pineapple ice, tells him, "Oh yes, that'll cut
the grease in your stomach" [EW, 88]) might serve one's purpose just
as well as the real thing, depending upon one's mood and what happens
to be on the menu that night.

The Global Village presented in Cage's narrative has no center: the Ceylonese restaurant in Boulder is no more peripheral than the Swiss chalet in
Ceylon; Jerusalem Artichoke may be ordered at the Moosewood Inn in
Ithaca, and fresh mangoes from India are served in Paris. Indeed, one's
dream recipe may turn up anywhere: in Cage's case, it makes its appearance in Room 135 of the Holiday Inn (city undesignated):

Four
cups of ground walnuts; 4 cups of
flour; 12 tablespoons of sugar; 2 2/3
cups of butter; 4 teaspoons of
vanilla. Form into circa 125
small balls. Bake at 350°
in motel oven. Now back to Room 135.
Roll in 1 pound of powdered sugar.
Nut balls.   (EW, 91)

These nut balls keep reappearing ("Variation 36" begins, "After Jean 'n'
I'd rolled one hundred / balls, I remembered I'd forgotten the vanilla"),
but fond as Cage is of this particular recipe, he is just as pleased to come
across "Excellent *tempura* (not greasy; flaky, delicate batter)" or to take
note of Cunningham's high-protein breakfast drink:

two
parts yeast, one part liver, one
part wheat germ, one part sunflower-
kernel meal, one part powdered milk (cold
pressed), pinch of kelp, one part lecithin,
one-half teaspoon powdered bone meal.
At home, mixed with milk and banana in a
blender. On tour USA, mixed with
milk in portable blender. On tour
elsewhere, mixed with yoghurt or
what-have-you.   (EW, 95)

Rules, that is to say, are always useful but one must retain one's flexi-
bility in applying them: "one does not seek by his actions to arrive at
the establishing of a school (truth) but does what must be done. One
does something else. What else?" (S, 68)

The final, or thirty-eighth, variation thickens the plot by a remarkable twist:

> "You go home now?" No; this ends the
> first of five weeks. Toward the
> end, Black Mountain didn't have a
> cent. The cattle were killed and the
> faculty were paid with beefsteaks. Chef
> in Kansas motel-restaurant cooked
> the mushrooms I'd collected. Enough
> for an army. They came to the table
> swimming in butter. Carolyn, who isn't
> wild about wild mushrooms, had seconds. I
> complimented the cook. How'd you know
> how to cook 'em? "We get them all
> the time: I'm from Oklahoma." There's a
> rumor Merce'll stop. Ten years ago, London
> critic said he was too old. He himself
> says he's just getting a running start.
> Annalie Newman says he's like wine:
> he improves with age.   (*EW*, 97)

The faculty at Black Mountain College are paid in beefsteaks because there is no money; the mushrooms Cage collects swim in butter; Cunningham is like wine: "he improves with age." How are we to interpret these overwhelming "what one eats is what one is" metaphors, when we remember that the man who is telling us this whole story is eating nothing but barley bread and brown rice?

A helpful perspective on this question is provided by the following exchange between Richard Kostelanetz and Cage:

Kostelanetz: But why don't you go yourself to every happening?

Cage: I've been telling you how busy I am. I barely have time to do my own work.

Kostelanetz: What I meant is, why do you go to one and not another? Because you happen to be in New York at that time?

Cage: Purely.

Kostelanetz: Do you walk out of one feeling happier that you went to that one rather than another?

Cage: The big thing to do actually is to get yourself into a situation in which you use your experience no matter where you are, even if you are at a performance of a work of art which, if you were asked to criticize it, you would criticize out of existence. Nevertheless, you should get yourself into such a position that, were you present at it, you would somehow be able to use it.

Kostelanetz: But does that alter the fact that you might have preferred going to a different happening?

Cage: That's not an interesting question; for you are actually at this one where you are. How are you going to use this situation if you are there? This is the big question. (*RK*, 28)

Which is to say, with reference to our text, that when one is engaged in eating, one enjoys what one eats, and when one is dieting, one finds a way to use that particular experience so that it will yield positive results. Now that Cage is on his macrobiotic diet, does he hold forth on the horrors of slaughtering cattle? No more than he objected to a vegetarian dance or to Merce's yeast-and-liver drink during his feasting days with the Cunningham troupe.

Where Are We Eating? and What Are We Eating? is thus, in a curious sense, an exemplary tale. The narrative reveals no psychological complexities, whether Cage's or anyone else's; it has neither a climax nor a turning point; it does not, for that matter, move toward an epiphany because our attention has been carried, so to speak, "not to a center of interest but all over the canvas and not following a particular path" (*YFM*, 31). Yet what seems to be a set of variations made up of "sheer multiplicity, unfocused attention, decentralization" (*RK*, 8) thickens the plot by layering its seemingly trivial data so as to arrest the attention, thus forcing us to rethink the meaning of its title. "EAT," we learn in "Variation 34," is the acronym of an organization called "Experiments in Art and Technology." "Merce," Cage remarks, "never got involved in it. David Tudor and I did" (*EW*, 95). Was it then a good thing to be, so to speak, part of EAT? Or is Cage to be defined by his new role as consumer of brown rice and seaweed? "The situation," as Cage says in his collage-essay on Jasper Johns, "must be Yes-and-No not either-or. *Avoid a polar situation*" (*YFM*, 79).

NOTES

1 "History of Experimental Music in the United States" (1958), reprinted in *Silence*, p. 68. The following abbreviations are used for Cage's works throughout this essay:

s   *Silence, Lectures and Writings* (Middletown, Conn.:
        Wesleyan University Press, 1961).

YFM   *A Year from Monday, New Lectures and Writings*
        (Middletown, Conn.: Wesleyan
        University Press, 1967).

M   *M, Writings '67–'72* (Middletown, Conn.:
        Wesleyan University Press, 1973).

EW   *Empty Words, Writings '73–'78* (Middletown,
        Conn.: Wesleyan University Press, 1979).

RK   *John Cage*, ed. Richard Kostelanetz (1970; New York:
        Praeger Publishers, Inc., 1974).

2   *Perspectives of New Music*, I (Spring 1963), p. 141.

3   Cited by Calvin Tomkins, "John Cage," in *The Bride and the Bachelors, Five
    Masters of the Avant-Garde* (New York: Penguin Books, 1976), p. 107.

4   *Tulane Drama Review*, X:2 (Winter 1965), p. 71. Subsequently cited as
    TDR.

5   For a good discussion of the analogies between contemporary art and
    science, see Michael Kirby, "The Aesthetics of the Avant-Garde" (1969), in
    Esthetics Contemporary, ed. Richard Kostelanetz (Buffalo, N.Y.: Prome-
    theus Books, 1978), pp. 36–70.

6   *The I Ching or Book of Changes*, the Richard Wilhelm translation from
    Chinese into German, rendered into English by Cary F. Baynes, Bollingen
    Series III (1950; Princeton: Princeton University Press, 1967), p. xxiii. I
    discuss the nonsensicality of Cage's Zen stories in the larger context of his
    performance aesthetic in my *The Poetics of Indeterminacy: Rimbaud to Cage*
    (Princeton: Princeton University Press, 1981), pp. 288–339.

7   For the sake of convenience, I have numbered the variations; similarly, in
    reproducing portions of the Kostelanetz interview, I normalize the format;
    Kostelanetz does not use names but italicizes his own questions, a device
    useful in a long interview but confusing in the case of brief quotations.

8   See, for example, "Four Statements on the Dance," in *Silence*, pp. 87–97.

10 The Word as Such: L=A=N=G=U=A=G=E poetry in the eighties

"oilfish" to "old chap" for "C"

Performing military service for the king and bearing a child have a common medieval root. The progression to this point is first academic, then technical. Textbooks give way to textiles which lead to T-formations and T-groups. We pause to add "th" and proceed through Mediterranean anemia, deep seas, Greek muses, pesticides, young shoots and the instinctual desire for death. It is there that we find "thane" to be followed by all manner of "thanks," including the "thank-you-ma-am"–a ridge built across a road so rain will roll off.

–Tina Darragh, *on the corner to off the corner*[1]

Carbon

But this is a false tart, the trap door insecurely latched, a tear in the velvet curtain. Yet the tear was but a drop of glycerine sliding down her cheek. Nonetheless skin is not porcelain, however it spots.

–Ron Silliman, *ABC*[2]

The Sheds of our Webs

Floating on completely vested time, a lacrity
To which abandon skirts another answer
Or part of but not returned.
Confined to snare, the sumpter portion
Rolls misty ply on foxglove, thought
Of once was plentitude of timorous
Lair, in fact will build around
It. Shores that glide me, a
Tender for unkeeping, when fit with
Sticks embellish empty throw. Days, after
All, which heave at having had.

–Charles Bernstein, *Resistance*[3]

215

But is it *poetry?* Tina Darragh's paragraph is a mock page from a dictionary; instead of "oilfish" to "old chap" (which is, of course, not under "C"), we are given a set of riddling permutations of words beginning with "t": "technical," "textbooks," "textiles," "T-formations," "T-groups." One or two phonemes (/k/, /kst/) can make all the difference. Add an "h" to "t" and you introduce a Greek element: "Mediterranean anemia" (evidently "thalamic hemorrhage"), "deep seas" ("thalassa," which gives us the word "Thalassian"), "Greek muses" (e.g., "Thalia"), pesticides ("Thalline"), "young shoots" ("thalluses"), and "the instinctual desire for death" ("thanatos"). Then "thane" and "thanks" and a "thank-you-ma'am" which, so the OED tells us, got its curious meaning ("a ridge built across a road so rain will roll off") from the fact that such a ridge or hollow in the road would cause "persons passing over it in a vehicle to nod the head involuntarily, as if in acknowledgement of a favour." (The first example cited by the OED is from Longfellow's *Kavanaugh* (1849): "We went like the wind over the hollows in the snow; / the driver called them 'thank you ma'ams,' because they made everybody bow.") And where does the "C" of the title come in? In the riddle of the first sentence, which pits "conscription" ("Performing military service for the king") against "confinement" ("bearing a child").

How curious, the text suggests, the vagaries of *words* that can, with the shift of a single phoneme or two, mean such different things as "thane" and "thanks"; with the addition of a suffix or two, turn "thanks" into "thanatos," or again, with the addition of a word or two, turn "thanks" into an idiom meaning ridge or hollow in the road. The signifier, it seems, is never merely transparent – a replica of the signified. The prefix "con," for that matter, generates life as easily as death.

Again, when, in the first line of "Carbon," Ron Silliman removes a single phoneme from a word ("false start" becomes "false tart"), he creates intriguing plot possibilities: to make a false start by falling through a trap door is one thing; to position a "false tart" in this setting, especially given the tear in the velvet curtain, quite another. But then "tear" (rip) becomes a teardrop, and one made out of glycerine at that. It is difficult, the text implies, to distinguish artifice from reality. Skin spots, porcelain spots; "Nonetheless skin is not porcelain."

Charles Bernstein takes this sort of word play a step further, almost to the point of unintelligibility. In "The Sheds of our Webs," neologisms abound: "a lacrity," "sumpter" ("marshy" or "low-lying" on the model of "sump"?), "plentitude." More important; grammatical position is frequently ambiguous: is "sheds" a noun or gerund ("sheddings")? "Abandon skirts" a verb followed by its direct object or a subject–verb clause? "Tender" a verb or adjective or noun? There is no way to be sure, especially since many of the words in ambiguous syntactic position are homonyms. Thus "vested" means (1) "conferred as a legal right" as well as (2) "wearing a vest"; and, what is more disconcerting, "tender," if a noun, can mean (1) "a formal offer to supply goods or carry out work or buy at a stated price"; (2) "a person who tends to look after something"; or (3) "a vessel or vehicle traveling to and from a larger one to convey stores or passengers etc.," more specifically, (4) "a car attached to a steam locomotive carrying fuel and water."

But is it not the function of syntax precisely to tell us which of these possible meanings is the appropriate one in the context? "Art," as Hugh Kenner puts it with reference to Williams' "The Red Wheelbarrow," "lifts the saying out of the zone of things said."[4] And the "saying," in the case of "The Sheds of our Webs," becomes a way of foregrounding the human need to escape confinement (the "plentitude of timorous lair"), the need to rid ourselves of our defenses, to shed our webs, which are also "sheds" in that, "Confined to snare," we hide within them. "Floating on completely vested time" is, after all, a way of skirting the issue with "a lacrity" rather than real conviction: "abandon skirts another answer" (or, abandon[ing] our skirts is an answer that brings in no returns). The poet opts for "Shores that glide me, a / Tender for unkeeping": he is, so to speak, the vessel that carries the cargo, even if others perceive it as an "empty throw." The thing is to make an imprint, to leave "Days, after / All, which heave at having had."

The prominent alliteration and assonance in these last lines, indeed, the highly formalized sound structure of the whole poem, with its stately diction and heavy stressing –

> Rólls mîsty plý on fóxglôve, ‖ thóught
> Of ónce was pléntitûde or tímorous
> Láir. . . .

recalls Hart Crane rather than, say, Williams. "Shores that glide me, a / Tender for unkeeping" is nothing if not Cranean even as Crane points back to the Yellow Nineties and to Swinburne. Indeed, in a curious way it is *fin de siècle* that the $L=A=N=G=U=A=G=E$ poetry of our own *fin de siècle* recalls in its renewed emphasis, after decades of seemingly "natural" free verse, on prominent sound patterning and arcane, or at least "unnatural," diction.

But of course the immediate impression likely to be produced by a Bernstein or Silliman poem is that Swinburne or Crane have somehow been put through the Cuisinart: what finds its way into the bowl looks,

at first sight, like so many chopped and hence unrecognizable vege-
tables. Faced with the syntactic and semantic difficulties I have been
describing, the reader may decide that "language-centered writing" is
little more than a clever hoax. What is the value, I have heard it asked,
of these little word games when we all know that the business of poetry
is to convey the concrete particulars of experience, the response of the
sensitive individual to the vagaries of human suffering and struggle?

In their more theoretical writings (essays, reviews, prose poems,
manifestos, interviews, and various hybrids of these) the Language poets have addressed themselves to precisely such questions. "Poetry and
philosophy," says Bernstein in a recent essay, "share *the project of inves-
tigating the possibilities (nature) and structures of phenomena,*"[5] an assumption shared by such otherwise diverse Language poets as Ron Silliman
and Lydia Davis, Clark Coolidge and Douglas Messerli, Lyn Hejinian
and Tom Raworth. I propose, therefore, to take up some of the central
theoretical assumptions that govern language-centered writing, assumptions that take us back into the poetry itself. But then, as the poets
repeatedly tell us, the distinction between theory and poetry is an arbitrary one anyway, even as generic and prosodic differentiation violates
the integrity of the text as "language-work." For Olson and Creeley,
"Form is never more than the extension of content." For the Language
poet, this aphorism becomes "Theory is never more than the extension
of practice."[6]

I

The "Language Sampler" appearing in the Winter 1982 *Paris
Review* bears the following headnote by Jonathan Galassi:

> One of the most frequently mentioned and least understood
> developments in American poetry in recent years has been the
> emergence of an ideologically, psychologically and linguisti-
> cally self-conscious movement, centered largely on the East and
> West Coasts, which some observers have dubbed Language
> Poetry. Like most pioneers in new literary directions, the Lan-
> guage Poets, for the most part, deny they belong to a formally
> constituted group and eschew the name imposed on them by
> casual critics. Nevertheless, for better or for worse, a shared
> tendency – or at the least, a common preoccupation with "the
> resonating of the wordness of language," as Charles Bernstein
> puts it – has been recognized by the outside world, and to some
> extent by many of these poets themselves.[7]

But how, the reader may well ask, can poetry by definition be anything but "language centered"? First and foremost, the distinction is between what Charles Bernstein calls in the introduction to the *Paris Review* "communication . . . schematized as a two-way wire with the message shuttling back and forth in blissful ignorance of the (its) transom (read: ideology)" and "a sounding of language from the inside, in which the dwelling is already / always given" (p. 75). And again, "The trouble with the conduit theory of communication (me → you) is that it presupposes individuals to exist as separate entities outside language and to be communicated *at* by language" (p. 78).

Since the rejection of the "conduit theory of communication" is at the very heart of Language Poetry, the concept needs clarification. In an essay called "Reading Cavell Reading Wittgenstein," Bernstein writes:

> The distortion is to imagine that knowledge has an "object" outside of the language of which it is a part – that words refer to "transcendental signifieds" rather than being part of a language which itself produces meaning in terms of its grammar, its conventions, its "agreements in judgment." Learning a language is not learning the names of things outside language, as if it were simply a matter of matching up "signifiers with signifieds," as if signifieds already existed and we were just learning new names for them. . . . Rather, we are initiated by language into a (the) world, and we see and understand the world through the terms and meanings that come into play in this acculturation. . . . In this sense, our conventions (grammar, codes, territorialities, myths, rules, standards, criteria) are our nature.[8]

This is not, Bernstein is quick to insist, a Derridean skepticism about the very possibility of "meaning":

> What Derrida ends up transforming to houses of cards – shimmering traces of life as insubstantial as elusive – Wittgenstein locates as *meaning,* with the full range of intention, responsibility, coherence, and possibility for revolt against or madness without. In Wittgenstein's accounting, one is not left sealed off from the world with only "markings" to "decipher" but rather *located* in a world with meanings to *respond* to. (LB, p. 61)

This is not the place to take up the knotty issue of Derridean versus Wittgensteinian language theory. Suffice it to say that Bernstein and his fellow poets take poetic discourse to be, not the expression in words of an individual speaking subject, but the creation of that subject by the particular set of discourses (cultural, social, historical) in which he or she functions. As Bernstein puts it in an interview with Tom Beckett for *The Difficulties:*

> It's a mistake, I think, to posit the self as the primary organiz-
> ing feature of writing. As many others have pointed out, a
> poem exists in a matrix of social and historical relations that are
> more significant to the formation of an individual text than any
> personal qualities of the life or voice of an author.[9]

More significant but not solely responsible "since in crucial ways a poem is as much a resistance (to the language as given) as a product."

What does this rejection of "the idea of individual voice as a privi-leged structure" mean in practice? Here is the opening stanza of Galway Kinnell's ".Memory of Wilmington" from the prize-winning *Mortal Acts, Mortal Wounds* (1980):

> Thirty-some years ago, hitchhiking
> north on Route 1, I stopped for the night
> at Wilmington, Delaware, one of those American cities
> that start falling apart before they ever get finished.
> I met, I remember, an ancient hobo – I almost remember
> his name – at the ferry – now dead,
> of course, him,
> and also the ferry –
> in great-brimmed hat, coat to his knees,
> pants dragging the ground, semi-zootish rig
> plucked off various clotheslines. I remember. . .[10]

From the vantage point of the Language poet, the implicit assumptions that inform a poem like this one are invalid. For Kinnell's premise is that there was a particular event (the meeting with the hobo) that took place at a particular moment in time (thirty-some years ago) in a particular place (Wilmington, Delaware), and that these "realities" exist outside language and, in Bernstein's words, "to be communicated *at* by lan-guage." That is to say, experience is prior to the language that communi-cates it: the story of the hobo exists in a mental realm waiting to be activated by the words of a poet who can somehow match signifier to signified, can characterize the hobo's outfit as a "semi-zootish rig / plucked off various clotheslines." Such reductive "portraiture," a poet-critic like Bernstein would argue, is a case of "fitting words into a pat-tern" rather than "actually letting it happen" (LB, p. 39) Or, as Lyn Hejinian puts it, it is a matter of seeking "a vocabulary for ideas" rather than "ideas for vocabularies" (LB, p. 29). In positing the self as the primary organizing feature of writing, Kinnell is bound by the inevitable restrictions of such watchwords as "I feel," "I see," "I know," "I remember," authenticity of feeling or memory being guaranteed by the poet's ability to specify, to match "image" to "idea":

> After he ate, I remember, the old hobo
> –*Amos!* yes, that was his name!–old Amos sang,
> or rather laughed forth a song or two, his voice
> creaking out slower and slower,
> like the music in old music boxes, when time slows itself
> down in them.   (P. 56)

Compare this memory of "old Amos" to the following passage from Ron Silliman's *Tjanting:*

> Performance piece: on a 5 buck dare my father sinks his hand into a vat of hot tar. In every telephone there were rooms. An audible marks the quarterback's despair. Day gradually steamd into night. Toothless man in a tweed cap, from wch a pigeon feather sticks. How before the new view soon bobbd into world. Anything might come next. The damp on the sitting steps finally soaked in. This is a weather report. Why remind it was important his shoelaces matchd himself? The violence of charm. To these almost too far apart bridges seemed instant.[11]

Here what Charles Bernstein calls "the conduit theory of communication (me → you)" gives way to a "sounding of language from the inside"; the poet's voice functions as no more than a marginal presence, splicing together the given "data" so as to articulate their meanings. A sentence like "Day gradually steamd into night," for example, is a stock "literary" phrase that expresses, not Silliman's uniqueness but, on the contrary, his familiarity with particular literary codes. There are kernels of similar cliché phrases in "How before the new view soon bobbd into world" and "The damp on the sitting steps finally soaked in." Again, the language of media communication appears in sentences like "This is a weather report" or, in garbled form, in "In every telephone there were rooms."

Interestingly, when a particular moment in the poet's own past is recalled–"on a 5 buck dare my father sinks his hand into a vat of hot tar"–the memory prompts, not personal revelation (Kinnell's "I remember those summer nights / when I was young and empty, / when I lay through the darkness, wanting, wanting . . ."), but the absorption of the subjective image into the larger field of public discourse: the "audible [that] marks the quarterback's despair" and the "rooms" (of vocal despair) inside "every telephone." The "Toothless man in a tweed cap, from wch a pigeon feather sticks" is itself a stock image to be found in novels like *Studs Lonigan,* novels in which old men whose shoelaces don't match sit on the back steps at night until the damp has "finally soaked in." But Silliman's "performance piece" will not allow us to read his text as a novel with a cast of characters, having such and such psychological traits. "Anything," as he puts it, "might come next." Indeed, the "real" and the "imaginary" inevitably fuse: "To these almost too far apart bridges seemed instant."

II

"A *tjanting,*" Barrett Watten explains in his introduction to Silliman's book, "is a drawing instrument used for handwork in batik. The pun is exact: *Tjanting* (chanting) would seem to follow its predecessor as an oral form (*Ketjak*), but is in fact written toward writing considered as itself. The trace of the hand on the surface, then, is the hero of the text." Silliman's poem thus challenges the familiar models of what the Language poets contemptuously call "ego organization." And if individual voice is no longer privileged, neither, says Bernstein in the *Paris Review* introduction, is any single mode: "Distinctions between essays and lyrics, prose and poetry are often not observed." And as a corollary:

> Issues of poetics, when not explicitly determining the genre of the work, often permeate its mode of address – a tendency that can pull the poem out of the realm of purely personal reference and into a consideration of the interaction among the seemingly competing spheres of politics, autobiography, fiction, philosophy, common sense, song, etc. . . . There is a willingness to use, within the space of a text, a multiplicity of such different modes, which counts more on a recognition of the plastic qualities of traditional genres and styles than on their banishment. (P. 76)

It is precisely this refusal to observe established "distinctions" (between essays and lyrics, between prose and poetry, between philosophy and poetry, between theory and practice) that has been called into question by critics of Language poetry. "Too bad that their poems aren't as interesting as their theories" is a common complaint; "this work is not poetry, it's prose" is another. The recently published

The $L=A=N=G=U=A=G=E$ Book may well reinforce these criticisms: The book has three sections, "Poetics and Language," "Writing and Politics," and "Readings" (reviews of collections of poems), none of which features poetry itself. And even Tom Beckett, in his interview with Charles Bernstein, feels called upon to remark: "Charles, one frequent criticism of many of the contributors to $L=A=N=G=U=A=G=E$ in general and you specifically is that the theoretical essays you write, say, are considered to be more 'alive' than your poems" (D, p. 37).

The question of genre as of "prose" versus "poetry (i.e., verse)" is indeed a problematic one. Shall we classify the books under review here as "poetry" simply because they are to be bought in poetry bookshops or ordered from poetry catalogues? The issue is hardly new: Gertrude Stein's *Tender Buttons* is in prose but it is not fiction; her "fiction" *Melanctha* is thinly veiled autobiography and its system of repetitions and phonemic recurrences (e.g., "Sometimes Melanctha was so blue that she didn't know what she was going to do") is closer to "verse" than to "prose." In the same vein, Lyn Hejinian's *My Life* and Lydia Davis' *Story,* both markedly influenced by Stein, fuse autobiography, reportage, fiction, and lyric, foregrounding phrasal repetition as a key element. Hejinian's *My Life* begins:

> *A pause, a rose*   A moment yellow, just as four years later,
> *something on paper*   when my father returned home from the
>   war, the moment of greeting him, as he
>   stood at the bottom of the stairs, younger,
>   thinner than when he had left, was purple –

though moments are no longer so colored. Somewhere, in the background, rooms share a pattern of small roses. Pretty is as pretty does. The better things were gathered in a pen. The windows were narrowed by white gauze curtains which were never loosened. Hence, repetitions, free from all ambition. The shadow of the redwood trees, she said, was oppressive. The plush must be worn away. On her walks she stepped into people's gardens to pinch off cuttings from their geraniums and succulents. An occasional sunset is reflected on the windows. A little puddle is overcast. If only you could touch, or, even, catch those gray great creatures.[12]

The italicized phrase in the upper left "box" – "*a pause, a rose, something on paper*" – will become a leitmotif later in the text (it first reappears on page 12 in the sentence, "A pause, a rose, something on paper, in a nature scrapbook"), but the "repetitions" are, in Hejinian's words, "free from all ambitions," for we never really learn what a pause, a rose, and something on paper have in common. "Pause" and "rose" have similar consonant endings; "pause" and "paper" begin with *pa*. On the opening page, the leitmotif seems to have something to do with the "pattern of small roses" on the nursery wallpaper, but the connection is never fully made, for the main thing is not the connotative value of roses or paper but the fact that the phrase itself goes through endless permutations, appearing each time in a new context. Thus, on page 21, we read: "I found myself dependent on a pause, a rose, something on paper. It is a way of saying, I want you, too, to have this experience, so that we are more alike, so that we are closer, bound together." The leitmotif, one surmises, of love, of paper valentines. But on page 29, the narrator declares, "I have been spoiled with privacy, permitted the luxury of solitude. A pause, a rose, something on paper" – the phrase now pointing, not to communion with the beloved other, but to the writer's need for self-sufficiency.

In the same vein, other phrasal units are reborn, either as headnotes, or within the text. "The windows were narrowed by white gauze curtains which were never loosened" becomes, on page 9, "At night, to close off the window from view of the street, my grandmother pulled down the window shades, never loosening the curtains, a gauze starched too stiff to hang properly down." The "shadow of the redwood trees" which is related metonymically to "those gray great creatures" which the child longs to "touch" or "catch" when the "little puddle is overcast," becomes, on page 7, "the overtones are a denser shadow in the room characterized by its habitual readiness, a form charged waiting," and on page 10, "The shadows one day deeper."

Embedded in this network of permutations, we find familiar proverbs and aphorisms, usually just slightly out of sync, as in the case of "Pretty is as pretty does" or "See lightning, wait for thunder" (p. 6), or again "You spill the sugar when you lift the spoon" (p. 7). We have all been told such things as "I'm not your maid I'm your mother," and "If we didn't have to eat we'd be rich" (pp. 26–27). The language of adults impinges on the child's world with all its prescriptions, admonitions, and "wisdom." But the child's world is itself a mass of contradictions: pronouns repeatedly shift so that we do not know whether a given "she" ("on her walks she stepped into people's gardens") is the poet or her mother or someone else. Moreover, the "lessons" given by the well-meaning adults defy all logic: "The shadow of the redwood trees, she said, was oppressive. The plush must be worn away." "The obvious analogy," we read in one of the most frequently repeated phrases, "is with music." In this sense, it is not clear whether someone is talking of "gutter or guitar," "cabbage or collage" (p. 22). "So much depends /

upon," Williams declared, "A red wheel / barrow." The narrator of *My Life* is not so sure. Again and again, we come across the unpunctuated question, "What was the meaning hung from that depend."

Hejinian's strategy is to create a language field that could be any-body's autobiography, a kind of collective unconscious whose language we all recognize. When a personal memory is presented – for example, "I was afraid of my uncle with the wart on his nose" – it is a total commmonplace. *My Life,* it seems, is not "mine" at all; the emphasis, in any case, is on writing itself, on the "life" lived by words, phrases, clauses, and sentences, endowed with the possibility of entering upon new relationships. At the same time, *My Life* conveys what the arche-typal life of a young American girl is like: "Even rain didn't spoil the barbecue, in the backyard behind a polished traffic, through a landscape along a shore" (p. 73). The contradictory spatial designations take us, so to speak, from the mountains to the prairies, to the oceans white with foam. And of course to the city with its "polished traffic" as well.

The fictions in Lydia Davis' *Story* present fewer surface difficulties. A tale like "The Fears of Mrs. Orlando" may initially strike us as Chek-hovian in its "realistic" detail about the habits of an elderly widow who lives alone and becomes so obsessed by groundless fears (of bad wiring, slick bathtubs, prowlers, muggers, getting on the wrong subway, odd noises) that finally she refuses to go out at all:

> Then she stays inside and just talks on the phone, keeping her eyes on the doors and windows and alert to strange shadows. The last thing is that she has gotten a goose into the yard. The goose honks at strangers and she herself does not go out except in the early morning to check for footprints.[13]

In Chekhov such details as the check for footprints serve to reveal individual psychology; in Davis' work, on the other hand, the emphasis is not on the pathos of the old lady's increasing isolation from reality but on questions of interpretation and inference. The Steinian narrator tells us, in short simple declarative sentences marked by phrasal repeti-tion, how Mrs. Orlando feels about danger and potential accidents, but we are privy only to the character's specific reactions to a given event, never to her inner consciousness. The narrator is aloof, detached, bland: a recorder rather than a participant, but a recorder who knows only what Mrs. Orlando herself knows, nothing further. Thus the daugh-ters, with whom Mrs. Orlando talks for hours on the phone, have no physical existence; they merely function to question the validity of what their mother tells them. The reader must play the same role:

One day she tells them a story over the telephone. She has been downtown shopping alone. She leaves the car and goes into a fabric store. She looks at fabrics and does not buy anything, though she takes away a couple of swatches in her purse. On the sidewalk there are many blacks walking around and they make her nervous. She goes to her car. As she takes out her keys, a hand grabs her ankle from under the car. A man has been lying under her car and now he grabs her stockinged ankle with his black hand and tells her in a voice muffled by the car to drop her purse and walk away. She does so, though she can hardly stand. She waits by the wall of a building and watches the purse but it does not move from where it lies on the curb. A few people glance at her. Then she walks to the car, kneels on the sidewalk and looks under. She can see the sunlight on the road beyond and some pipes on the belly of the car: no man. She picks up her purse and drives home.

Her daughters don't believe her story. They ask her why a man would do such a peculiar thing in broad daylight. They point out that he could not have simply disappeared then, simply vanished into thin air. She is outraged by their disbelief and does not like the way they talk about broad daylight and thin air.   (Pp. 71–72)

Because the incident is recorded in the third person and present tense, we have the sense of confronting unmediated reality. It is as if we were watching a film: woman leaves car and goes into fabric store, woman looks at fabrics, woman takes a couple of swatches in her purse and comes out of store. Accordingly, when we read, "As she takes out her keys, a hand grabs her ankle from under the car," it appears to be simple fact. Even when the purse, dropped on the ground, remains where it was, there is no evidence that the "attack" was Mrs. Orlando's fantasy. Therefore, when the nameless and faceless "daughters" respond in disbelief and "talk about broad daylight and thin air," we tend to take Mrs. Orlando's side. For who has more "evidence," the old woman who sticks to the "facts" or the daughters who use clichés like "simply vanished into thin air"?

"Ordinary language," says Maurice Blanchot in a famous essay that Lydia Davis has translated,[14] "is not necessarily clear, it does not always say what it says; misunderstanding is also one of its paths. This is inevitable. Every time we speak we make words into monsters with two faces, one being reality, physical presence, and the other meaning, ideal absence." Such "misunderstanding" inherent in "ordinary language" is the impetus behind Davis' own compositions, for example, "Story," which begins with the sentence, "I get home from work and there is a message from him: that he is not coming, that he is busy" (*Story*, p. 27).

How the "I" responds to this "message" from the man she evidently loves to the point of obsession is now relayed in three chilling pages. The "I" acts: She phones, goes to his house, comes back, goes again, finds him, questions him, tries to understand what is really going on with "his former girlfriend." At the end we know no more than at the beginning even though a series of specific but contradictory incidents has taken place:

> The fact that he does not tell me the truth all the time makes me not sure of his truth at certain times, and then I work to figure out for myself if what he is telling me is the truth or not, and sometimes I can figure out that it's not the truth and sometimes I don't know and never know, and sometimes just because he says it to me over and over again I am convinced it is the truth because I don't believe he would repeat a lie so often. Maybe the truth does not matter, but I want to know it if only so that I can come to some conclusions about such questions as: whether he is angry at me or not; if he is, then how angry; whether he still loves her or not; if he does, then how much; whether he loves me or not; how much; how capable he is of deceiving me in the act and after the act in the telling.   (P. 30)

The irony here is that the either-or answers and arithmetical ratios ("how much") the narrator demands are not to be found. Interpretation of what seem to be simple "facts" ("So they went to the movies"; "he had returned from buying beer") can never yield up "the truth." Yet—and this is the success of Davis' "Story"—one tries to "figure it out" nevertheless. And ultimately it is the hermeneutic puzzle that becomes the obsession.

Davis' fictions thus deal with the realm of language and logic, the domain of information theory, evidence, and inference. These are not "poems" in the strict sense, but, as short verbal compositions that relentlessly juxtapose and permutate a limited corpus of verbal elements, they are not, strictly speaking, "stories" either. "Texts," in the sense of Beckett's "Texts for Nothing," is probably the best term. Clark Coolidge's *Mine: The One that Enters the Stories*[15] falls into the same category, as do such hybrid pieces as Alan Davies' "Private Enigma in the Opened Text" in *The $L=A=N=G=U=A=G=E$ Book*.[16]

But whatever the generic category, the important distinction to be made is not between "story" and "prose poem" or "story" and "essay" but, as Charles Bernstein points out, between "different contexts of reading and different readerships" (D, p. 35). To read such "writerly" texts as Hejinian's *My Life* or Davis' *Story,* is to become aware of what the Language poets call "the rights of the signifier."[17] Again, to "lay bare the device," a term the Language poets have borrowed from the Russian Futurists, does not necessarily mean to write in verse rather than prose, or to write lyric rather than "essay" or "manifesto." It means only that "the Word as Such" – what the poets Khlebnikov and Kruchenykh called, in the title of their manifesto of 1913, *Slovo kak takovoe*[18] – becomes the primary poetic determinant.

III

To emphasize the Word as Such is, inevitably, to pay special attention to sound patterning, to phonemic play, punning, rhythmic recurrence, rhyme. It is a paradox of language-centered writing that, despite its frequent recourse to prose rather than verse, and its refusal to separate "philosophy" from "poetry," sound structures are heavily foregrounded. This is not, of course, coincidence: a violation of "normal" language habits is in itself a commentary on these habits – in this case, the recourse to the frequently bland free verse that currently passes for "poetry." As Charles Bernstein puts it in the introduction to the *Paris Review* "Language Sampler":

> . . .there is a claim being made to a syntax . . . of absolute attention to the ordering of sound's syllables. . . . Not that this is "lyric" poetry, insofar as that term may assume a musical, or metric, *accompaniment* to the words: the music rather is built into the sequence of the words' tones, totally saturating the text's sound. (P. 76)

A good example of such saturation can be found in Douglas Messerli's *River to Rivet:* here is "When the Wind Blows," subtitled "a lullaby":

> slow grain to insistence, lust
> er of facts click
> & gone. that quick
> ens every vessel, transport
> ing the temptation to "stand your
> ground" into earth
> quake & bolt against

to from. certain
sentiments settle
back with the sediment
losing track
of actions, sleep
ing straight as a rock
bed that sudden
ly rattles right
into rhythm, training
what minds trick
with the flickers of hearts
to spare
the child despair.[19]

Here the title, which is, of course, the third line of "Rock-A-Bye
Baby," generates the momentum of the poetic discourse. The wind
blowing stirs up the "slow grain to insistence": whether the lullaby is
sung on shipboard (the wind "quickens every vessel" in its path, making
it mandatory to "stand your ground") or on dry land (the scene of
"earth / quake"), it causes a change of heart. "Certain / sentiments
settle / back with the sediment / losing track / of actions." The cliché of
sleeping like a rock gives way to the "rock / bed that sudden / ly rattles
right / into rhythm." One thinks of Yeats' "The Second Coming":

> The darkness drops again. But now I know
> That twenty centuries of stony sleep
> Were vexed to nightmare by a rocking cradle . . .

But here, the adults are sensible: They rely on "minds trick / with the
flicker of hearts / to spare / the child despair."

In "When the Wind Blows," pun, allusion, and rhyme are embedded
in a series of syntactically ambiguous phrases and sentences. Is "slow"
in the first line a noun or a verb? What is the referent of "that" in line 3?
Again, the breaking up of words into component syllables creates
puzzles: are we talking of "lust" or "luster" (which is itself a pun
meaning "one who lusts" or the noun for "shine"), "earth" or "earth-
quake," "bolt" ("lock the door") or "bolt" ("run for it")? Not only are
words cut at line ends but we hear the echo of familiar phrases: "click /
& gone," "losing track" (Denise Levertov's poem by this title), "sleep /
ing straight as a rock," "the flickers of hearts."

Rhyme, alliteration, assonance, consonance, repetition – all these are
prominent in "When the Wind Blows," but sound recurrence as such is
not what distinguishes this poem from any number of poems that have

nothing to do with the Language movement. Rather, we might say that here the sound structure is generative. A "vessel," for example, is obviously a form of "transport": add an "ing" and the ground shifts to the particular emotional response ("temptation") produced. Again, the proverbial wisdom of "stand your ground" brings to mind "earth" and "earth / quake" (the impossibility of standing one's ground), but when "quake" is separated from "earth" it becomes a verb that goes with "bolt." "Sentiments settle / back with the sediment" because the phoneme *se* in the first two words demands this conclusion. The same is true of "rattles right / into rhythm" and then of "trick" / "flick" and "spare" / "despair." Messerli's syntax has no truck with what Yeats called "the natural words in the natural order"; on the contrary, it is the sound associations here that domesticate the "lust / er of facts" and determine the nature of the "lullaby."

A poem like "When the Wind Blows" thus marks a turn away from the process poetics of the postwar era, from the "I do this, I do that" mode of Frank O'Hara and the New York school. For here the attempt is not to articulate the curve of a particular experience but to create a formal linguistic construct that itself shapes our perception of the world around us. If John Ashbery is an important precursor of Language poetry, it is the Ashbery of "The Tennis Court Oath" rather than of "Self-Portrait in a Convex Mirror."

Take, for example, Charles Bernstein's recent poem "Dysraphism," which appeared in *Sulfur*, 8 (1983). Here is the poet's note on his title:

> "Dysraphism" is actually a word in use by specialists in congenital diseases, to mean dysfunctional fusion of embryonic parts – a birth defect. . . . "Raph" of course means "seam," so for me disraphism is mis-seaming – a prosodic device! But it has the punch of being the same root of rhapsody (*rhaph*) – or in Skeats – "one who strings (lit. stitches) songs together, a reciter of epic poetry," cf. "ode" etc. In any case, to be simple, Dorland's [the standard U.S. medical dictionary] does define "dysrhafia" (if not dysraphism) as "incomplete closure of the primary neural tube; status dysraphicus"; this is just below "dysprosody" (sic): "disturbance of stress, pitch, and rhythm of speech."[20]

Bernstein's sensitivity to etymologies and latent meanings is reflected in the poem itself, which is an elaborate "dysfunctional fusion of embryonic parts," a "disturbance of stress, pitch, and rhythm of speech" in the interest of a new kind of urban "rhapsody." The "mis-seaming" of the poem brings together the life of the entire city – let us say New

York – with its overheard conversations, advertising slogans, Wall
Street jargon, medical terminology, TV clichés, how-to manuals, remembered proverbs, wise sayings, and nonsense rhymes. Like Joyce's
"Aeolus" chapter in *Ulysses,* it playfully exploits such rhetorical figures
as pun, anaphora, epiphora, metathesis, epigram, anagram, and neolo-
gism to create a seamless web of reconstituted words:

> The pillar's tale: a windowbox onto society.
> But heed not the pear that blows in your
> brain. God's poison is the concept of
> conceptlessness – anaerobic breath.
> No less is culled no more vacated – temptation's
> flight is always to
> beacon's hill – the soul's
> mineshaft.
> *Endless strummer.* There is never annul-
> ment, only abridgment. The Northern Lights is
> the universe's paneled basement. Joy
> when jogged. Delight in
> forefright.   (P. 41)

This is not nonsense talk, the collaging of whatever bits and pieces
happen to enter the poet's consciousness. Rather, "Dysraphism" violates standard language so as to foreground the discourses actually operative on contemporary writing: the "literary" ("pillar's tale" for
Chaucer's "Miller's Tale"), the "sociological" ("a window[box] onto
society"), the recourse to proverbial wisdom ("But heed not the
pear . . ."), the obsession with film titles (*Endless S[tr]ummer*), book
titles and publishers' blurbs ("Joy when jogged" for "the joy of jog-
ging" or "Delight in / forefright" rather than "foreplay"). Instructions
to the waiter or waitress new on the job ("Fill / the water glasses – ask
each person / if they would like / more coffee, etc.") alternate with
parodies of medical textbooks ("vaccination of cobalt emissaries preg-
nant with bivalent expasperation, protruding with inert material") and
the lingo of the business conference ("It's a realistic package, it's a /
negotiable package, it's / not a final package").

"Dysraphism" thus presents the reader with a world in which the
articulation of an individual language is all but prevented by the official
discourses that bombard the consciousness from all sides. "Blinded by
avenue and filled with / adjacency," "Arch or arched at," how do we
avoid speech as mere repetition? Perhaps, the poem implies, by de-
composition and recharge – in this case, particularly the recharge of
sound. For the psychological self-projection ("Twenty-five years ago I

walked . . ." "It was that night I knew . . .") of most contemporary free
verse, Bernstein substitutes the overdetermination of sound. Sometimes
we hear a quasi-Elizabethan iambic pentameter ("that hits the spring to
sing with sanguine bulk"), sometimes the tunes of Tin Pan Alley ("No
where to go but pianissimo"), everywhere the chiming of rhyme: "Mo-
rose or comatose," "Best of the spoils: gargoyles," "Reality is always
greener / when you haven't seen her." "Prose / pose" "Poem, chrome,"
"*A fleet of ferries, forever merry.*" Words, that is to say, are not dependable
when it comes to signification, but the play of their sounds is endlessly
pleasurable. "Thread / threads the threads, like / thrush. thrombolytic
casette." Or, as we read on the poem's last page:

> That is, in prose you start with the world
> and find the words to match; in poetry you start
> with the words and find the world in them.   (P. 44)

In a world "Riddled / with riot" (a play on Yeats' "Riddled with light" in
"The Cold Heaven"), "there is always something dripping through," if
we can find it. Otherwise, "We seem to be retreading the same tire / over
and over, with no additional traction."

IV

The unmasking of contemporary discourse in poems like
"Dysraphism" is, of course, far from innocent. Both in San Francisco
and New York, the Language movement arose as an essentially Marxist
critique of contemporary American capitalist society on behalf of young
poets who came of age in the wake of the Vietnam War and Watergate.
Thus a third of *The L=A=N=G=U=A=G=E Book* is taken up by
discussions of poetry and politics, discussions laced with the names of
such Marxist critics as Althusser, Macherey, and Jameson. In an essay
called "Disappearance of the Word, Appearance of the World," Ron
Silliman gives us the classic Marxist position espoused by many of the
Language poets.

Silliman takes as his epigraph Marx's famous statement (1859): "The
mode of production of material life conditions the social, political and
intellectual life process in general. It is not the consciousness of men
that determines their being, but on the contrary, their social being that
determines their consciousness." Applied to poetic language, this
becomes:

> (1) the stage of historical development determines the *natural*
> laws (or if you prefer the terminology, the underlying struc-

tures) of poetry; (2) the stage of historical development determines the natural laws of language; (3) the primary impact on language and language arts, of the rise of capitalism has been in the area of reference and is directly related to the phenomena known as the commodity fetish. (LB, p. 122)

Whereas early tribal societies preserved the "expressive integrity of the gestural nature of language" (what may look like "nonsense" syllables to us), "what happens when a language moves toward and passes into a capitalist stage of development is an anaesthetic transformation of the perceived tangibility of the word, with corresponding increases in its descriptive and narrative capacities, preconditions for the invention of 'realism,' the optical illusion of reality in capitalist thought" (LB, p. 125). Language, under capitalism, is thus "transformed (deformed) into referentiality": it becomes merely transparent.

The same point is made in related essays by Bruce Andrews, Barrett Watten, Charles Bernstein, and others. As Steve McCaffery declares in his manifesto "Intraview": "[The] linguistic promise that the signified gives of something beyond language i've come to feel as being central to capitalism (the fetish of commodity). . . . To demystify this fetish and reveal the human relationships involved within the labour process of language will involve the humanization of the linguistic Sign by means of a centering of language within itself" (LB, p. 189).

This argument for "the rights of the signifier" has been questioned by such older (and perhaps wiser) poets as Jackson MacLow, himself a writer on the Left who is an important precursor of the Language movement. In an essay called "Language-Centered," MacLow observes that the "brilliant, seemingly Marxist, attack on reference as a kind of fetishism contributing to alienation . . . is a dangerous argument, easily turned against its proponents. What could be more of a fetish or more alienated than slices of language stripped of reference?"[21]

Precisely. If language were really stripped of its referential properties (and, of course, as MacLow reminds us, it cannot be since "all signs point to what they signify"), "language poetry" would be no more than a mandarin game, designed to entertain an elitist coterie. Indeed, MacLow rightly points out that it would be more correct to call this a "perceiver-centered" rather than a "language-centered" or "non-referential" poetry, in the sense that "the larger part of the work of giving or finding meaning devolves upon the perceivers" (OL, p. 26). But even then the question remains whether the calling into question of "normal" language rules, or received discourses that I have been describing is a meaningful critique of capitalism.

For one thing, what the Language poets call late monopoly capitalism is never compared to the economic system of existing Marxist countries – the Soviet Union, China, Cuba, and their satellites. "The rise of capitalism," writes Silliman, "sets the preconditions for the rise of the novel, the invention of the optical illusion of realism, the final breakdown of gestural poetic forms" (LB, p. 126). Where does the rise of communism fit into this picture? Is Silliman implying that in contemporary China, "the optical illusion of realism" has given way to a valorization of "gestural poetic forms"? Or is the very opposite not the case in countries that can only tolerate socialist realism? Indeed, the transparency of the signifier, its loss of power to *be* in its own right, seems to me the very hallmark of discourse in the literary journals of, say, East Germany.

Still, poets like Silliman and Bernstein are on to something important when they lament the "invisibility" of language in our "literary" culture. "The words," says Silliman sadly, "are never our own. Rather, they are our own usages of a determinate coding passed down to us like all other products of civilization" (LB, p. 167). The dominance of a sophisticated technology, whether under capitalism or socialism, means that language is always in danger of becoming commodity. Those of us who have taught courses on poetry are familiar with the student with a very high IQ, say a computer science major, who cannot make anything of a poem like Blake's "London" because he or she cannot conceive of a linguistic or social context in which one might refer to a soldier's "hapless sigh" as "Run[ning] like blood down palace walls." In the discourse of medical text books or legal briefs, such statements simply make no sense.

There are two ways of responding to this situation. One may, as do the bulk of "creative writing" teachers and students in workshops across the country, turn one's back on contemporary technology and write "personal" poems in which an individual "I" responds to sunsets and spiders and moths flickering on windowpanes or remembers a magical incident that occurred on a fishing trip with Father. Or one can take on the very public discourses that seem so threatening and explore their poetic potential. To do this is to recognize that "I look straight into my heart & write the exact words that come from within" (LB, p. 39) is, strictly speaking, impossible, for the "exact words that come from within" are already coded by the historical and social context in which they function.

This is the situation explored by the British poet Tom Raworth, a kind of elder statesman to the Language movement, in his remarkable poem *Writing*.[22] The frontispiece of this oversize book is a sonagram of Raworth's own voice, recorded at the Exploratorium in San Francisco. This visual representation of vocality has a nice irony for, as the poem itself will suggest, the poet's voice is constantly displaced by the process of writing itself. Each page of the unpaginated text has four columns of minimal lines (they average four or five syllables), resembling ticker-tapes; the first such "tape" begins:

> spears of laughter
> hiss for a time
> then clank across
> leaving flakes of rust
> to fox pages
> as the sepia picture
> goes full color
> and begins to move
> but for now
> we get the idea
> birds' eye view
> see the words try
> to explain what
> is going in there
> an imagined book
> coming in to focus
> the scene
> in which the book rests
> is stationery
> only
> within the moving picture

The self tries to find some ordering principle that might contain the particulars of experience, but even "as the sepia picture / goes full color" and comes into focus, even as "the words try / to explain what / is going in there," the "scene" dissolves and becomes a "moving picture." Coherence cannot be had but as the "tape" is played, images and memories crowd the mental field with all the momentum of a television set tuned to three channels at the same time or one telephone conversation that crosses another. Indeed, if we read across rather than down, we are placed in this double or multiple bind. The phrase "as the sepia picture" can also be read across:

> as the sepia picture   i can hold   under ground steam
>   instead of read

Or again, "coming in to focus" (line 16) points horizontally to "blue and red," "flickers in as," and "rooms leading into others" – which makes perfectly good sense as an account of film unreeling. The "frame" of the motion picture is repeatedly violated.

The refusal of a coherent voice can, of course, lead to monotony and formlessness. If *Writing* is a straightforward transcription of whatever comes to Raworth's mind, why should we care to read it? Because, I would say, this particular transcription of experience and memory allows language to create its own vectors. Here is a section called "HAPPY BIRTHDAY BING" that superimposes on the voice of the narrator, that of the Great Crooner, Bing Crosby:

> clarity of another mind
> spinning so I see through
> too, to a view
> of rearrangements
>
> i could set back
> this against black
> it glows   he knows
>
> light has been caught
> and as i explain
> i want to feel this pain
>
> no longer
> die, nerves, burn out
> release me   how my shout
> drifts through that whirring mind

Here the Crosby swing rhythms cross the poet's own locutions so as to give us a memorably absurd picture of the popular music of the World War II years ("it glows   he knows"; "die, nerves, burn out / release me   how my shout"). After fourteen such parodic lines, the bubble suddenly bursts:

> lies
> lies
> pictured as a bent photograph
> etched
> on a two way mirror
> eggshell
> endless words
> how i see
> is alien

> you sing a little
> then i sing a little
> every time
> we say goodbye
> what do you battle
> for
> to be best
> you
> as a better me
> i agree
> to show you what i see
> egg   moon   acquent   apolune
> pivot
> on the front step with

Like a double exposure, this passage presents us with a Bing Crosby tap dancing his way down the front steps, crooning, "Every time we say goodbye," even as the missing second and fourth lines of this particular song ("I start to cry a little"; "I start to die a little") find their way into the tuneful words "egg   moon   acquent   apolune," the apolune being the point in a body's orbit about the moon where it is farthest from the moon's center and hence an image of dislocation, absence, the place, so to speak, where the falcon cannot hear the falconer.

The reader expects some sort of closure at this point but there is only "pivot." Writing is inevitably repetition, but each repetition reveals something else. As Charles Bernstein puts it in a poem called "Sprocket Damage":

> What happens opens up into what
>   happens the next time.[23]

Or, as Ron Silliman playfully paraphrases Freud so as to avoid the familiar id and ego, "When words are, meaning soon follows. Where words join, writing is" (LB, p. 16).

NOTES

1   *on the corner to off the corner* (College Park, Md.: Sun & Moon Press, 1981), p. 7.
2   *ABC* (Berkeley: Tuumba, 1983), unpaginated.
3   *Resistance* (Windsor, Vt.: Awede, 1983), unpaginated.
4   *A Homemade World. The American Modernist Writers* (New York: Knopf, 1975), p. 60.

5   "Writing and Method," *Poetics Journal*, 3 (May 1983), 7.

6   See Charles Bernstein, "Interview with Tom Beckett," *The Difficulties: Charles Bernstein Issue*, ed. Tom Beckett, Vol. 2, no. 1 (Fall 1982), 35.

7   *Paris Review*, 86 (Winter 1982), 75.

8   *boundary 2*, 9 (1981); rpt. in excerpted form under the title "The Objects of Meaning," in *The L=A=N=G=U=A=G=E Book*, ed. Bruce Andrews and Charles Bernstein (Carbondale: Southern Illinois University Press, 1984), p. 60. This text is subsequently cited as LB.

9   *The Difficulties: Charles Bernstein Issue*, 41. Subsequently cited as D.

10   *Mortal Acts, Mortal Wounds* (Boston: Houghton Mifflin, 1980), p. 55.

11   *Tjanting* (Berkeley: The Figures, 1981), introduction unpaginated. Page references refer to Silliman's text.

12   *My Life* (Providence, R.I.: Burning Deck, 1980), pp. 5–6.

13   *Story and Other Stories* (Great Barrington, Mass.: The Figures, 1983), p. 74.

14   "Literature and the Right to Death" (1949), *The Gaze of Orpheus and Other Literary Essays*, trans. Lydia Davis; ed. P. Adams Sitney (Barrytown, N.Y.: Station Hill Press, 1981), p. 59. Station Hill has also published Lydia Davis' translation of Blanchot's novel *Death Sentence* and a bilingual edition of *The Madness of the Day / La Folie du Jour*.

15   *Mine: The One that Enters the Stories* (Berkeley: The Figures, 1982).

16   See LB, pp. 7–10.

17   See Nanon Valaoritis, Introduction to "Poésie Language USA," *Change*, 41 (Paris: Seghers, March 1981), 159. The section devoted to "Language Poetry" in this issue is on pp. 151–88.

18   See Vladimir Markov (ed.), *Russian Futurism: A History* (Berkeley: University of California Press, 1968), pp. 129–31.

19   *River to Rivet: A Manifesto* (College Park, Md.: Sun & Moon Press, 1984), p. 17. Together with *Dinner on the Lawn* and *Some Distance*, this volume constitutes the three-volume *River to Rivet: A Trilogy* (1984).

20   *Sulfur*, 8 (1983), 39.

21   *L=A=N=G=U=A=G=E*, 4(1981), ed. Bruce Andrews and Charles Bernstein (*Open Letter*, Fifth Series, No. 1), 23. Subsequently cited as OL.

22   *Writing* (Berkeley: The Figures, 1982), unpaginated.

23   *Islets/Irritations* (New York: Jordan Davies, 1983), p. 5.

Index

Boldface is used to distinguish major references.

Abrams, Meyer, 177
Ahearn, Barry, 199–200n32
Aiken, Conrad, 99, 100; "Illusions," 96–98
Aldington, Richard, 94
Alpert, Barry S., 72n28
Ammons, A. R., 175
Andrews, Bruce, 233
Antheil, George, 61
Antin, David, 26n48, 48, 70n5, 147, 148, 154n9, 183, 190; "the death of the hired man," 192–96
Apollinaire, Guillaume, 8, 22–23
Aristotle, 152, 157, 161, 180
Armajani, Siah, 192–93 (ill.), 195
Arnold, Matthew, 7, 178, 197–98n10
Arp, Hans, 44
Ashbery, John, 23, 148, 168, 188, 189, 230; "They Dream Only of America," 161–63; *Three Poems,* ix, 145–46, 153n9, 190
Auden, W. H., 178, 187–88

Balla, Giacomo, 40, 71n20
Barthes, Roland, 70
Baudelaire, Charles, *Le Spleen de Paris,* 158
Beaujour, Michel, 180, 189
Beckett, Lucy, 2–3
Beckett, Samuel, ix, **135–54;** *Enough,* 139; *How It Is,* 139, 144, 152, 153n8; *Ill Seen Ill Said,* **135–54;** *Imagination Dead Imagine,* 142; *The Lost Ones,* 142; "Texts for Nothing," 227; *The Unnamable,* 143; *Whoroscope,* 152
Beckett, Tom, 220, 223

Bernstein, Charles, x, 217, 218, 219–20, 221, 222, 223, 228, 233, 234, 238n6; "Dysraphism," 230–32; "The Sheds of our Webs," 215–17; "Sprocket Damage," 237
Bernstein, Michael A., 16, 27n62, 181–83, 186
Berry, Eleanor, 118n43, 134n16
Binyon, Lawrence, 59
Blackmur, R. P., 23–24n3
Blake, William, 5, 6, 23, 177, 178; "London," 234
Blanchot, Maurice, 226, 238n14
BLAST, 37, 39, 49, 50, 51, 71n18, 72n31
Bloom, Harold, ix, 2–3, 4–6, 10, 14, 21, 23, 25n38, 27n68, 148, 174–75, 176, 180, 182, 187
Blunden, Edmund, 178
Bly, Robert, 152, 171n7
Bodenheim, Maxwell, 96
Booth, Wayne, 151–52, 173
Borroff, Marie, 19
Bozzola, Angelo, 71n21
Brancusi, Constantin, 44, 46
Braque, Georges, 35
Breslin, James E. 99, 117n27
Bridges, Robert, 74, 77
Brodkey, Harold, 153n4; "Sea Noise," 136–38
Brodsky, Horace, 46, 49, 54
Brooke-Rose, Christine, 2, 14, 22
Bruns, Gerald L., 152n12
Brzeska, Sophie, 54, 55, 70, 73n37
Buffet-Picabia, Gabrielle, 101
Burgess, Anthony, 85

Burnham, Jack, 46
Bush, Ronald, 73n36
Buttel, Robert, 9, 25n27
Byron, George Gordon, Lord, 177, 180

Cage, John, viii, x, 35, **61–70**, 73n44, 73n45, 147, 152, 170, 183, 189, 190, 196, **201–14**; *Empty Words,* 207; "Erik Satie," 61; "For William McN. who studied with Ezra Pound," 61; "Mosaic," 63–69; "On Robert Rauschenberg, Artist and His Work," 62; *Silence,* 201–02, 203, 205; "36 Mesostics Re and not Re Duchamp," 206; *Where Are We Eating? and What Are We Eating?,* 207–13; *A Year from Monday,* 202
Cameron, Sharon, 15, 159
Cannell, Skipwith, 96
Carne-Ross, D. S., 9–10, 22, 25n40
Carrà, Carlo, 40, 42
Carruth, Hayden, 99, 104
Cawein, Madison, 92
Cendrars, Blaise, 194–95
Charles, Daniel, 196
Chekhov, Anton, 225
Cianci, Giovanni, 71n10, 72n22
Clausen, Christopher, 151–52, 154n17, 172–73, 175, 178, 181, 186, 190, 196, 197n2, 198n13
Cohn, Ruby, 138
Cole, Roger, 71n8
Coleridge, Samuel Taylor, 14
Collins, William, 177
Conarroe, Joel, 173
Cook, Albert, 25n36
Coolidge, Clark, 218, 227
Cork, Richard, 39, 44, 71n8, 72n21, 73n38
Corman, Cid, 200n34
Corti, Maria, 26n42, 175
Cowper, William, 177
Crane, Hart, 158, 217
Creeley, Robert, 148, 190, 218; *A Day Book,* 147
Crosby, Bing, 236–37
Cunningham, Merce, 207, 208, 210

Darragh, Tina, *on the corner to off the corner,* 215–16
Davenport Guy, 2, 10, 20, 22, 148–52, 183; "Au Tombeau de Charles Fourier," 148–50; "Ernst Machs Max Ernst," 150, 152
Davidson, Michael, 148, 190; *The Prose of Fact,* 147

Davie, Donald, 2, 10, 13, 14, 17, 20, 21, 22, 26n55, 71n9
Davies, Alan, 227
Davis, Lydia, 190, 218, 226, 238n14; "The Fears of Mrs. Orlando," 225–26; *Story,* 223, 225, 228; "Story," 227
de Man, Paul, 197n7
Dembo, L. S., 119–20, 126, 131–32, 133n3, 133n9
Derrida, Jacques, 219
Deutsch, Babette, 1
Dickinson, Emily, 23, 156
Djikstra, Bram, 101, 117n26
Dodge, Mabel, 103
Doggett, Frank, 25n27
Donne, John, 177
Donoghue, Denis, 18, 19, 26n57, 27n68
Doolittle, Hilda (H. D.), 93, 100, 116n15
Dorn, Ed, 161; *Slinger* viii, ix, 164–68
Duchamp, Marcel, 101, 105, 206
Duncan, Robert, 148

Ede, H. S., 55, 73n37
Einzig, Barbara, *Disappearing Work,* 147–48
Eliot, T. S., 23, 74–76, 156, 178, 179
Ellmann, Richard, 81, 86n2, 86n7, 87n7
Elsen, Albert E., 72n29
Emerson, Ralph Waldo, 3, 14, 17, 23
Ernst, Max, 154n16
Espey, John, 23n3

Fenollosa, Ernest, 11, 12
Fletcher, John Gould, 94
Ford, Ford Madox, 50, 52, 54, 78
Fraser, Kathleen, *Each Next,* 147–48
Fredman, Stephen, 153n9, 188–89, 192
Frost, Robert, 23, 156, 157, 178, 193–95; "Mending Wall," 193
Frye, Northrop, 15, 135, 142–43, 153n2, 189

Galassi, Jonathan, 218
Gall, Sally M., 25n40
Gaudier-Brzeska, Henri, **33–60,** 70n1; *Birds Erect,* 44–46 (ill.); *The Boy with a Coney,* 51–52, 53 (ill.); *Charm,* 33, 34 (ill.); *The Dancer,* 35–37 (ill.); *Hieratic Head,* 56, 57 (ill.), 59–60; *Red Stone Dancer,* 42–44 (ill.); 51–52; *Stags,* 37 (ill.); "VORTEX GAUDIER BRZESKA" 51–54
Gerber, John W., 90, 115n7
Gilbert, Stuart, 86n2
Ginsberg, Allen, 23, 156
Glasheen, Adaline, 87n9

Gleason, H. A., 134n12
Goethe, Johann Wolfgang von, 156
Gray, Thomas, 177
Grogan, Ruth, 117n27

Hall, Donald, 173
Hardy, Thomas, 178
Hartman, Charles O., 107–08, 114n2, 153n4
Hartman, Geoffrey, 3, 21
Heal, Edith, 114n1
Heine, Heinrich, 180
Hejinian, Lyn, x, 218, 220; *My Life,* 223–25, 228
Herbert, George, 141, 177
Hesse, Eva, 11–12, 22, 40, 71n19
Hollander, John, 201–02, 204
Hoyt, Helen, 96; "Damask," 96–98

Jabès, Edmond, 70
Jarrell, Randall, 1
Johns, Jasper, 62
Johnson, Lionel, x
Johnson, Samuel, 177
Joyce, James, ix, 39, 231; *Finnegans Wake,* 83–85; letters, **75–87;** *Ulysses,* 140
Jung, Carl, 206

Kandinsky, Wassily, 49, 73n35
Kearns, George, 12, 25n34
Keats, John, 6, 14, 21
Kenner, Hugh, 2, 8–9, 10, 12, 13, 14, 17–18, 22, 23, 27n68, 35, 71n9, 72n31, 90, 111, 116n18, 133n11, 153n8, 217
Kermode, Frank, 2, 4, 14, 16, 17, 21, 25n27
Khlebnikov, Velimir, 228
Kinnell, Galway, "Memory of Wilmington," 220–21
Kirby, Michael, 214n5
Koch, Kenneth, 148
Kostelanetz, Richard, 61, 73n45, 203, 204–05, 212–13, 214n7
Krauss, Rosalind, 46–48, 63
Kreymborg, Alfred, 96
Kruchenykh, Alexey, 228
Kumin, Maxine, 173
Kutnik, Jerzy, 189

Laughlin, James, 113, 118n40
Lawrence, D. H. 178
Le Guin, Ursula, 170, 171n16
Leibowitz, Herbert, 116n11
Levertov, Denise, 229
Levy, Mervyn, 44

Lewis, C. Day, 178
Lewis, Wyndham, 39–40, 42, 46, 48, 51, 71n21, 72n31; *Timon of Athens,* 41 (ill.)
Litz, A. Walton, 3
Lord, Albert, 158
Lowell, Robert, 156, 157
Loy, Mina, 96
Lukacs, Georg, 181

McCaffery, Steve, 233
MacKaye, Percy, 92
MacLow, Jackson, 233
Mallarmé, Stephane, 176, 177, 178, 179, 180, 186, 198n18, 199n19, 199n20
Mariani, Paul, 114n2, 115n10, 116n15
Marinetti, F. T., 39, 42, 56, 60, 71n21
Markov, Vladimir, 238n18
Marx, Karl, 232
Materer, Timothy, 39–40, 46, 71n8, 72n24
Merrill, James, 23, 188
Messerli, Douglas, 39, 71n10, 72n31, 218, 230; *River to Rivet,* 228; "When the Wind Blows," 228–30
Miller, J. Hillis, 2, 6, 14, 24n19, 122, 124
Molesworth, Charles, 153n9
Monroe, Harriet, 114n2, 116n15, 133n4
Moore, Henry, 46
Moore, Marianne, 95–96, 116n20, 178
Morris, Adelaide Kirby, 9, 25n27

Nelson, Cary, 115n5
Norman, Howard, *The Wishing Bone Cycle,* 169–70

O'Connor, William Van, 1
O'Hara, Frank, ix, 148, 159–61; "Poem (Lana Turner has collapsed!)," 159–61, 230
Olson, Charles, 22, 61, 107, 148, 167, 218
Oppen, George, viii, ix, **119–34;** *Discrete Series,* 123, 124, 126, 131; "The Forms of Love," 131–32, 134n16; "Her ankles are watches," 128–30; "Images of the Engines," 132; "Near your eyes," 127–28; "She lies, hip high," 123–26, 128, 133n10; "A Theological Definition," 130–31
Oppen, Mary, 124
Owen, Wilfred, 178

Paige, D. D., 86n1
Palgrave, F. T., 176–77, 178, 179; *The Golden Treasury,* 176, 177, 178
Pastan, Linda, 173

Pater, Walter, 5, 70, 199n18
Pearce, Roy Harvey, 25n27
Perkins, David, 23n3, 115n3
Peterson, Walter, 117n39
Picabia, Francis, 101, 103, 105; *Ici, C'est Ici Stieglitz/Foi et Amour*, 101–03 (ill.), 104
Picasso, Pablo, 35, 46–49, 101, 103; *Violin*, 46–48 (ill.)
Pike, Kenneth, 108
Pinsky, Robert, 138
Poe, Edgar Allen, 158
Pope, Alexander, 177
Pound, Ezra, viii, ix, x, **1–27, 33–73,** 93–94, 95–96, 116n14, 116n16, 119, 148, 156, 178, 181, 182, 183, 186, 188, 196, 199n27; *The Cantos*, viii, 12, 17, 19–20, 22, 33, 60, 61, 76, 77, 78, 83, 186; *Canto LXII*, 78–80, 83, 85, *Canto LXXXI*, 3, 9–12, 15–16, 19–20, **30–32;** *Gaudier-Brzeska*, **33–73,** 76; letters, **74–87;** "A Retrospect," 13
Powell, James A., 25n40
Power, Kevin, 133n6

Quinn, Sr. Bernetta, 1

Rabaté, Jean-Michel, 29n62
Rauschenberg, Robert, 35, 62–63, 69, 73n46; *Fossil for Bob Morris, N.Y.,* 63, 65 (ill.)
Raworth, Tom, 218, 234; *Writing,* 235–37
Ray, Man, 101
Read, Forrest, 87n7
Rich, Adrienne, 23, 157
Ricoeur, Paul, 157
Riddel, Joseph N., 24n3
Rodin, Auguste, 35–37; *The Burghers of Calais,* 37, 38 (ill.)
Roethke, Theodore, 156
Rosenblum, Robert, 70n5
Rosenthal, M. L., 11
Rothenberg, Jerome, 70, 86n3, 148, 188
Rubin, William S., 117n28

Sandburg, Carl, 100
Sayre, Henry M., 115n4, 117n27, 189, 200n44, 200n45
Schieffer, Reinhold, 120, 133n5, 133n9
Schneidau, Herbert, 12–13, 71n9
Schoenberg, Arnold, 63–69
Scholes, Robert, 157, 161
Schwitters, Kurt, 23, 184
Seitz, William C., 70n4

Severini, Gino, 56–59, 73n38; *Portrait of Marinetti,* 56, 58 (ill.)
Shaffer, Peter, 152
Shattuck, Roger, 70n5
Shelley, P. B., 177, 178
Sieburth, Richard, 69
Silliman, Ron, x, 217, 218, 232–33, 234, 237; "Carbon," 215–16; *Tjanting,* 221–22
Singh, G., 26n60
Sitwell, Edith, 178
Snyder, Gary, 170
Sorrentino, Gilbert, 70, 186–87
Stein, Gertrude, 103, 149, 163, 223, 225; "Milk," 190–92, 193; *Tender Buttons,* viii
Steinberg, Leo, 35
Stephens, Alan, 117n36
Stevens, Wallace, ix, **1–27,** 96, 130, 156, 157, 158, 178, 179, 198n14, 198n15; "It Must Give Pleasure," **28–30;** *The Necessary Angel,* 7–8, 18; *Notes toward a Supreme Fiction,* 3–6, 15–17, 19, 24n3
Stieglitz, Alfred, 101, 103, 105
Strand, Mark, 175
Sullivan, J. P., 22
Sutton, Walker, 104, 108, 114n2
Swinburne, Algernon C., x, 217

Tashjian, Dikran, 101, 117n26
Tate, Allen, 1
Terrell, Carroll F., 86n6
Thirwall, John C., 114n2, 117n33
Thompson, James, 177
Tisdall, Caroline, 71n21
Todorov, Tzvetan, 177
Tomkins, Calvin, 214n3
Townley, Rod, 115n10
Turner, Victor, 157

Ulmer, Gregory, 23
Updike, John 152

Valéry, Paul, 8
Varèse, Louise, 171n6
Vendler, Helen, 2, 3, 6–7, 13, 14, 17, 21, 23, 198n15

Wagner, Linda, 114n2
Wallace, Emily Mitchell, 115n7, 116n12, 116n14, 133n7
Watten, Barrett, 222, 233
Weatherhead, A. Kingsley, 117n36
Weaver, Mike, 114n2, 133n4
Wees, William, 39, 71n10, 72n21

Weiss, Theodore, 1
Wescher, Herta, 70n5, 72n33
Whitman, Walter, 162
Wilde, Oscar, x
Williams, William Carlos, ix, 1, 8, 23, 27n70, 40, 55, **88–118,** 119, 124, 129, 132, 133n4, 148, 178, 183, 189, 217, 225; *Al Que Quiere,* 99, 100, 101, 105, 116n21; "The Attic Which Is Desire," 113–14; *The Autobiography of William Carlos Williams,* 92; "Between Walls," 105–07, 109, 113, 122–24, 126; "For Eleanor and Bill Monahan," 108; "Gay Wallpaper," 122; "Good Night," 103–05; *Kora in Hell,* viii, 61, 101, 113, 148, 154n12; "Love Song," 97–98, 100, 104–05, 116n21; "Nantucket," 121–23, 126, 130; "The Nightingales," 88–90; "Of Asphodel, That Greeny Flower," 108–10; *Paterson,* 110–13; *Poems,* 92; "Post-lude," 93; "The Revelation," 94–95, 101; *Spring and All,* 105, 110; *The Tempers,* 92, 93, 100; "This Is Just To Say," 90–91; "The Young Housewife," 99–100, 117n25

Winters, Yvor, 2, 24n4
Wittgenstein, Ludwig, 219
Wolmark, Alfred, 49, 54
Wordsworth, William, 6, 174, 178
Wright, James, 159, 160, 165; "Snow-storm in the Midwest," 155–56, 162, 163–64, 168

Yeats, W. B., vii–x, 17, 23, 35, 129, 156, 157, 158, 178, 182, 197, 230, 232; "The Second Coming," 229

Zukofsky, Louis, 183–87, 199n32; *"A,"* viii; *"A"-1,* 184; *"A"-12,* 183–86